Violence, Ritual, and the Wari Empire

BIOARCHAEOLOGICAL INTERPRETATIONS OF THE HUMAN PAST:
LOCAL, REGIONAL, AND GLOBAL PERSPECTIVES

UNIVERSITY PRESS OF FLORIDA

Florida A&M University, Tallahassee
Florida Atlantic University, Boca Raton
Florida Gulf Coast University, Ft. Myers
Florida International University, Miami
Florida State University, Tallahassee
New College of Florida, Sarasota
University of Central Florida, Orlando
University of Florida, Gainesville
University of North Florida, Jacksonville
University of South Florida, Tampa
University of West Florida, Pensacola

Violence, Ritual, and the Wari Empire

A Social Bioarchaeology of Imperialism in the Ancient Andes

Tiffiny A. Tung

FOREWORD BY CLARK SPENCER LARSEN

UNIVERSITY PRESS OF FLORIDA

Gainesville/Tallahassee/Tampa/Boca Raton
Pensacola/Orlando/Miami/Jacksonville/Ft. Myers/Sarasota

First cloth printing, 2012

First paperback printing, 2013

Library of Congress Cataloging-in-Publication Data

Tung, Tiffiny A.

Violence, ritual, and the Wari empire : a social bioarchaeology of imperialism in the ancient
Andes / Tiffiny A. Tung ; foreword by Clark Spencer Larsen.

p. cm. — (Bioarchaeological interpretations of the human past :
local, regional, and global perspectives)

Includes bibliographical references and index.

ISBN 978-0-8130-3767-7 (cloth: alk. paper)

ISBN 978-0-8130-4473-6 (pbk.)

1. Huari Indians—Antiquities. 2. Huari Indians—Funeral rites and ceremonies.
3. Social structure—Peru. 4. Human remains (Archaeology)—Peru. 5. Human skeleton—
Analysis—Peru. 6. Imperialism—Social aspects—Peru. 7. Social archaeology—Peru—Peru.
8. Excavations (Archaeology)—Peru. I. Title.

F3430.1.H83T86 2012

985'.01—dc23   2011037498

The University Press of Florida is the scholarly publishing agency for the State University
System of Florida, comprising Florida A&M University, Florida Atlantic University, Florida
Gulf Coast University, Florida International University, Florida State University, New College
of Florida, University of Central Florida, University of Florida, University of North Florida,
University of South Florida, and University of West Florida.

University Press of Florida

15 Northwest 15th Street

Gainesville, FL 32611-2079

http://www.upf.com

For Steve

&

Dedicated to the memory
of Phillip Walker

Contents

Figures

Tables

Foreword

The Bioarchaeology of Wari Imperialism

Among the most interesting of the complex societies that arose in ancient South America was the Wari Empire, the first to emerge, rise, and fall in the Andes. During its reign from approximately AD 600 to AD 1000, this empire and the political forces that organized and maintained it had gained influence over a vast expanse of territory, certainly rivaling any other empire in size and scope in the New World and many in the Old World. Tiffiny Tung, one of a group of scholars with interests in the interface between biology and culture in archaeological settings, presents in this book her compelling investigation of the powerful influences of social and political forces on life in this remarkable setting. She accomplishes this via the study of mortuary traditions and the remains of persons who in life were players in the remarkably complex social, economic, and political Wari network. Tung addresses the overarching questions surrounding this extraordinary empire: How did the Wari pull off the building of such an extensive empire? What behaviors and actions did they employ to build and maintain the empire some eight hundred years before the rise of the later Inka Empire?

Bioarchaeology—the study of human remains from archaeological contexts—provides an essential avenue for investigating these questions. In her study, Tung takes on the labyrinth of social and cultural data from this setting in particular and social theory in general to identify, interpret, and inform our growing understanding of Wari society. Following a comprehensive overview of theoretical issues regarding states and empires and a discussion of the Wari Empire, Tung presents key bioarchaeological analyses of demographic profiles and strontium isotope ratios from burials, placing the populations in context with regard to community organization. She shows that the heartland site of Conchopata was not a cosmopolitan center to which foreigners migrated but was instead an exclusive settlement comprising locals. She also applies an analysis of ancient mtDNA to document kin patterning and mortuary traditions in a selected series.

Military actions, in addition to being well represented in a variety of iconographic representations, are evident in skeletal trauma and the analysis of trophy heads such as Tung uses in this volume to show that violence was sometimes employed in the expansion and rule of the Wari Empire by a political and ritual elite.

Like many cultures around the world, the Wari were trophy-takers, using heads of victims as a marker of conqueror-vanquished interactions. Some of those conquered by the Wari were represented by their heads, which were integrated into elaborate rituals that showcased military achievements. In support of this model, Tung's analysis of strontium isotope data provides clear evidence that most trophy heads were not from bystanders who had their heads taken. Rather, they were from those captives—usually men—taken from distant lands being conquered. This well-crafted integration of trophy, trauma, and iconographic data provides a picture of male behavior whereby the state and the individual acted together in creating a distinctive masculine identity in the heartland of the empire, an identity that was often in the service of state goals.

The larger picture that emerges frames identity in several contexts: the individual, the military, and those responsible for ritual. Critical to understanding the policies promulgated by the empire is the centrality of two key classes, namely, a military class that conducted all matters of subjugation through violence and a ritual class that oversaw ceremonies and rituals that contributed to the rise, spread, and maintenance of the Wari Empire.

This study is at the foundation of how socially, politically, and economically contextualized bioarchaeology contributes to an understanding of complex, imperialistic societies, past and present. Human skeletons provide a remarkably rich data set at the level of both individual and community. At the aggregate, population level, we learn how a state affected the lives of its players. Additionally, even while the remains of the deceased present a normative picture in the collective, they also present us with the variability of social and behavioral circumstances that contributed to shaping the lives, livelihoods, and conditions of those once living. As this study so well demonstrates, the integrative nature of bioarchaeology offers new perspectives for understanding key aspects of past social behavior, community organization, and the rise and maintenance of states and empires. This bioarchaeological investigation provides new opportunities and new directions for addressing fundamental issues and concerns in anthropology, underscoring the power of integrative science in developing an understanding of the human condition and the social forces that shape it.

Clark Spencer Larsen
Series Editor
Bioarchaeology Research Laboratory
Ohio State University

Preface

A goal of this book is to implement what I call a "bioarchaeology of imperialism," which aims to document how archaic states and empires affected demographic profiles, community organization, population health, incidences of violence, and funerary and ritual treatment of human bodies. I propose that premodern states and the expansion of these entities affected morbidity patterns and rituals involving the body in profound ways for both conquering and subject populations. A staggering amount of previous archaeological research demonstrates that many other aspects of social and political life can be strongly impacted by imperial policies and practices (see Alcock et al. 2001; Feinman and Marcus 1998), so this is likely to also hold true for biological health status and the ways in which people, through their bodies, were socially molded and manipulated for imperial ends. However, in studies of ancient empires, a bioarchaeological perspective is still lacking. Thus, this book builds on those foundational archaeological studies of empire and offers a complementary yet distinctive view gleaned from hundreds of human skeletons evaluated in their mortuary and ritual contexts.

A bioarchaeological perspective on imperialism is ideally suited for documenting particular aspects of health and lifeways of peoples who left no written record. In bioarchaeology, the human skeletal remains are the record; they are the bony diary of people's lives. Bioarchaeological inquiry can tell us about the lived experiences of people from the prehistoric past; it provides a direct means of analysis by focusing on the human body itself. The skeletal indicators of age, sex, pathological lesions, bone fractures, and postmortem modifications to the body are analyzed because they show how human bodies were inscribed with individual actions, and they show how social structures and the environment may have profoundly affected one's behavior and health. Bioarchaeological data reveal such things as the demographic makeup of families and communities, which can be used to examine the form and nature of community organization. Skeletal data, in conjunction with archaeological context, also disclose information about dietary practices, disease load, and the physical traumas that people endured, whether at the hands of an attacker or as a result of hard, physical labor. Together, these data can be used to reconstruct narratives about an individual, burial group, family, and community. This in turn allows scholars to reconstruct how lives were experienced during particular swaths of time: in this case, during a time of state rule and imperial domination in the ancient Peruvian Andes.

Although human skeletal remains are commonly examined to assess aspects of health and disease—tasks that are undertaken in this work—this study is also concerned with how the human body (and representations of it) is inscribed with meaning; this complementary aspect of skeletal analysis brings us closer to understanding the lived experience of populations from the distant past. Thus, by fully integrating skeletal and contextual data, this book aims to provide insights into both "health, disease, and diet" (sensu Larsen 1997) and the "body as material culture" (sensu Sofaer 2006). While these two aspects of the human body in prehistory have traditionally been approached separately, I illustrate how they are mutually constitutive by showing how archaeological bodies (mummies and skeletons) were inscribed with traces of biological status and cultural identity. Data obtained from archaeological bodies can thus be marshaled to address a variety of anthropological questions, such as how ancient imperial expansion affected both biological and social aspects of people's lives.

In writing about how individuals and communities were affected by Wari imperialism, I present the data and interpretations in some detail, for I want the correlates and the analytical and interpretive process to be transparent, both for the experienced bioarchaeologist and for the student of anthropology. I devote a chapter to each category of data, showing how they support or refute particular hypotheses, and I include interpretations that are informed both by the patterns in osteological data and by the all-important archaeological context. When the osteological and archaeological data can support alternative interpretations, I indicate what those might be. Thus, for some readers, my interpretations may not seem conclusive enough. However, given the nature of equifinality that arises with some categories of osteological and archaeological data, I have opted to include alternative interpretations rather than exclude them. I hope that my future research and studies by other scholars eventually produce more conclusive data, which will in turn lead to more questions.

Every so often in this book, I make analogies to modern state institutions or social circumstances that are reminiscent of what I have observed in Wari society. This is not meant to overemphasize parallels between the past and present or argue that ancient state institutions had the same organizational and monitoring qualities of those in the present. Rather, it is meant to illuminate how some state and social institutions—from tribute systems and state-supported militarism to patriarchy—shaped the lives of the Wari and how they structure our lives today. In my teaching, I have found that analogies of that sort help students to understand ancient societies, while also shining a spotlight on our own. My goal is to educate students and researchers about Wari society specifically, and about human societies more generally. To that end, I occasionally make analogies between societies of the past and present.

The Study of Imperialism

My interest in how imperial expansion affects the lifeways of conquered peoples has roots in both my scholarly and my family life. Some of my fascination with how empires impact the lives of those they conquer derives from stories from my father and his sisters, who endured attacks and invasion by the Japanese military while youths in China in the late 1930s to 1940s. After my paternal family left Beijing for Jiangxi province, enticed by a nice position for my grandfather as the director of the government's Farm Institute, they eventually fled the region when the Japanese invaded and bombed that area. They moved to the outskirts of Chongqing in Sichuan province, and when the Japanese military planes arrived there too—devastating Chongqing with bombs—my family relocated once again, this time to a more rural farming area.

The stories of the bombing raids are poignant: fleeing from the house to the lake to avoid bombings; my father carrying his little sister, who had polio, while running from attack; learning to identify the sounds of Japanese planes and estimate how long before the attack ("they fly slower when loaded down with bombs"). My father and aunts ended many of these stories with, "Most Americans have no idea what it's like to be invaded and colonized by a foreign power." That statement has stayed with me as I try to document and understand what it is like for a people to be conquered by another, whether today, 60 years ago, or 1,200 years ago.

Acknowledgments

The data presented in this book results from some 40 months of field and lab work in Arequipa and Ayacucho, Peru. The work was supported by various granting agencies to which I am extremely grateful. Those include the following: Fulbright IIE Fellowship, Wenner-Gren Foundation for Anthropological Research (Grant No. 6680 and 8169), National Science Foundation (BCS-0118751, Physical Anthropology Division), Sigma Xi Grants in Aid of Research, UNC–Chapel Hill Latané Summer Research Grant, Vanderbilt Interdisciplinary Discovery Grant, and Center for American Overseas Research Council Grant. I was also given precious time to analyze data, rethink some of my interpretations, and write them up with the support of a Faculty Leave Fellowship from Vanderbilt University.

In addition to the generous financial support from various sources, many people aided in the development of ideas presented in this book. Early support and encouragement from Phil Walker and Katharina Schreiber laid the foundation for my interests in bioarchaeology and Andean archaeology, and I am grateful to them for setting me on this path.

Clark Spencer Larsen was generous with his time and provided me with important feedback as I developed this project in the late 1990s. I am grateful for the encouragement and support he has provided me over the years. Brian Billman enthusiastically supported me as I began this research, and he was instrumental in guiding me as I prepared for directing my first archaeological excavation at the site of Beringa in the Majes valley. Bruce Winterhalder gave me excellent feedback as my research ideas were developing; there is no doubt that Bruce's guidance and wise insights have improved my scholarship. Dale Hutchinson, Margie Scarry, and Vin Steponaitis also assisted me in the early phases of this process, and all of them were a key source of ideas and support.

My lab and fieldwork in Peru would not have been possible without the generous support and collaboration of many people from several research projects. Anita Cook invited me to participate in the Conchopata Archaeology Project in Ayacucho in 1999, and shortly thereafter, Anita Cook and William Isbell, codirectors of the project, entrusted me with complete access to all of the Conchopata human skeletal remains, field notes, and field photos. I am grateful to them for entrusting me with this important skeletal sample. Their support for my research has been unfailing. Anita and I have had many invigorating discussions about the Wari, and she has always been generous in sharing her vast knowledge of Wari society with me; her insights have greatly improved my study. Bill always encouraged vigorous exploration of all avenues of research, as well as open debate of our interpretations. His great breadth of knowledge contributed much to my understanding of Andean archaeology, Wari imperialism, and the ways in which I interpret some of the findings. This book would not have been possible without Anita and Bill's support, and I am forever grateful to them. José Ochatoma and Martha Cabrera, professors at the Universidad Nacional de San Cristóbal de Huamanga (UNSCH), likewise gave me access to human skeletal remains that they excavated from Conchopata; I thank them for entrusting me with the bioarchaeological analysis of those remains. They have also provided much logistical support for my projects in Ayacucho, giving me lab space at the university to analyze the skeletal remains, assisting me with paperwork at the National Institute of Culture in Ayacucho, and hosting me at dinners during the many months that I have lived in Ayacucho. I cherish both their scholarly insights and their friendship.

Other members of the Conchopata Archaeology Project provided invaluable support and assistance while I was in the field and lab in Ayacucho. Warm thanks go to my friends and colleagues Catherine Bencic, David Crowley, Greg Ketteman, Juan Leoni, Charlene Milliken, Nikki Slovak, and Barbara Wolff. I thank Juan Carlos Blacker for allowing me to use his fantastic map of Conchopata, and I gratefully acknowledge Greg Ketteman for his detailed field notes on the trophy heads from the circular ritual structure. Juan Leoni generously offered his insights about the pre-Wari (Huarpa) period. Lorenzo Huisa Palomino and Jimmy Jauregui Suarez assisted me in the UNSCH lab and helped keep all of the bone boxes in order; I greatly appreciate their help and friendship. Gloria Suarez Fuentes kept me and my students well fed while living in Ayacucho, and we are all grateful for those scrumptious meals made with love and lots of *ají*. I also thank Caroline Yezer and Jessaca Leinaweaver for sharing their house in Ayacucho with me. In later years, Barbara Wolff and I shared a research house; not only was she a great housemate, she also helped me find many detailed field notes. Her uncanny ability to locate obscure field forms still inspire awe, and I am grateful for all of her assistance, ranging from logistical to technical and intellectual.

In the Department of Arequipa, my research was made possible by the support of Karen Wise and Augusto Cardona Rosas, codirectors of the Center for Archaeological Research in Arequipa (CIARQ). Karen first invited me to participate on a CIARQ archaeology project in 1998; I warmly thank her for providing me with opportunities to conduct research in the Arequipa region. Augusto Cardona provided assistance through many stages of my research endeavor; he visited several sites with me in the Majes valley in 1998 and 1999 when I was trying to locate a Middle Horizon site with a mortuary component. Augusto also allowed me to use CIARQ excavation equipment during my excavations at Beringa. Finally, Augusto provided me with lab space at CIARQ for analysis of the Beringa remains. I am extremely appreciative of the support that Augusto, Karen, and CIARQ have provided.

Additionally, many people at the Institute of National Culture (INC) in Arequipa contributed to the success of this research project. Pablo de la Vera Cruz introduced me to the site of La Real in 1998, and the INC-Arequipa granted me permits to transport the human skeletal remains from the municipality in Aplao (in the Majes valley) to the INC in Arequipa. Pablo de la Vera Cruz and the INC also gave me permission to analyze all of the La Real human remains and provided me with the excavation field notes. I warmly thank Pablo for allowing me to study this significant skeletal collection. Others at the INC-Arequipa also made my research possible; Marco López Hurtado, Lucy Linares Delgado, and Cecilia Quequezana all ensured that I had access to the La Real skeletal collection while it was stored at the INC-Arequipa. I thank all of them for their support and friendship. Finally, I owe the INC-Arequipa director, Luís Sardón Cánepa, a great thanks for showing interest in my research and approving my various requests. I also send a heartfelt thanks to Willy Yépez Alvarez, a professional archaeologist who excavated the site of La Real, for providing me with sketch maps of the site and additional field notes.

A great part of this research project would not have been possible without the hard work of dozens of individuals who participated on my excavation project at Beringa in the Majes valley. I directed the Proyecto Bio-arqueológico y Arqueológico de Valle de Majes in agreement with the Instituto Nacional de Cultura under legal permit, Resolución 615 (year 2001). Ana Miranda Quispe was the codirector of this project, and she spent long hours collecting much of the ceramic data and photographing the ceramics; I gratefully acknowledge her participation. Bruce Owen contributed his expertise to the Beringa project by collecting much of the ceramic data and organizing the entire ceramic database; his work has made an invaluable contribution to the Beringa project. My thanks also go to Adan Umire and Cara Monroe for their excellent illustrations of ceramics from Beringa. Randi Gladwell, the faunal specialist, produced an incredibly detailed inventory of the Beringa faunal remains, providing important information regarding the Beringa menu; I am grateful for all of her hard work, both in the field and in the lab. I also thank Gina Quinn, the textile specialist, who cleaned and inventoried the Beringa textiles. Yenny Ihue Umire inventoried the plant remains; I warmly thank her for her contribution to this research project. I also want to acknowledge Karen Reed and Erika Simborth Lozada for producing the Beringa site map. I especially owe a debt of gratitude to Mirza del Castillo Salazar for all of her long hours assisting me in the osteology lab. I treasure her friendship and hope that this book reflects favorably on her hard work and dedication to the Beringa Bioarchaeology Project.

My heartfelt thanks go to all of the members of the Beringa Bioarchaeology Project, including Mirza del Castillo Salazar, Aubrey Cockrill, David Crowley, Diana Durand, Brian Finucane, Dennis Geldres, Randi Gladwell, Joe Griffin, Yenny Ihue Umire, Kelly Knudson, Samantha Lawrence, Aurelio López, Evelín López Sosa, Virginia Lorena, Lorena Macedo, Virginia Mayorí Valencia, Ana Miranda Quispe, Andre Marín, Ricardo Marín, Percy Marín, Augusto Marín, Cara Monroe, Bruce Owen, Meryl Owen, Andy Peterson, Gina Quinn, Arnold Ramos Cuba, Gino Rosas, Karen Reed, Bill Ross, Abi Schuler, Erika Simborth Lozada, José Tito, Adan Umire, Steve Wernke, and Maria Magdalena Ydme. The excavations at Beringa were made possible through the gracious hospitality and support of Julio Zúñiga and Derby del Castillo. The project team lived at Julio and Derby's farm, and they prepared our meals and rented me one of their trucks and a raft. Without their raft, we could not have reached the site of Beringa during the first part of the field season, when the river level was still high. I am also grateful to community members of the town of Huancarqui, who built us an impressive footbridge across the Majes River once the water level dropped, enabling us to access the site with greater ease. After the terrible earthquake in June 2001, they built us another footbridge, so we could continue with the excavations. I thank the *apus* that we stopped work early that day to attend an agricultural festival, so we were not on the road when it was pounded by boulders and washed into the river.

Many of the ideas presented in this book have grown out of conversations that I have had with many friends and colleagues, including Valerie Andrushko, Deborah Blom, Ann Kakaliouras, Corina Kellner, Celeste Gagnon, Patricia Lambert, Christina Torres-Rouf, John Verano, and Phil Walker. I particularly want to thank Phil, Deborah, Valerie, and John with whom I have had extended discussions regarding cranial trauma. Early conversations with John Janusek influenced my thinking on issues related to violence and ritual battles; I thank him for encouraging me to explore the relationship between them. In Arequipa, CIARQ was always a bustling *tambo* full of fascinating researchers. I thank the following people for providing hours of lively discussions on Andean scholarship while living and working at CIARQ: Augusto Cardona, Miriam Doutriaux, Randi Gladwell, Justin Jennings, Kelly Knudson, Enrique (Kike) López Hurtado, Giancarolo Marconi, Clory Orbegosa, Bruce Owen, Felix Palacios Ríos, Erika Simborth, Nico Trepcevich, Steve Wernke, Patrick Ryan Williams, and Willy Yépez.

The first batch of samples for strontium isotope analysis was done by Kelly Knudson and Douglas Price at the University of Wisconsin–Madison, where the samples were initially prepped. Kelly Knudson and Paul Fullagar then processed them at the Isotope Geochemistry Laboratory at UNC–Chapel Hill. Subsequent samples were processed by Kelly Knudson and her students at the Archaeological Chemistry Lab at Arizona State University. I thank all of them, especially Kelly, for promptly and reliably processing the samples from Conchopata.

Obtaining the mtDNA from the Wari-era skeletal samples was certainly a team effort. I extend a heartfelt thanks to Marshal Summar for donating isolated lab space and equipment for the ancient DNA extraction; his enthusiasm for the project was infectious, and his relentless pursuit for better techniques greatly improved the project. I also thank Brian Kemp for his untiring efforts to obtain ancient mtDNA from Wari (and post-Wari) skeletal samples. As a postdoctoral fellow supported by my Vanderbilt Interdisciplinary Discovery Research Grant, he brought his excellent lab and research skills to Vanderbilt; this led to novel genetic data and many spirited discussions on Wari society (and Wari collapse, which will be discussed in other publications).

Since joining the faculty at Vanderbilt University, I have had the pleasure of working with excellent students and colleagues. My scholarship has benefited from lively discussions—both in informal settings and at our South American Anthropology Discussion Group—with Beth Conklin, Tom Dillehay, Lesley Gill, John Janusek, and Steve Wernke. I also thank Steve Wernke for creating many of the fantastic maps for this book.

Many students have joined me in the field and assisted in cleaning, labeling, reconstructing, inventorying, and photographing bones from the site of Conchopata. Their assistance has been invaluable, and I want to thank each of them: Susan Braunlin Geiger, Mirza Del Castillo, Catherine Domanska, Danielle Kurin, Luciana Mendola, Emily Sharp, Allison Sherill, K. C. Smith, and Samantha Summar.

As the book manuscript took form, I received valuable input from a variety of friends and colleagues. I am extremely grateful to Christina Torres-Rouff and Debra Martin for reading the entire manuscript and giving thoughtful feedback. Their suggestions and keen insights have improved the book greatly; we in the bioarchaeological community are fortunate to have such fine colleagues. I thank Elaine Tung for her comments on the preface and Patrick Inman for his edits on the earliest version of chapters 4 and 5, as well as another chapter on physiological health that I ultimately decided to cut. I also thank Ann Kakaliouras, who read an early version of the introduction and provided suggestions on its organization. Finally, I want to thank editors John Byram and Kara Schwartz at the University Press of Florida for their thoughtful suggestions on the organization of the book, and I send a huge thank you to Sally Bennett for her copyediting suggestions and her superb attention to the details of the data.

I thank my parents, Elaine and Paul Tung, for supporting my academic endeavors from the earliest stages and on. Finally, Steve Wernke deserves the greatest acknowledgment for his untiring support for my research; I greatly appreciate the time he has dedicated to discussing various aspects of my research. My scholarship benefited from his wise insights and impressive intellect, and he kept me sane with his charming sense of humor.

Although we do not know what the Wari called themselves, I would like to think that this book tells part of their story. It is dedicated to them.

- 1 -

Introduction to Wari

Approximately 1,400 years ago, two women were buried at the Wari site of Conchopata in the central Peruvian Andes. One was painstakingly covered in rich, red cinnabar and buried with other individuals in an elaborate mausoleum filled with beautifully decorated ceramics and gold, silver, and copper artifacts. She had lived until her fifties, and she showed no signs of trauma or disease. The other woman was buried alone, the only artifact a ceramic sherd under her head. She too had lived until her fifties, but she had suffered a life of abuse and hard labor; this was evident in her numerous skull fractures, broken ribs, and arthritis of the arms, back, and hips. These two women provide a glimpse of life under Wari imperial rule, and they reveal how Wari policies and practices could differentially affect people's lives. How was Wari imperial society organized such that these women experienced such dramatically distinct lifeways while living in the same community? And how did Wari imperial expansion structure health outcomes and lived experience for others in the Wari domain? These are important questions to ask because they reveal the ways that imperial policies can affect people's lives, and how people's actions can simultaneously structure imperial policies and practices, either today or in the distant past.

This book addresses those and related issues from a bioarchaeological perspective, using data from the human skeleton to examine how the first expansive empire in South America structured demographic profiles and community organization and altered people's exposure to violence. The relationship between violence and imperialism is explored in detail in this book, evaluating how militarism was employed in the expansion and maintenance of the Wari Empire and how attitudes about violence structured people's lifeways more generally. Indeed, the second woman's injuries described above were likely related to Wari attitudes toward some categories of women and about aggression and the role of violence in Wari society.

The Wari Empire was the first of its kind in the Andes of South America. The capital city—the site of Huari—was a large urban center covering some three to five square kilometers in the Ayacucho Basin (see figure 3.1), from where it expanded to incorporate spatially disparate groups in southern, northern, and coastal Peru. Prior to the time of Wari florescence circa AD 600, no other Andean polity had achieved such widespread influence over such a vast geographical area. The footprint of Wari imperialism can be seen in the Wari-style architecture at distant sites—patios surrounded by narrow rectangular buildings, niched halls, and D-shaped buildings used for rituals (Cook 2001; Isbell 1991; Schreiber 1992)—as well as in the transformation of landscapes, often to increase agricultural output (Valencia Zegarra 2005; Williams 2002). Wari influence also altered mortuary traditions in some regions; in Nasca, multiple burials with Wari artifacts were placed in sepultures, a change from preceding Nasca mortuary traditions in which single interments were the norm (Isla Cuadrado 2009). Throughout much of the Peruvian Andes, material culture was also transformed, as new Wari icons were integrated into ceramics, textiles, metals, and other media. Attaining this kind of depth and breadth of influence was no easy task, yet as I will argue, military activities, elaborate rituals, and the savvy integration of the two aided Wari leaders in creating an expansive empire for the first time in South America, eight hundred years before the rise of the well-studied Inka Empire.

In fact, much of Inka statecraft was built on that of the Wari, in terms of both the material (for example, road systems) and the ritual, including such practices as human sacrifice and the display of human body parts as trophies. Although there is a long history of human sacrifice and trophy taking in the ancient Andes (Tung 2007a; Verano 1995), Wari leaders, and subsequently the Inka (Ogburn 2007), combined these ritual acts with military actions and represented them in elaborate iconography as a way to legitimize their rule. I argue later that the destruction of particular bodies—both "real" bodies and representations of them—reified notions of Wari imperial supremacy and control.

The bioarchaeological study presented here examines the body both in terms of its physiology and in the ways it can be used as political and social currency. That is, the archaeological body is examined to reconstruct individual and population morbidity profiles and the ways that rituals of the body can shape the individual and society. Bodies were manipulated—dismembered and transformed—in the service of the state and as a dramatic way to control the populace. The manipulation of bodies also served the interests of those who engaged in the practice—the military agents and ritual specialists—whose actions were celebrated and valued in Wari society. The mutually benefiting aspects of particular practices thus ensured their ongoing performance, which helped to sustain Wari political authority for nearly four centuries and provided individuals in Wari society with important social and political roles. In turn, acts associated with those roles aided in maintaining Wari imperial dominance, and as a practice-based perspective would suggest, those actions ensured that the roles of military and ritual specialists were continually institutionalized. In this way, we can see the mutual constitution of the individual and society and agency and structure realized through military and ritual acts. As I discuss later, other mundane activities of daily life reveal other ways that Wari citizens were made and Wari society was constituted.

Theoretical Overview

Throughout the book, I employ a perspective that views imperial authority as a strong structural force in individual and community life—particularly in terms of shaping community organization, health outcomes, and likelihood for violence—with an agency-oriented approach that recognizes the role of individual and group action in shaping imperial policy specifically, and society more generally. In other words, Giddens's (1984) ideas on the recursive nature of agency and structure, of individual and society, are at work in this research—a theory of society that is sometimes difficult to integrate into studies of peoples that lived thousands of years ago. Nonetheless, this research strives to identify ways that individuals constituted society and how society shaped individuals, a quest that benefits from the bioarchaeological toolkit. Bioarchaeology, with its analytical focus on the body, is ideally suited to identify the health and lifeways of a person and recognize the role of the individual—all kinds of individuals, not just political leaders—in generating social norms, performing identity, and contributing to other aspects of society.

However, I also recognize that certain individuals are better positioned to embody authority and shape society (Sewell 2005), a perspective that may be viewed as "top-down," in which political leaders and other elites are seen as better positioned as architects of political and cultural norms and ways of being. A top-down view, particularly in studies of centralized states, is often described as part of a neoevolutionary framework that (overly) highlights the singular authority of political elites and the coercive nature of the state (Feinman and Marcus 1998), but that should not make it wholly incompatible with agency-oriented ideas about how society is constituted. Thus, although I agree with Sewell (2005) that some in society are better situated to effect change or enforce the status quo, I do not view those privileged persons as the sole generators and enforcers of behavioral norms, social identities, ideologies, or other facets of society. All actors play a role, and they are constantly in dialogue, mutually (re) generating social norms and deviations from them.

For bioarchaeology, this is important because it reveals the larger social orbit that can aid in understanding how, for example, violence emerges. Do the cranial fractures on an old female reflect—and then simultaneously generate—social norms about how women or the elderly in Wari society are to be treated? Or do those violence-related injuries represent a social transgression on the part of the attacker? If the former, Wari imperial policy that promoted the abduction of women may have contributed to the cruel treatment of some women in Wari communities. This exemplifies what I mean when I suggest that imperial policies and practices can profoundly shape the lives of ruling and subject peoples. But it is not a one-way path of influence. Imperial policies, community attitudes, and individual actions are all intertwined, each giving form to the other in a mutually constitutive manner. Bioarchaeology, then, with its ability to document lifeways at individual and population-level scales, is well suited to evaluate the recursive nature of individual and society and of agency and structure. It is also ideal for obtaining a "bottom-up" perspective, showing how all kinds of individuals can shape society. Thus, bioarchaeology, with its traditional strengths in document-ing the biological condition of humans, is also excellent for understanding as-pects of the complex social world in which humans live. In the study presented here, I aim not only to illuminate details about the Wari Empire and the role that violence played during its expansion and long-term rule, but also to show how bioarchaeology is embedded in the larger anthropological project to under-stand individuals and society and how both are constituted.

Book Organization

In the following chapter (chapter 2), I present the theoretical frameworks that inform this study, discussing general theories of states and empires and how those particular forms of political organization might structure health outcomes for particular segments of society. I also present an overview on theories about violence and warfare, and I discuss the oft-cited relationship between militarism and imperial expansion and how those linkages can be detected in the skeletal record. Additionally, I argue that analysis of skeletons and associated contexts can aid in clarifying the details of the recursive relationship between social struc-ture and individual agency. For example, data on the frequency and patterning of violence-related trauma, weaponry, and militaristic iconography provide in-sights on how social norms—or attempts to create them—may have shaped the likelihood that an individual would engage in violent acts, and reciprocally, how the practice of violence structures social norms and sets a precedent for ways of being in Wari society. I argue that certain kinds of violent acts served the interests of the state while simultaneously providing a path to power for those who performed the state-sanctioned violence and for those who celebrated the violent exploits.

Chapter 3 is an overview of the current state of knowledge on the Wari Empire. I summarize previous findings and explain how those earlier studies shaped the research program presented in this book. I also present background information on each of the three study populations in this study: one population from the site of Conchopata in the Wari imperial core and two archaeological populations from the sites of Beringa and La Real in the Majes valley of southern Peru, a region in the southern periphery of the Wari domain.

In chapter 4, I present data on the age-at-death and sex profiles at each site to reconstruct aspects of community organization. When I inquire about the form of "community organization" at a particular site, I am evaluating such things as whether, for example, the population was organized around small family units with a mother and father and offspring; a polygynous household with a man, several wives, and offspring; or a large group of related individuals with several generations living together and sharing resources and responsibilities. In addition to presenting the demographic profiles of particular tombs at Conchopata, I interpret ancient mtDNA results from a small subsample from Conchopata to begin addressing issues of kin-based burial traditions.

Documenting the sex profile is also essential for evaluating specific aspects of community organization. For example, a skewed sex profile with significantly more men than women may signal that a work party temporarily lived at the site, laboring on state projects. In contrast, a significant dearth of male skeletons may suggest that they were buried in an unexcavated portion of the site, revealing sex-specific mortuary practices. Conversely, it may signal that men were more mobile and died in distant locales, never to be properly buried in their natal settlement.

Through a study of the demographic profiles of Wari-era communities, I show how Wari imperial policies may have structured community organization, by encouraging (or forcing) temporary or permanent population movement to and from a settlement. As the demographic data reveal, there are atypical sex profiles at the heartland site of Conchopata and the hinterland site of La Real, intriguing observations that require further explanation. Indeed, in light of the military iconography in the Wari heartland, it may come as no surprise that the unequal sex distributions at the two sites may be related to militaristic activities, an idea that I explore in chapter 4 and the concluding chapter.

In chapter 5, I present data on violence-related trauma and accidental injury. The former data set is particularly essential for examining whether militarism and violence were central components of Wari imperial expansion and rule. Moreover, the heartland versus hinterland comparison that I employ in this book permits insights into how the era of Wari imperial rule differentially affected rates and kinds of violence for each community. Did Wari imperial authority aid in stabilizing tensions between communities, leading to a *pax Wari*, or enforced peace, throughout parts of the imperial domain? Or did the imperialistic enterprise intentionally employ militaristic strategies that resulted in trauma and death for particular groups? It is also possible that Wari policies inadvertently led to tensions and conflict by reshuffling political alliances and trade networks, essentially destabilizing regions both within and on the edges of the Wari imperial domain. The skeletal and iconographic evidence, as I discuss later, overwhelmingly indicates that militarism was an integral part of Wari imperial strategies for expansion and rule. The sex-based differences in violence-related trauma are also evaluated to explore gender roles in Wari society and examine how they differ in the heartland versus the hinterland.

Chapter 6 follows with a description of Wari trophy heads from Conchopata, a body of evidence that more fully explicates the role of militarism and violence in the Wari Empire. This is further exemplified by the strontium isotope data from the trophy heads and burials, which demonstrate that most trophy heads were from captives taken in foreign locales. Those individuals were not local ancestors who were dismembered and transformed into trophies, an interpretation that is well supported not only by the skeletal and strontium isotope data but also by the iconography. Integrated analysis of the trophy heads, skeletal trauma, and iconography also reveals how masculine identity may have been constructed in Wari society: an identity shaped by militaristic acts and trophy taking that served the interests of the Wari state, while also creating ways for individuals to author and reaffirm their high-status roles in Wari society.

The production of trophy heads, however, did not result purely from militaristic activities; ritual specialists also played an integral role in the creation of these icons of Wari authority. Given the perceived supernatural abilities of the ritual specialists, they transformed humans into trophy heads, likely making them cathected objects in the process. Simultaneously, those extraordinary trophy head objects reified the supernatural qualities of the ritual specialists. Thus, through the anthropogenic objects known as trophy heads, we see pathways to military and ritual authority for individuals, and we witness how particular social roles shaped Wari society and Wari imperial policies. Thus, through a discussion of warriors and ritual specialists, I explore the process of their identity construction in Wari society, while also showing how their practices simultaneously generated and reaffirmed the social structures that shaped their actions. In short, a study of these particular classes of persons reveals the recursive interaction between the individual's actions, the social structures that shape those actions, and how the actions shape the social structures.

I conclude the book in chapter 7 by integrating various lines of data—presented here and elsewhere—to reconstruct how Wari imperial policies and practices structured Wari health and lifeways, and how actions by individuals shaped Wari society and the Wari Empire. One of the conclusions that I advance is that the creation of a military class tasked with conducting and overseeing violent activities, combined with the creation of a ritual class that managed the ceremonial and ritual activities, was a crucial component in the expansion and maintenance of the Wari Empire.

A Few Words about Terms

Defining the terms *population* and *community*, as used in this study, is crucial because these can be differentially conceived in distinct settings and among different academic disciplines. The skeletal remains that derive from one archaeological site are referred to as one "population," even though the skeletal sample may not accurately represent the once-living population from which it was drawn (Paine and Boldsen 2002; Sattenspiel and Harpending 1983). (The chapter on demography explains this further and describes which sites are likely representative of the once-living group and which are not.) The term *community* can be a referent for several distinct concepts (Anderson 1991), and in the Andes it may refer to individuals who belong to a community organized beyond the level of the settlement. For example, the Andean concept of *ayllu* (an extended group of biological and fictive kin who share a common ancestor, real or imagined) can denote community membership at the suprasettlement level; thus, individuals from several sites may belong to the same ayllu. However, based on current data discussed here, there are no means to identify community membership at the suprasite level during the Wari era, so archaeological site affiliation is the defining criterion for community membership. In short, *community* is synonymous with *population* in the context of this study, unless otherwise noted.

I use the terms *the empire* and *the state* throughout the book, and although the phrases seem to reference a nonspecific, amorphous, acorporeal entity, I recognize that empires and states (the state is a subcategory of empire) and their policies and practices are created and maintained by individuals and human-made institutions populated by people. Yet, what distinguishes this level of organization from so-called pre-state-level societies is the potential disembodiment, or perceived disembodiment, of authority as it occurs through institutions. Individuals are cognizant of and personally experience the ways in which state structures and formal state institutions affect their lives, their family, and their community without necessarily having to place that authority in one particular person. (Think of the seemingly acorporeal entities known as the U.S. Internal Revenue Service [IRS] or even "the administration" at a large public university, though Uncle Sam and chancellors are meant to figuratively or literally personify those institutions.) Thus, I use phrases such as *the Wari Empire* and *the Wari state* as shorthand, while risking criticism for not always explicitly situating authority in the bodies of state agents (people). Having said that, when I think the data can point to an individual, a particular class of individuals, or even the abstract notion of an individual or group that is involved in certain tasks or responsible for particular events, I label them and describe them as such.

Bioarchaeology of Imperialism and Violence

Bioarchaeology—the study of human remains and associated contexts recovered from archaeology sites—is well suited to examine how ancient forms of imperialism shaped the health outcomes and lifeways of individuals in an imperial domain. It is also ideal for evaluating the relationship between imperialism and violence, for the human skeleton serves as a bony diary of a person's lived experience, including such serious incidences as violence. Violence—common though it may be in some societies—is an extraordinary act; it represents someone's attempt to kill another human being, or at least seriously harm them. How and in what social contexts is violence wielded, and to what ends? How was violence used in the ancient Andes, particularly during the rise and rule of the Wari Empire?

These questions are explored by analyzing skeletal trauma, trophy body parts, and, to a lesser degree, iconography. Data sources such as these have long been a fundamental part of research on violence and warfare (Martin and Frayer 1997; Verano 2001a). Those osteological data provide the foundation for documenting the frequency and population distribution of violence, and when integrated with other data sets, they permit a richly textured view of ancient life. Complementary data on demographic structure, health profiles, dietary practices, and material culture further illuminate the conditions that may have contributed to a violent act against a single person or systemic violence aimed at an entire subgroup. Although this book focuses primarily on the relationship between violence and imperialism as seen through skeletal trauma and trophy heads, I also include information on the population composition of the three Wari-era communities. Moreover, the data presented here are part of a larger research agenda that strives to examine various facets of life during periods of ancient imperialism. In other words, this study is part of a broader goal aimed at developing a bioarchaeology of imperialism, an area of study that uses its ideally suited focus on the human body to understand how imperial policies and practices affect individual and community life, and how individual actions shape imperial structures.

The Bioarchaeology of Imperialism

While the ways that modern states affect our lives today is quite apparent—from the taxes or state university tuitions we pay, to the safety of the foods and water we consume, to the likelihood that some will go to war—their effects remain poorly understood for many ancient states in the Americas. This study aims to ameliorate this shortcoming by showing how imperial processes and state structures affected the lives of people living in the pre-Hispanic Andes during the time of Wari imperial rule. This requires a comprehensive approach that I call "the bioarchaeology of imperialism," which examines the biological and social effects of imperial processes among the conquering and conquered groups, as well as those communities that are incompletely integrated into the imperial domain. Through a study of the human skeleton and its context, we can gain clearer insights into the lifeways of individuals who experienced significant changes in the social and political order and evaluate how particular social processes affected individual persons, groups of people, and whole communities. How did imperial policies structure the demographic makeup of a community, and how did imperial practices contribute to the prevalence of violence for particular groups of people? How did connections to imperial trade networks shape a community's access to exotic goods, which in turn may have altered their standing in a region? Could those new alliances also create new foes, contributing to intraregional conflict, not just conflict with the expanding empire? This book explores these and related questions to clarify understandings of Wari imperialism specifically and gain insights into imperial processes and effects more generally.

Imperial practices and their effects can vary within and between communities, so one of the goals of a bioarchaeological study of imperialism is to document how they vary. For example, an imperial polity might use military force in one region, which can lead to increased bodily injury and premature death among some, while in another region the expanding state may initiate increased trade networks leading to greater access to foodstuffs, exotic items, or other goods. In this way, we can see how imperial policies may have a negative impact in one arena and a positive outcome in another. To say that imperialism leads to variable outcomes is not enough—of course it can. But how does it vary? Does risk for violence increase while malnutrition decreases? Does it vary from person to person based on age, sex, or social status, or vary between entire communities based on their particular connections with the state? For example, militaristic activities or resource extractive policies could potentially lead to overall negative effects for an entire community, where little to no variation is seen between subgroups. Moreover, perceptions of a particular outcome as either positive or negative may differ depending on the circumstances. For example, is the outcome positive if an Andean community gains more access to the socially valued crop maize even though its use as a staple crop can sometimes lead to depressed nutritional health? Or that militarism increases risk for injury and early death but provides warriors with a path to power and status? Clearly, the people who lived in the Wari realm did not measure quality of life strictly based on counts of infant deaths, pathological lesions, or cranial fractures. Nevertheless, those skeletal observations are one of the best means to re-create their lifeways and begin to comprehend their life experiences.

Theoretical Frameworks for Seeing Empire from Bottom to Top

The policies and practices of states and empires have the potential to affect subjects' lives in profound ways, both in the modern era and in the ancient past. Through social and political institutions that are peopled by individual agents, states and empires are variably successful at achieving a variety of tasks and promoting or inhibiting particular behaviors by the populace. State authorities may collect tribute and help provide staple goods for all or some of the people, and they may prescribe what is legal or appropriate to eat and drink. This can affect the nutritional health status of the populace. State and imperial authorities may also institute policies that can lead to injury and death of many subjects, including systems of corporal punishment, judicial killing, and the sanctioning of war. State leaders can organize and manage public works projects too, ensuring that infrastructure is in place to support the productive activities of its populace. Powers such as these demonstrate that states and empires have the potential to be far-reaching and influential, profoundly affecting the lives of people that they attempt to claim within their realm.

However, the reach of state and imperial authorities may also be limited and spotty, and the policies and influence can be fully or incompletely embraced, renegotiated and incorporated with local policies, or totally rejected. People of various statuses and personal qualities are differentially affected by state and imperial policies, and diverse individuals or groups of people can also variously affect state and social structures (see Brumfiel 1992; Sewell 2005:127). For this reason, it is essential to document the categories and classes of people within an imperial domain and examine how they are affected by—and how they affect—the community, society, and structures of power in the state. And while families and communities can engage in practices that challenge state and imperial policies, actions by the populace may nonetheless be arbitrated through larger imperial agendas that may be to the detriment of local peoples. For example, imperial policies that hinder the production or distribution of nutritional foodstuffs will disproportionately impact the young, the elderly, and the ill; nutritious calories are a must for all, but especially so for developing or frail and healing bodies. Yet in recognizing that local groups can sometimes find ways to mitigate the potentially negative effects of state decisions, we can envision cases in which locals creatively secure access to more resources and enact a more equitable distribution of foods. This is only one of the many ways that top-down imperial policies may be mediated through local people acting in particular social circumstances and environmental contexts.

The reverse is true too: action from the "bottom up," say, local decisions about preferred trade routes, local agricultural practices, or the appropriateness of particular marriage partners, can shape imperial policies and the ways that imperial elites might interact with local leaders. Although local agricultural practices might dictate the ongoing production of certain crops, imperial engineering projects, such as the Wari-orchestrated water canal systems in the middle Moquegua valley (Williams 2002), might increase crop output for storage, feasting events, or tribute to imperial elites. In this way, we can see how imperial and local interests intertwine, leading to negotiated outcomes, both intended and unintended. Some of the unintended consequences might include reduced nutritional status, resulting from the homogenization of crop production, and thus, loss of diversity in the diet. Other outcomes might include the development of a military class, as individuals initiate resistance to, or collaborate with, imperial forces. In this context, we can identify how a novel social class was constituted and, through bioarchaeological analysis, evaluate how the constitution and performance of that particular social role shaped the health status and lived experience for an individual or subgroup.

Bioarchaeology is well suited to examine the lifeways of individuals from ancient communities, which also aids in a privileged perspective from the bottom up. Bottom-up perspectives more readily identify the interests and actions of various individuals and the resulting contentiousness and cooperation that constitute society (Bourdieu 1977; Giddens 1984). That is, through direct skeletal evidence, we can observe ways that individuals constitute society through their actions, whether in terms of how infants are cared for or in terms of how violence is enacted against others. And with population-level skeletal data and other insights from the archaeological record, we can also view how society structures normative behaviors and common health profiles, as well as deviations from them.

State and imperial regulations, or the lack thereof, also interact with more personal qualities to structure health outcomes and access to resources, political power, and social networks. These personal traits interacting with state policies can also shape economic, occupational, and marriage opportunities (Sewell 2005:124–25). For example, a woman's kinship network may structure her access to potential marriage partners, and a person's age, sex, or health status can affect his or her ability to use political or violent means to challenge nascent or well-established state systems. Take, for example, the premise that men in many societies may be better positioned to gain access to military training and technology, as well as the attendant powers and obligations that come with those associations. By virtue of a particular personal quality—what we identify as a person's sex, for example—we can witness how social forces shape some of the opportunities available to that individual. Another example can be seen in how certain anomalous birth characteristics may predispose a person to a particular role in society. For example, in Inka society, dwarves were often perceived to have supernatural qualities, and they often became ritual specialists or court attendants tasked with significant ritual and ceremonial obligations (Rowe 1966). In contrast, some physical traits that a community identifies as abnormal (such as birth defects and acquired injuries) may push them to the margins of society, negatively impacting both their social and their biological well-being.

Although I note the ways in which certain personal characteristics or bodily conditions can affect one's role in society, these traits and the social structures that shape the outcomes are not predetermined. Discursive interactions between individuals and social structures have the potential to both reproduce state and social structures and transform them in novel ways. That is, while structures place "constraints on human agency," they are simultaneously enabling (Giddens 1976:161), providing the means and methods for carrying out particular acts. Sewell (2005) explains this further, noting that Giddens's conception "implies that those agents are capable of putting their structurally formed capacities to work in creative and innovative ways. And if enough people, *or even a few people who are powerful enough*, act in innovative ways, their action may have the consequence of transforming the very structures that gave them the capacity to act" (Sewell 2005:127; italics mine). This indicates that certain individuals are better positioned to benefit from particular state and societal structures, while others are not, and suggests that some are also better able to maintain the status quo or enact change, adjusting circumstances to their preferences. These variable potentials to act and react likely had serious implications for one's health status, family organization, and risk for violence.

Theoretical Frameworks for Seeing Empire from Heartland to Hinterland

This study categorizes skeletal populations into those from the Wari heartland (imperial core) and those from the Wari hinterland (periphery), which might suggest a perspective situated in world systems theory (Wallerstein 1974b) with a dominant core exerting control and extracting resources from groups in the semiperiphery and periphery. As Stein (2002) notes, our analytical vocabulary—terms like heartland versus hinterland and core versus periphery—presupposes "an inherently unequal relationship where the former controls, or at the very least, influences the latter" (Stein 2002:904). While previous archaeological research of the Wari Empire suggests that the Ayacucho Basin served as a political and social center from which policies were crafted and put into practice, this investigation attempts to identify how groups in the periphery determined the nature of interregional interaction and how peripheral groups could undermine the dominance of the imperial core. At the least, particular local ideologies and practices would have required the imperial center to reformulate policies and enact new methods of sociopolitical integration or resource extraction, if those were indeed imperial goals. Furthermore, the interaction between core and periphery need not have been based upon continuous marked inequalities that were characterized by unbalanced extraction of labor and resources and general exploitation of peripheral populations (Sinopoli 1994). Peripheral regions also gained access to previously rare goods through their interaction with the imperial center, and they may have promoted the desirability of particular goods for consumption by those in the imperial heartland.

When Wallerstein initially crafted his world systems theory, he did so to analyze the economic connections between modern nation-states (or ill-defined boundaries of world regions) and explain structural global inequality that arose in the European colonial era around the early 16th century. Archaeologists then built on those ideas to investigate the political economy of archaic states and empires (Abu-Lughod 1989; Kohl 1987; Mathien et al. 1986; Plog 1983), despite Wallerstein's initial claims that a world system did not exist prior to the end of the 15th century. (In this, he does not mean "world" system as encompassing the entire globe; rather, he is stressing that the modern global economic system is "larger than any juridically-defined political unit" [Wallerstein 1974a:15]). He later recognized that studies of precapitalist systems may benefit from a world systems approach, while also providing insights into the development and effects of recent and modern world systems (Wallerstein 1990).

Despite critiques of world systems theory (Kohl 1987; Simpson 1990; Stein 2002), one of its basic tenets—core-periphery inequality—sets up expectations regarding how the process of imperialism might contribute to institutionalized social hierarchy and its attendant inequalities. In the field of bioarchaeology, documenting social inequalities is of paramount interest, as this has been shown to have a profound impact on one's morbidity, such as through access to nutritious foodstuffs, succumbing to infectious disease, or exposure to violence.

A serious problem with world systems theory, however, is the overemphasis on the power of core populations, elites in particular, to author and promote social inequality. These inequalities do not emerge solely at the hands of a core elite well situated within a state apparatus, nor are various kinds of inequalities fully realized, despite concerted efforts by some to create marked disparities in health, wealth, and status. This is because—and critiques of world systems theory have contributed much to this recognition—peripheral populations are not merely subordinate homogenous masses wholly subjugated by a dominant core. Rather, various factions have the capacity to author distinct policies and carry out unique practices that may or may not be aligned with the core or the dominant class (Brumfiel 1996; Brumfiel 2001; Joyce 2003). Thus, a study of archaic forms of imperialism must recognize the creative and generative role of both core and peripheral polities. This dovetails with general understandings of how structure and agency are at play in human societies, showing the recursive interaction between imperial policies that can structure human behavior, and individual agency that is both reflective and generative of larger societal structures.

Ongoing negotiations between ruling and subject classes destabilize the notion of an imperial core as the sole and determinative author of ideology and policy promulgated to subjects in the periphery. As noted above, while imperial policies can contribute to structural constraints for those living in an imperial domain, those structures and how individuals respond to and challenge them simultaneously enable action. These actions by various peoples, in turn, create the social and political structures that guide, restrict, and generate human agency. In this way, it becomes clear that elites in the imperial core are not the only actors playing a role in the process of imperial expansion and governance. This is not to assume that there is parity in all categories of interaction, nor is it to assume that the core is dominant in all of them; instead, researchers should examine the process of interactions and evaluate their outcomes. As a bioarchaeological investigation, this work is particularly interested in the biocultural effects of those interactions.

In this discussion, I have likened imperial policies to structure, which in turn limits and enhances the agency of humans within the imperial realm. But this is somewhat misleading. I do not mean to suggest that imperial policies and programs are *the* structuring components in society. To the contrary, numerous factors structure society; religious affiliation, shared histories or landscapes, and common ideologies can structure behaviors, just as one's age or sex can shape actions and opportunities. That is, because social structures that constrain and enable action are diffuse, permeating society at all levels, the imperial agenda is not the only thing that guides individual behavior and determines outcomes. The family (however defined), peer groups, the local community, trade communities, and beyond can all circumscribe and enable human agency, and, recursively, individuals can affect societal structures at a variety of levels. Thus, one goal of this study is to identify how this process occurs, particularly during a time of imperial expansion.

A Social Bioarchaeology

Rather than viewing the human body solely as a fixed, biological, presocial being, social bioarchaeology is an approach that more accurately reflects the biological and social conditions that shaped the lives and health profiles of ancient peoples. Through the integration of bioarchaeological data (demographic, paleopathological, genetic, isotopic, and so forth) with data on material culture and insights from theories on the evolution of disease, middle range theory, and structuration theory, among others, a social bioarchaeological framework documents disease and trauma prevalence, evaluating their epidemiological factors, and examines how community health and demography can shape social dynamics and political organization. Recursively, it also evaluates how social and political structures shape disease and demographic profiles. It is an explicit recognition that social and historical circumstances can structure health outcomes and show, for example, how a particular subgroup or specific individual is at higher risk for violence-related trauma, accidental injury, infectious disease, osteoarthritis, or iron-deficiency anemia.

Although the genetic profile and biological condition of an individual certainly shape susceptibility to infectious disease or sensitivity to bone fractures, there are other social factors that structure particular states of health and how a community might define and respond to disease and violence. On the one hand, data on age and sex profiles and morbidity levels are important in and of themselves, for they reveal significant information about fertility, mortality, and the distribution and evolution of disease. On the other hand, these observations provide more than biological health data; they are instrumental to understanding the social organization and political structure of ancient societies. Without information on sex ratios (and biological affiliations), we could never begin to reconstruct family organization in prehistoric populations, whether as a polyandrous family group, a heterosexual and (presumably) monogamous mating pair, an extended family group of biological kin and affines, or some other family form.

In other words, bioarchaeologists should use the demographic, morbidity, and other skeletal data to reconstruct the social dynamics and political organization of past populations, moving the discipline beyond traditional reports on age and sex ratios and skeletal lesion frequencies. Because the broader summaries and interpretations are typically left to the principal investigator (usually an archaeologist) (Sofaer 2006), skeletal data are often interpreted by someone other than the bioarchaeologist, which can sometimes lead to incomplete integration of skeletal data with the larger corpus of site and regional data. This is not to suggest that archaeologists have done a disservice to skeletal studies; to the contrary, the majority of archaeologists have gone to great lengths to include osteologists and other specialists on projects. Rather, bioarchaeologists need to increase involvement in research programs from early development of research agendas to the broad-scale interpretations. This particular approach follows in the footsteps of Buikstra's important call to get bioarchaeologists "out of the appendix and into the dirt" (Buikstra 1991) and Sofaer's eloquent argument for bioarchaeologists to engage more fully in the anthropological interpretations of the osteological data (Sofaer 2006).

This study strives to address those calls and uses bioarchaeological methods to identify demographic and morbidity profiles and examine how they correlate to particular social and environmental contexts. Thus, in subsequent chapters I report age-at-death and sex distributions, combined with preliminary mtDNA data on haplogroup identification and strontium isotope ratios to distinguish between locals and foreigners. I also examine how population profiles differed between the heartland and hinterland communities, data that are used to evaluate the various forms of family structure and community organization within the Wari world.

The frequency and distribution of skeletal trauma, both intentional and accidental, are also presented to infer how violence and physical activity were patterned during the time of Wari imperialism. For example, if Wari imperial strategy used militarism to expand, or if the expansion contributed to social unrest and conflict, then there should be evidence for violence-related trauma. Similarly, if Wari militarism included prisoner capture and trophy taking, likely tools of imperial expansion, then there should be nonlocal individuals present at heartland sites and physical remains of trophy heads and other trophy body parts.

A social bioarchaeological approach aims to document more than the health outcomes of imperial policies and practices. It strives to demonstrate how the body is an agent and a tool in the development and implementation of imperial policy. That is, while imperial practices may mark the body—literally, in terms of skull fractures that may represent warfare instigated by the state, chop marks that indicate sacrifice for imperial agendas, or skeletal lesions that reflect poor nutrition resulting from unfair food distribution policies— the body also serves as a type of currency in imperial and local community agendas.

The body is the locus through which agendas are constructed and contested, and, as bioarchaeologists, we have privileged access to those narratives. For example, we can inquire how warriors were made, how their bodies were put in service of the state, or how they may have challenged state authority. In answering those questions, we can see how bioarchaeology reveals how bodies, both living and dead, may have been used for political and other ends. For example, powerful militarized bodies and the subservient prisoners that were portrayed in Wari art may have their corporeal counterpart in the scarred skeletons of Wari warriors and dismembered bodies of captives. This would demonstrate that some Wari individuals engaged in violent behaviors and provide glimpses into how individual aggressiveness was either a pathway to authority or a marker of social ostracism. Further, the bioarchaeological, artifactual, and iconographic data can be used to examine whether individual aggressiveness was actively promoted in Wari communities and linked to militarism and other state goals. State-sponsored celebrations of violent exploits, the privileged placement of dismembered bodies, and artistic representations of those acts could have been powerful means for communicating particular ways of being in Wari society. Thus, through a contextualized analysis that views the body as both a product of behaviors and a generative force in shaping social norms, we can more fully realize a bioarchaeology that is about both inferring human behavior through a reconstruction of health, disease, and diet (sensu Larsen 1997) and inferring political, social, and economic agendas in which the body is a form of material culture (sensu Sofaer 2006).

Violence

The analysis of violence-related trauma is one of the most important avenues of bioarchaeological inquiry; it has the potential to reveal how and why violence was used against another person to kill or injure. It can be one of the most revealing in terms of understanding ancient social organization, attitudes about gender roles and class divisions, and the role of the state. All morbidity data are important pieces of the bioarchaeological puzzle, but data on violence-related trauma are particularly revealing. For example, while some skeletal lesions indicate nutritional deficiency, the causes of poor nutrition may be unclear. They could be from widespread crop failure, poor food distribution, or intentional food hoarding meant to harm certain individuals. Data on violence-related trauma, in contrast, tell a story of direct action that was intended to harm or kill another person. The intensity and intentionality of this particular kind of action should not be overlooked. It is one of the best and most direct connections that we have for understanding the intentions of past peoples and inferring significant details about the societies in which the violence emerged.

Imperialism and Violence

The process of state and imperial expansion may have created a social environment conducive to high levels of violence and skeletal injury, possibly generated by warfare or other forms of interpersonal or intergroup conflict. Several scholars working in the materialist framework have attributed the rise and expansion of states to warfare (Carneiro 1970; Cohen 1984; Fried 1961; Hassig 1988), positing that the state develops from contestation over access to productive land and resources, particularly in environmentally circumscribed zones (Carneiro 1970), while others suggest that although warfare was not the prime mover in state development and expansion, it still contributed in significant ways (Webster 1975). In the northern Andes, Dagget (1987) has argued that warfare contributed to increasing sociopolitical complexity and state development, conclusions that are primarily based on settlement pattern data, defensible site locations, and defensive architecture. In the Inka Empire, military power as a means for imperial expansion has been documented both ethnohistorically and archaeologically (Bauer 1992; D'Altroy 1992; Earle 1997). However, while these important studies on the Inka have demonstrated the connection between increasing social control and the threat or actual use of force, direct evidence of violence in the form of skeletal trauma is still wanting (but see Andrushko 2007 for Inka studies). Analysis of data on violence-related skeletal trauma remains the most convincing method for evaluating the relationship between violence and both state formation and imperial expansion and for exploring how violence structures political organization and the contours of society.

Prior to this study, archaeological research had shown that the development and expansion of the Wari Empire may have included militarism, combined with religio-ideological indoctrination (Isbell and McEwan 1991a; Menzel 1964; Menzel 1977; Schreiber 1992), which was ultimately backed by "an administratively and militarily strong Huari" (Isbell and McEwan 1991a:7). Lumbreras (1974) also noted the role of Wari militarism as a means of expansion and suggested that the Wari conquerors exerted domination by force and squelched foreign lifeways, thereby leading to a despotic regime headed by a strong, centrally controlled Wari administration. To assess these claims of militarism and conflict in Wari expansion, archaeological and osteological data sets should be evaluated. For example, data on settlement patterns, defensible site locations, and defensive architecture can elucidate how and to what extent particular communities were concerned with issues of defense (Allen and Arkush 2006; Arkush 2008). However, these archaeological characteristics, as essential as they are, do not indicate whether physical conflict in fact took place. Skeletal trauma, in contrast, is an excellent proxy for ascertaining the frequency of violence among members of a community, and data on the age and sex of those with trauma give insight into the nature and social contexts of the violence.

Violence at Imperial Margins

Although warfare and raiding are often linked to expanding states, violence need not be confined to the conqueror and conquered; violence between indigenous groups within or at the edges of the imperial domain may emerge or become heightened as a result of changes ushered in by imperial influence in a region (see Ferguson and Whitehead 1992). In archaeological contexts, conflict between conquerors and the conquered versus conflict between neighboring conquered groups can be difficult to discern. Nevertheless, the studies in the volume edited by Ferguson and Whitehead (1992) send a cautionary message; the presence of skeletal trauma among subject populations does not necessarily imply that it was directly perpetrated by agents of the imperial power (nor does the violence-related trauma mean that physical conflict was present prior to the arrival of the imperial or colonial influence). Rather, the social upheaval and physical conflict between indigenous groups may have been instigated by new imperial policies and practices that destabilized preimperial/precolonial relations, even in areas where no direct imperial presence is evident.

Violence in Various Contexts

Violence-related skeletal trauma is often linked to warfare, including battles, raids, massacres, and sieges, between autonomous political groups, particularly when the trauma coincides with a time of imperial expansion. However, violence may emerge in a variety of contexts, not just battles or raids. Other categories of violence can include domestic violence, corporal punishment, physical conflict resolution (such as club fights), and ritual battles, all of which can lead to serious bodily injury (Chagnon and Bugos 1979; Conklin 2001; Counts et al. 1999; Martin 1997; Smith 2003; Verano 1995; Walker 2001). Documenting the frequency and locational distribution of wounds on the body, as well as distinguishing between lethal versus nonlethal wounds, can aid in discerning between types of violent encounters. Also, comparing male and female skeletal wound frequencies and patterns provides insight into the social contexts in which violence occurred (Lambert 1994; Robb 1997; Walker 2001; Wilkinson and Van Wagenen 1993).

Warfare

Violence that occurs in the context of warfare can lead to serious bodily injury and sometimes death because attacks in war are often undertaken with lethal intent. As such, embedded projectile points (Lambert 1994; Tomasto 2009) or perimortem fractures to the skull may be good evidence for warfare, especially if a sizeable percentage of draft-age males exhibit those wounds (Walker 2001). But not all warfare injuries are necessarily lethal; good defenses and treatment can lead to survival and healed wounds. If sublethal trauma is sustained in war, then healed wounds may reflect warfare battles or raids earlier in a person's life (Walker 1989). Again, the frequency and age and sex distribution of cranial trauma can aid in evaluating whether injuries were sustained in war (for example, cranial trauma among young to midadult males). The spatial distribution of wounds can also aid in interpreting the context; anterior head wounds in particular are often interpreted as evidence for battle injuries in which combatants squared off face-to-face (Lambert 1994; Walker 1989, 2001; Webb 1995).

Additionally, victims may exhibit healed injuries if the intent of the assailant was prisoner capture and not (immediate) death. Some cultural groups, such as the Aztecs, focused on capturing prisoners alive for later sacrifice and the creation of war trophies (Hassig 1988). Thus, evidence for sacrifice and the presence of trophy body parts may suggest that war-related activities occurred, followed by elaborate rituals involving human sacrifice and bodily dismemberment for the purpose of making war trophies.

Physical Conflict Resolution

The importance of documenting injury traits, and their various causes, is illustrated in a study by Lambert (1994:119), in which she suggests that the prehistoric Chumash from southern California engaged in face-to-face fighting akin to physical conflict resolution. She notes that the perimortem cranial fractures were distinct in "severity and intent from the sub-lethal [cranial] wounds"; the perimortem wounds were larger and concentrated on the side and posterior of the cranium, while sublethal wounds were smaller and located on the anterior. Moreover, based on the association of projectile point injuries and perimortem head trauma, Lambert (1994:119) suggests that "when a lethal blow was administered, the lethality of the blow was intentional rather than accidental." In the case of the nonlethal head wounds, their patterned location on the frontal bones of males suggests that they were received in standardized face-to-face combat (Lambert 1994; also see Walker 1989), similar to nonlethal conflict resolutions, such as club fights, practiced by the Jalé of New Guinea (Koch 1974), the Yanomamo of Venezuela (Chagnon 1992), and the Oro-Warí of the Brazilian Amazon (Conklin 2001). Lambert's (1994) study eloquently demonstrates how data on wound frequency, wound type (that is, nonlethal versus lethal), and the spatial distribution of wounds (where the wounds are located on the body) can be marshaled to reconstruct levels of violence, intentionality, and the cultural context in which violent encounters occurred.

Ritual Battles: Tinku

Ethnographic studies in the Andes have also documented a form of ritual battle known as *tinku* in the Peruvian and Bolivian Andes (Allen 1988; Bolin 1998; Brachetti 2001; Gifford et al. 1976; Hartmann 1972; Orlove 1994; Sallnow 1987; Schuller and Petermann 1992; Schultz 1988) and *juego de la pucara* (game of the fortress) in Ecuador (Chacon et al. 2004). During tinku, two communities converge to engage in violent battles in which one of the goals is to shed the blood of an opponent. Although these ritual battles sometimes lead to deaths, the acts are primarily sublethal and are meant to release blood as an offering to the earth for a bountiful harvest; the ritual battles are scheduled to correspond with festivals or the maize harvest (Bolin 1998; Gifford et al. 1976; Hartmann 1972; Orlove 1994).

While physical fights are certainly key components of tinku, it is not perceived to be entirely hostile by the participants, because this ritualized joining together of opposites is meant to maintain balance and harmony (Allen 1988; Bolin 1998; Gifford et al. 1976; Hartmann 1972). As one of Bolin's informants from Chillhuani (in the Peruvian highlands) states, the tinku "is not done in the mood of hostility. Instead it causes solidarity. It brings fertility for all" (Bolin 1998:95). Nevertheless, the fighting can be brutal, and while the ultimate goal is harmony, the proximate goal that brings this about is bloodshed and prisoner taking. Based on his observations of tinku in Ch'iaraje (southern Peruvian Andes), Orlove notes that "the goal of the fighting was to take prisoners. . . . [T]here had been several such prisoners who had been taken to the lands of the other side, stripped, beaten and killed. [T]he prisoners corpses [were] sometimes decapitated" (Orlove 1994:135). Killings are often perpetrated in response to killings from the previous year; thus, there appears to have been an element of revenge in this cyclical event (Orlove 1994).

Tinku typically involves men who square off in face-to-face fighting or hurl stones at each other with a sling (Allen 1988; Bolin 1998; Gifford et al. 1976; Hartmann 1972; Orlove 1994; Schuller and Petermann 1992; see figure 5.20). Women occasionally participate in the battles and are sometimes taken as prisoners, but this is relatively rare (Allen 1988; Bolin 1998; Schuller and Petermann 1992). The fighting can be vicious and the injuries serious, often resulting in severe head trauma (figure 5.20). While some of the ethnographic literature emphasizes killings during tinku, most injuries are nonlethal (Allen 1988; Arkush and Stanish 2005; Bolin 1998; Chacon et al. 2004; Hartmann 1972; Orlove 1994; Schuller and Petermann 1992; Schultz 1988). These ethnographic and historical data remind us that ritual battles similar to tinku could have occurred prior to Spanish conquest. If so, then these ethnographic studies, coupled with biological and archaeological data, may give clues to ancient behaviors.

Corporal Punishment

Empires have legal codes that proscribe some behaviors and define social practice, and transgressions may be met with punitive actions, such as corporal punishment. According to historical accounts, the Inka Empire, which flourished four centuries after the decline of the Wari, used corporal punishment to prosecute what was deemed inappropriate behavior (Cobo 1892 [1653]:3:xxi, xxvii, 238, 240–41; Moore 1958; Murúa 1946 [1590]:xx, 70, 211, 213; Valera 1945 [1585]:58). Physical punishment included hanging, whippings, and lethal and nonlethal stonings. The latter would have occasionally generated bone fractures, particularly on the cranium, and would, therefore, be visible in the skeletal record. Punishable offenses that warranted stonings included hunting without permission (Cobo 1892 [1653]:3:xxi, xxvii, 241), a poorly executed labor project (Murúa 1946 [1590]:xx, 70), disobeying a native nobleman (*curaca*) (Cobo 1892 [1653]:3:xxi, xxvii, 240), rape of a virgin (Valera 1945 [1585]:58), and stealing food from a non-Inka (Cobo 1892 [1653]:3:xxi, xxvii, 240). A curaca could also be punished by blows with a stone if he ordered an imperial subject to death without obtaining proper authority (Murúa 1946 [1590]:xx, 213, 238). The punishment could also vary depending on one's sex and familial status. If a man fled his hometown, he could be stoned to death, while a childless woman could be hanged for the same offense, but a woman with children received some other unspecified punishment (Moore 1958; Murúa 1946 [1590]:xx, 211).

Although nothing is known of Wari judicial practices, a study of Wari-era skeletal trauma should consider the possibility that some wounds were inflicted as a state- or community-sanctioned punishment. Notably, if this was a practice sanctioned by the Wari state, then perhaps this partially formed the foundation for later Inka laws and associated forms of corporal punishment.

The Wari Empire in the Andean World

The Wari Empire expanded from its capital, the site of Huari, in the Ayacucho Basin of modern-day Peru to encompass huge swaths of Andean lands, from pockets of coastal regions to vast sections of productive midvalley agricultural lands and smaller areas of high-altitude mountain zones. Before the Middle Horizon (see table 3.1), no other Andean society had achieved such widespread influence, nor had any group distributed its telltale architectural and iconographic styles to such far-flung Andean regions. Wari administrative sites and architecture in distant locales—from Cerro Baúl in the Moquegua valley of southern Peru to Pikillacta in the Cusco region and Viracochapampa (and other smaller Wari sites) in Huamachuco of northern highland Peru—all point to conquest, collaboration, and/or incorporation of groups that lived far from the Wari imperial heartland. The widespread distribution of Wari textiles and ceramics and the occasional Wari-style trophy head outside of the imperial core further demonstrate Wari's influence in a vast region, while also showing various levels of interaction with the imperial center. The overall process of Wari imperial expansion—even with its variable intrusion and influence—would have reshuffled local, regional, and supraregional political, social, and economic networks, profoundly affecting conquering and subject groups and perhaps those on the margins (see Barfield 2001; Ferguson and Whitehead 1992).

In recognition of the fact that empires rarely use one monolithic strategy to incorporate other communities into their domain, this study aims to document

Table 3.1. Andean chronology

Time period	Dominant polities	Dates
Late Horizon	Inka	AD 1450–1532
Late Intermediate Period	Regional polities	AD 1000/1100–1450
Middle Horizon	Wari and Tiwanaku	AD 600–1000/1100
Early Intermediate Period	Regional polities	AD 1–550/600
Early Horizon	Chavín	800 BC–AD 1

variability in imperial and local policies and practices, and how they differentially impacted Wari-era groups. To that end, this study takes a comparative approach, examining life- and deathways in the imperial heartland and the southern hinterland. What were those effects for various peoples living in distinct areas of the Wari realm? And how did peoples' actions and reactions affect the nature of Wari governance and strategies of control?

Much of the recent information regarding Wari imperialism and its effects derives from archaeological data, such as that culled from analysis of architecture, settlement patterns, and portable material culture. Scholars working in the Andes have shown that there were concomitant changes in iconography, architecture, urban planning, settlement patterns, and other aspects of material culture during the Wari era, all of which have served to elucidate social and political transformations that may have been instigated by the Wari (Cook 1992, 2001; Czwarno et al. 1989; Isbell 1984; Isbell and Cook 1987; Isbell and McEwan 1991; Isbell and Schreiber 1978; McEwan 1996; Schreiber 1992, 2001; Stone-Miller and McEwan 1990; Treacy 1989; Williams 2001). Despite these pioneering and foundational investigations, however, no studies have analyzed Wari-era skeletal remains from both heartland and hinterland populations to assess their population profiles, forms of social organization, prevalence of violence, and rituals of the body. This means that we have an incomplete picture of the important cultural and biological changes related to the rise and dominance of the Wari. Thus, this bioarchaeological study contributes new, yet complementary, insights into how the first instance of imperialism in the ancient Andes affected individual and community lifeways.

Although the southern, highland Andes was home to the Tiwanaku state, which became a powerful polity approximately fifty or a hundred years before the Wari, those political elites do not appear to have created expansionist policies like those of the Wari, such that large groups of unrelated, distant populations were brought within the Tiwanaku political sphere. Data on settlement patterns, material culture, cranial modification styles (Torres-Rouff 2002), and migration patterns as gleaned through artifactual and settlement pattern data (Goldstein 2005) and strontium isotope analysis (Knudson et al. 2004) suggest that Tiwanaku's sphere of control was less extensive and hegemonic than that of the Wari. These differences in state strategy, and the ability to carry out expansionistic policies, suggest that Wari state leaders and other Wari agents with decision-making power were the first to develop and execute policies that called for large-scale expansion and incorporation of other communities.

Of course, this does not mean that the Wari always successfully implemented their imperial policies, nor does it mean that the Wari attempted to conquer or incorporate all groups in the Andean region. Rather, the key point here is that from the seventh to 11th centuries AD, there was a new level of political and social integration never before witnessed in the Andes. This major sociopolitical transformation thus necessitates an investigation of the process, and how these changes affected Andean lifeways, and how Andean lifeways affected this change.

The development of Wari imperial policies and the means for implementing them would not have arisen in isolation. Surely, Wari and Tiwanaku heavily influenced one another, each contributing to the other's state policies and variable successes in implementing and adapting them (Janusek 2008). Furthermore, Wari and Tiwanaku shared some cultural material styles and aspects of religion and ideology (Cook 1994), and they also affected each other's settlement patterns and landscape transformation projects, particularly in the Moquegua valley of southern Peru (Williams and Nash 2005). In light of their contemporaneity but distinct policies on expansion, conquest, and state governance more generally, the question arises: how did Wari state leaders and others in Wari society initiate and maintain widespread influence and conquest over particular communities?

It is no easy task to convince others to adopt new social practices, whether consuming different foods and drink, burying your dead in a new way, or engaging in violent acts or formalized warfare. Similarly, the group that Wari leaders were attempting to incorporate may have been disinclined to adopt new material goods for a variety of reasons, ranging from different aesthetic preferences to reluctance to assume new social practices that the novel icons or objects were meant to generate (for example, new weapons for more-lethal violence, more irrigation canals for increased production of crops for tribute, or iconographic representations of new deities that were to be incorporated into, or to replace, existing belief systems). Although I have noted these changes in terms of Wari state agents attempting to integrate (or force) these upon new populations, local groups could have sought these novel symbols and practices on their own accord. That is, Wari symbols and practices may have been adopted by other populations for reasons of personal preference, usefulness, and/or a desire to associate oneself with the meanings and perhaps status-enhancement qualities that could be tied to particular objects, icons, or foods. In either case—imposition by Wari state agents or independent adoption by other groups—many people during this era (at least more than in any preceding time) would have seen and experienced a relatively more Wari-dominated world, and this likely had a profound impact on many people's lives.

What, then, were those effects, particularly in terms of community health and rituals involving the body (for example, mortuary rites and trophy head display)? The remaining chapters aim to examine those questions, but first, I briefly summarize the history of Wari studies that have brought scholars to the point where nuanced questions about imperial and local policies and practices and their consequences can be examined.

The Wari Study Samples

To gain insights into how the process of Wari imperialism affected the lives of people within the Wari sphere, I analyze skeletal populations from both the imperial heartland and the southern hinterland; this provides the necessary data sets to evaluate how the Wari Empire may have differentially affected morbidity, mortality, and rituals of the body (funerary and other). In turn, this allows for a greater understanding of the methods and effects of ancient imperial expansion. To this end, I examined 621 skeletal individuals, not all of which were complete, from three sites: one in the Wari heartland and two in the southern hinterland (figure 3.1).

> Conchopata: a large, urban Wari site in the Ayacucho Basin (that is, the
>   Wari heartland)
> Beringa: a village site with domestic and mortuary contexts in the middle
>   Majes valley
> La Real: a ceremonial and mortuary site also in the middle Majes valley

Given the importance of archaeological context, each site is discussed in detail below.

Discovering Huari and the Wari Empire

The term *Wari* means honored ancestor (Schreiber 2001) and appears to have been attributed to the capital site after it was initially called Viñaque by Spanish chroniclers. Two spellings are used to refer to this ancient society: Wari and Huari. In this study, I follow Isbell's designation, in which *Wari* refers to the culture (for example, Wari Empire, Wari communities, Wari ceramics) and *Huari* refers specifically to the archaeology site—the capital of the Wari Empire—located in the Department of Ayacucho.

When the Spanish chronicler Pedro de Cieza de León encountered ancient ruins in the central Andes, near the modern city of Ayacucho, he was correct in attributing them to a pre-Inkan society. After Cieza de León's 16th-century visit to those impressive structures, the site remained virtually unknown until Julio Tello published images of stone statues from Huari in his book *Antiguo Perú* (1929) and described the site in a Lima newspaper article in 1931 (Tello 1970). Two decades passed before archaeological investigations began at Huari

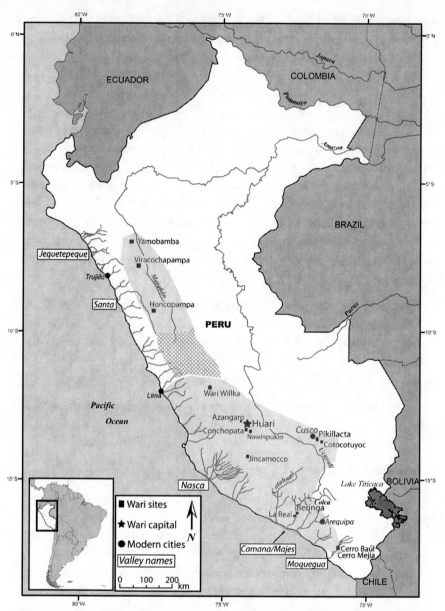

Figure 3.1. Map of Peru. Shaded areas show regions within the Wari Empire. The checkered area is an understudied zone, so Wari presence there is unclear.

(Bennett 1954; Rowe et al. 1950). As a result, the Wari Empire is relatively understudied compared to the Tiwanaku polity and the later Inka Empire (AD 1450–1532). Moreover, intensive violent conflict between the Maoist rebel group the Shining Path (*Sendero Luminoso*) and the Peruvian military from the late 1970s to the early 1990s prevented many foreign scholars from conducting research in Ayacucho, where numerous Wari sites are located. Faculty and students from the local university (Universidad Nacional de San Cristóbal de Huamanga), however, conducted limited, small-scale excavations during this time, contributing important insights into our understanding of Wari society. In 1992, the Shining Path leader, Abimael Guzman, was captured, and relative stability returned to the central Andes. With this, numerous excavations at Wari heartland sites were initiated, rapidly increasing our knowledge of this Middle Horizon empire and its people. This study is part of that second wave of research in the Ayacucho Basin.

Wari within the Andean Chronology

Human populations have occupied the Andes for at least twelve thousand years, and during the past three thousand years the region has been characterized by cycles of "horizons"—times of widespread homogeneity in art, architecture, and culture, interspersed with periods of distinct, heterogeneous cultures (table 3.1) (Willey 1991). One of these horizons is characterized by the rise and spread of the Wari Empire (and the rise of the Tiwanaku state in the southern Andes). Before detailing the specific era of Wari imperial influence, I briefly describe the preceding horizons and periods.

The Early Horizon (800 BC–AD 1) was the first time that an artistic theme, or horizon style, was widely dispersed in the Andes. The particularly common icon—a "staff deity"—was representative of a unified cultural tradition stemming from the pilgrimage center at the northern highland site of Chavín de Huantar (Burger 1992), and it surpassed local boundaries and unified distinct areas in ways that had never before been experienced.

As influence from Chavín began to wane, independent polities arose with distinct artifactual styles that were not unified by any one cultural theme. This time, known as the Early Intermediate Period (EIP) (AD 1–600), was characterized by several powerful regional polities, such as the Gallinazo-Moche on the north coast (Bawden 1996; Bourget 2006) and the Nasca culture on the south-central coast, from where the famous Nasca trophy heads and beautiful polychrome ceramics derive (Silverman and Proulx 2002; Vaughn 2004).

During the EIP, Huarpa society occupied the central highland Andes of the Ayacucho Basin, eventually giving rise to what we now call the Wari Empire. This intermediate period was characterized by numerous non-nucleated habitations and large sites, some of which have been interpreted as possible political-ritual centers, a few of which later grew into Wari settlements (Leoni 2004). Lumbreras originally called Huarpa a state-level society (Lumbreras 1974) but later reevaluated the data and concluded that its sociopolitical organization was organized more like a "chiefdom" (Lumbreras 2000a). Recent excavations at the

Huarpa site of Ñawinpukio in Ayacucho reveal some degree of social differentiation expressed through spatial organization and architectural differences (Leoni 2004), but those differences were minor compared to the subsequent Wari era.

Around AD 550–600, Huarpa society underwent significant cultural and political changes that led to the emergence of Wari, or a proto-Wari phase, and not surprisingly, some Huarpa cultural traits persisted into the Wari era. Leoni (2004) notes that Ñawinpukio maintained its centrally located sacred Huarpa buildings even as Wari structures were built at the site; this is a rarity in multicomponent Huarpa/Wari sites. Leoni interprets this as a way that local Ñawinpukio inhabitants could maintain their distinctive identity while in the folds of the "powerful Huari [Wari] state authority" (2004:3). In short, archaeological evidence from the Ayacucho Basin suggests that Huarpa sites coalesced around the beginning of the seventh century AD, resulting in settlements with Wari characteristics (Lumbreras 2000a,b; Schreiber 2001), even while some local, smaller sites attempted to retain aspects of their earlier pre-Wari identity (Leoni 2004).

The coalescence of Wari authority in the central Andes, and eventually in other Andean regions, contributed to a time of relative cultural unity during the Middle Horizon (AD 600–1000). This time was characterized by homogeneity in art, architecture, and sociopolitical organization that reached from parts of modern-day Bolivia and northern Chile in the south to parts of northern Peru (figure 3.1). These pan-Andean changes stemmed from two major cultural spheres: Wari in the Ayacucho Basin and Tiwanaku in the southern Andes of the Lake Titicaca Basin (figure 3.1). These two dominant polities appear to have controlled separate geographical regions, except in the Moquegua valley of southern Peru where Tiwanaku and Wari settlements coexisted (Feldman 1998; Moseley et al. 1991; Williams 2001; Williams and Nash 2005).

Around AD 1000–1100, the Wari Empire and the Tiwanaku state declined, and in the wake of this power void several sovereign regional polities once again developed. This era, known as the Late Intermediate Period (AD 1000–1450), lasted until the rise of the Inka Empire, when the Inka expanded out of the Cusco valley, rapidly conquering the largest territory and incorporating the greatest diversity of people of any Andean polity (Bauer and Covey 2002; D'Altroy 2002). The Inka Empire flourished until shortly after the arrival of the Spanish in 1532.

History of Wari Studies

The history of Wari studies has already been well described by Isbell and McEwan (1991a), so here I briefly summarize it and refer readers to Isbell and

McEwan for a more detailed overview. Before archaeologists recognized Wari as an independent, expansive empire, and prior to its identification as the source of a widespread ceramic tradition, many believed that Wari was a branch of Tiwanaku. The similarities between Wari and Tiwanaku iconography, though sometimes presented in different media, led many to posit that coastal Wari ceramics were part of the Tiwanaku tradition. Specifically, Wari ceramics from the site of Pacheco in the Nasca drainage and from other south and central coastal sites were initially called "Coastal Tiwanaku." This reflected their presumed connection to the site of Tiwanaku.

After analyzing several ceramic collections, Julio Tello correctly noted as early as the 1930s that the Coastal Tiwanaku style was derived from the massive, urban site of Huari, not Tiwanaku (Isbell and McEwan 1991a). However, he wrongly suggested that the entire Nasca style (AD 1–600), which actually predated Wari, also grew out of the Wari ceramic tradition. Isbell and McEwan (1991a) note that this miscalculation overshadowed his correct assessment, thus requiring two more decades before the coastal styles were correctly attributed to Wari styles and another few years before Wari was recognized as an independent, conquest empire.

John Rowe (1956) was the first to suggest that Wari and Tiwanaku were distinct states and to posit explicitly that the site of Huari may have been the source for the intrusive styles found throughout vast regions of the Andes. He noted that the "Tiahuanacoid Huari pottery which appears intrusive in local sequences ... suggests a parallel with the homogeneity [and distribution] of Inca pottery" (Rowe 1956:150). In other words, the vast distribution of the "Tiahuanacoid Huari" styles indicates that whatever site was the source, it must have represented an expansive empire akin to the Inka. He suggested that "the most likely candidate in our present state of knowledge is Huari, which is the largest and most spectacular site where the right kind of pottery is found" (Rowe 1956:150). Thus, the notion was born that Wari was an expansive empire responsible for the wide distribution of Wari-derived ceramics and architecture. This also implied that the site of Huari (and neighboring Wari sites) was the source of a political administration capable of expanding and maintaining the first expansive state in the Andes, six centuries prior to the Inkas.

Competing Models to Explain Wari Political Organization

Rowe's assertion that Wari was an expansive empire has been widely supported by archaeological data from subsequent excavations and surveys, and ongoing studies continue to undergird his early claims. Nevertheless, two major interpretations persist regarding the political organization of Wari: Wari was one of many autonomous Andean polities during the Middle Horizon with no great power over any other region; and Wari was a politically centralized state and expansive empire that incorporated numerous communities into its domain.

Autonomous Polities during the Middle Horizon

The first interpretation views Wari as one of many independent polities that flourished during the Middle Horizon. Supporters of this perspective doubt that the Wari sphere of influence was geographically great or ideologically dominant (Bawden and Conrad 1982; Conrad 1981; Donnan and Mackey 1978; Shady Solis 1989; Shimada 1990). Bawden and Conrad argue that "Middle Horizon unity has been greatly exaggerated, and we should probably think in terms of a series of regional states or spheres of influence" (1982:31). This was echoed by Czwarno and colleagues, who stated that the Middle Horizon "may have represented the florescence or consolidation of a number of autonomous states, of which Wari was one . . . [and] no particular state was pre-eminent over the others" (Czwarno et al. 1989:138).

Isbell and McEwan (1991a) note that this view finds support among many Andeanists who work in the northern regions of Peru. That is, those scholars see no evidence for direct Wari control in the north and argue that northern indigenous polities maintained local control during the Middle Horizon. Although the site of Viracochapampa in Huamachuco in the northern highlands was built in the Wari masonry style, some have long argued that the site cannot claim Wari as its architectural prototype (Conrad 1981; Moseley 1978:530). Similarly, John Topic classifies it as a "hybrid Huamachuco-Huari site," not a "totally intrusive [Wari] site" (J. R. Topic 1991:161). (But see his postscript [J. R. Topic 1991:163 and discussion below] noting a smaller Wari masonry building near the site.) If Viracochapampa is not a site of Wari masonry style, then this might suggest that Wari leaders did not have direct control over populations and land in these northern regions, a pattern that fits with what Schreiber (1992) describes as a Wari mosaic of control throughout parts of the Andes: direct control in some areas, indirect in others, and interactions of parity in yet other regions. In contrast to the northern coast and highlands, other Andean regions show intrusive architectural styles suggestive of Wari control (Anders 1989; Glowacki 2002; Schreiber 1992; McEwan 2005; Williams 2001; Williams and Nash 2006; and see discussion below).

The notion that several autonomous polities existed during the Middle Horizon includes a multitude of views on the nature of their interactions. For example, John and Teresa Topic have suggested that the site of Huari and related Wari sites were a confederation composed of kin groups and lineages (J. R.

Topic 1991; Topic and Topic 1985, 1992; T. L. Topic 1991), while Ruth Shady has posited that Wari was not expansionist but rather engaged in long-distance trade with distant polities, each of which maintained autonomy (Shady and Ruiz 1979; Shady Solis 1982, 1988). Another related view has identified Huari and other important Middle Horizon sites as a group of somewhat autonomous oracles. The site of Pachacamac just south of Lima may have been the primary oracle with a loosely connected hierarchy of provincial and local shrines distributed across the landscape (Shea 1969). Although details of the nature of interaction between Middle Horizon polities differ, the general idea among these scholars is that no polity was dominant over another.

Wari as a Politically Centralized State and Expansive Empire

The variation in Wari influence from region to region is not surprising. As noted above, the Wari maintained a "mosaic of control" throughout the Andean landscape, and it varied depending on both Wari and local strategies for interaction (Schreiber 1992). Thus, some regions closer to Ayacucho (for example, the site of Jincamocco in the Sondondo valley and Pataraya in the upper stretches of Nasca [Edwards 2010; Schreiber 1998]) may have been more intensively integrated into the Wari world, such that local peoples were heavily involved in agricultural production for the state. Farther south, in the Moquegua valley, architectural, artifactual, and food remains demonstrate a strong Wari presence in which new irrigation canals were constructed to enhance agricultural production for the Wari state (Williams 2002) and the political-ritual Wari center of Cerro Baúl was built atop a massive mesa with sweeping views of the valley (Feldman 1998; Williams 2001; Williams and Nash 2006).

While Wari influence may have been more limited in northern Peru—or at least different relative to other Andean regions—the evidence for Wari imperialism in other parts of the Andes is striking. A large group of scholars, myself included, identify Wari as a politically centralized, expansive state with an extended administrative structure and its capital at the site of Huari (Brewster-Wray 1989; Cook 1992, 2001; Cook and Glowacki 2003; Feldman 1989; Isbell 1984; Isbell and Cook 1987, 2002; Jennings and Craig 2001; Larco Hoyle 1948; Lumbreras 1974; McEwan 1983; McEwan 1991; Meddens 1991; Moseley et al. 1991; Ochatoma and Cabrera 2002; Schreiber 1987; Schreiber 1992, 2001; Tung 2003, 2007b; Williams 2001; Williams and Nash 2005). Archaeological and, as I show in subsequent chapters, osteological evidence demonstrate that the Wari Empire expanded from the Ayacucho Basin to incorporate a mosaic of regions in the Andes, particularly those areas to the south, southeast, and southwest of the imperial heartland. Some have suggested that Wari expansionism stemmed from religious indoctrination (Menzel 1964), while others point to militaristic actions (Feldman 1989; Isbell 1991; Larco Hoyle 1948; Menzel 1964:67; Rowe 1956). Both strategies, among yet-unidentified others, were likely employed by Wari state agents, showing a savvy implementation of political strategy depending on local circumstances, state goals, resources, and personal qualities of individuals from the local and state communities.

Recent analyses of Wari heartland iconography particularly support the idea that militarism played a strong role in Wari state expansion. State-produced polychrome ceramics from the sites of Huari and Conchopata depict Wari warriors wielding weapons, carrying armor, and holding trophy heads and prisoners, images that suggest that agents of the Wari state (political elites and ceramic artisans, among others) were engaged in the promotion of a military ideology and perhaps the creation of an actual military (Ochatoma and Cabrera 2002; Ochatoma et al. 2008). Based on these intriguing data, a main goal of this study is to use data on skeletal trauma and trophy heads to evaluate whether militarism and violence were crucial components in Wari expansion and control.

This study's focus on the biocultural effects of ancient imperialism requires that the archaeological evidence demonstrating that Wari was an expansive state be summarized and evaluated, as I do in the passages that follow. Additionally, as I show in later sections of the book, the osteological data further support previous data sets that demonstrate that Wari was indeed a politically centralized state with policies and practices aligned with goals of imperial expansion.

Origins of the Wari Empire

Although details regarding key aspects of the cultural and ideological origins of Wari remain elusive, there are several well-founded explanations, none of which are mutually exclusive of the others. In the infancy of Wari studies, the southern capital of Tiwanaku was thought to be the source of particular material manifestations of Wari ideology, in particular the religious icon known as the "Front Face Staff Deity." Menzel (1964:67) suggested that Wari developed out of the Tiwanaku religious tradition, either through direct indoctrination or through Wari pilgrims who visited Tiwanaku and returned with the religio-cultural messages from the south. She reasons that the introduction of these foreign traditions ushered in major cultural changes and the creation and expansion of the Wari Empire. However, Isbell and Cook (2002) suggest that religious iconography used by both Wari and Tiwanaku may derive from some older, shared source. In this case, significant aspects of Wari iconography would not be considered derivative of Tiwanaku, nor would Tiwanaku ideology have initiated the Wari cultural horizon. A yet-undiscovered source may have been the origin for the distinctive Wari-Tiwanaku Middle Horizon style. Finally, as noted above, the origins of the Wari Empire are seen to have emerged from the preceding Huarpa society in the Ayacucho Basin.

The Temporal and Spatial Aspects of Wari Development and Expansion

The Wari Imperial Core

Andean scholars once suggested that Wari did not initiate imperial expansion until AD 700–750 and that the Wari Empire collapsed two centuries later, circa AD 900 (Menzel 1964, 1968). However, new evidence indicates that Wari expansion to distant regions may have begun earlier (around AD 600) and lasted longer (until AD 1000–1100), both in the imperial heartland and in the southern hinterland (Ketteman 2002; Malpass 1998; Tung 2007c; Williams 2001). In particular, new radiocarbon dates from the two Wari hinterland sites in this study indicate that Wari expansion to the south occurred around AD 650 (Tung 2007c).

In the Wari heartland, the capital site of Huari grew out of preceding Huarpa hamlets and villages, coalescing into a large capital city about three to five kilometers in size (Isbell et al. 1991). Architectural groups include large, ceremonial complexes that feature D-shaped ritual structures, such as those seen at the sectors of Vegachayoq Moqo (Bragayrac 1991) and Monqachayoq (Solano and Guerrero 1981), large and beautifully constructed mortuary complexes (for example, Cheqo Wasi and Monqachayoq), and residential and production areas (for example, Moraduchayoq [Isbell 1997b]). The site was home to urban elites, craft specialists, ritual specialists, farmers (Isbell 1997b, 2001a; Schreiber 2001), and other social classes that have yet to be identified based on empirical evidence.

Twelve kilometers south of the capital, the Wari site of Conchopata also developed out of preceding Huarpa settlements (figure 3.2) (Blacker 2001; Isbell and Cook 2002). Wari characteristics in iconography and architecture were visible at Conchopata by about AD 600, around which time the site began to develop into the second city in the Wari imperial core (Isbell and Cook 2002; Silverman and Isbell 2002). The Wari occupation at Conchopata continued until approximately AD 1000 (Isbell and Cook 2002; Ketteman 2002). (Conchopata is described in more detail below.)

Additional Wari sites and several Wari administrative centers are located throughout the central highland Andes, demonstrating the extent and intensity of Wari control in this region (Anders 1991; Isbell 1977; McEwan 1996; Ochatoma and Cabrera 2001; Schreiber 1991b; Schreiber 1992). The site of Azángaro, located 15 kilometers northwest of the Wari capital, appears to have been constructed around the ninth century AD to facilitate oversight of irrigation

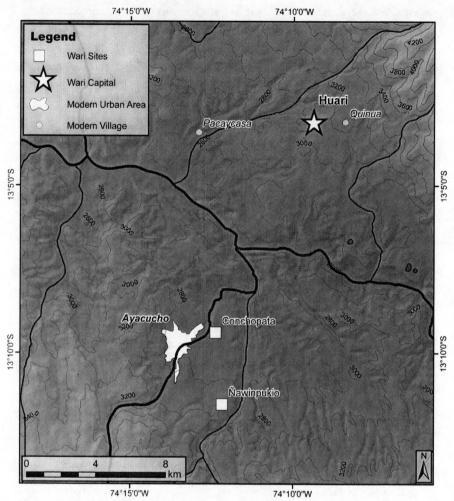

Figure 3.2. Map of Ayacucho Basin. (By S. A. Wernke.)

networks and agricultural production; it also may have served a calendrical/ceremonial purpose within the Wari Empire (Anders 1991:168). Jargampata, located about 25 kilometers east of Huari, is the smallest of the Wari centers in the core, likely serving as an agricultural collection center with local peasants producing for the Wari state (Isbell 1977:56). The small Wari sites of Aqo Wayqo and Trigo Pampa, also located in the Ayacucho Basin, show domestic and mortuary components and were probably residential sites for peasant agriculturalists who provided agricultural resources to the Wari state (Ochatoma and Cabrera 2001:197–98).

In the more distant Sondondo valley (formerly referred to as the Carhuarazo valley), about 125 kilometers south of Huari, the site of Jincamocco was constructed in the late eighth century AD (+100 years) (Schreiber 1992:193). Based on a survey of the valley and excavations at Jincamocco, Schreiber describes the site as "a regional administrative center, [and] the focus of Wari control over this valley" (Schreiber 1992:258).

Wari in the Northern Andes

In the north, indigenous groups, particularly local elites, maintained some level of autonomy during the Middle Horizon, but there is ample evidence that Wari intruded into the local scene and harnessed local labor for the construction of buildings in the Wari-masonry style. The site of Honcopampa, located along the western slopes of the Cordillera Blanca (figure 3.1), appears to have been a Wari administrative site with Wari-style patio groups and D-shaped structures in the Purushmonte central sector of the site; these architectural features are signatures of the Wari Empire (Isbell 1989).

Farther north, the large site of Viracochapampa in Huamachuco was apparently constructed in the Wari architectural tradition (T. L. Topic 1991), leading some to insist that this large but uncompleted site illustrates Wari administrative presence in the region (Jennings and Craig 2001; Schreiber 1992). John Topic (1991), however, initially downplayed the Wari architectural traits as evidence of Wari control but later noted in a postscript "that a small compound built with Huari-style masonry is present in the maize growing area" (J. R. Topic 1991:163), perhaps as a strategy to control the production and distribution of this socially valued crop. Furthermore, he states that "appreciable concentrations of Huari pottery" were recovered from the site of Cerro Amaru, across the Rio Grande from Viracochapampa (J. R. Topic 1991:141). While foreign pottery alone does not signify imperial control, its intrusion into the local style, combined with Wari architecture in maize-rich growing zones, points to Wari administrative presence in the north, or at least a very strong influence.

Wari in the Southeast and in the Southern Andes

To the southeast of the Wari heartland, in the modern Department of Cusco, the second largest site in the Wari Empire—Pikillacta—was constructed as an administrative site complete with elite residences and ceremonial sectors (McEwan 1991:117), though "the site never reached its full potential; three of its four sectors were left unfinished, having been only minimally occupied" (Glowacki 2005:120). Nonetheless, Pikillacta shows "extensive Wari presence" around AD 600–700 (Glowacki 2005:123).

Seventeen kilometers southeast of Pikillacta there was "an extensive Huari occupation of the Huaro Valley" that predates Pikillacta and may have served as the "primary Huari settlement of the Cuzco region throughout the Middle

Horizon" (Glowacki 2002:269). One of the sites in the valley, Hatun Cotuyoc, may have been the residence for the Wari labor force; the site of Qoripata was likely the Wari administrative center from which agricultural projects were managed; and three sites in the northern area of the valley that housed temples and the main cemetery were perhaps religious precincts (Glowacki 2002:282–83). Wari's focus eventually shifted from the Huaro valley to the Lucre Basin, where Pikillacta is located.

Wari presence also stretched to the southwest of the capital to *yungas* (midvalley) and coastal areas, including the Nasca drainage. Although Wari iconography was greatly influenced by cultural media of the earlier Nasca culture (Menzel 1964), the direction of influence began to change around the mid-seventh century AD, as the Wari Empire incorporated populations from Nasca into its domain. This was concomitant with the decline of the Nasca polity around the end of the seventh century AD, as suggested by major changes in ceramic designs and settlement patterns (Silverman and Proulx 2002). In particular, the Wari site of Pacheco was established, serving as an offering site and pilgrimage center or major oracle. Here, nearly three tons of Wari ceramics, including oversized Wari ceramic urns, were intentionally smashed in rituals, marking a new ritual practice in the region that was introduced by Wari highland neighbors to the east (Menzel 1964).

After Pacheco was abandoned in the early Middle Horizon, the Wari coopted an area in the upper Nasca valley, where a small Wari enclosure, Pataraya, marked the limits of Wari control in the Nasca drainage (Schreiber 1999:169, 2001:90). Inhabitants at Pataraya were heavily involved in textile production, and according to Edwards (2010), the area is ideal for cotton production and may explain Wari investment in the region. Pataraya and the nearby site of Incawasi may well have been important Wari sites that helped to secure steady and reliable access to cotton for Wari textile production (Edwards 2010).

Additionally, there was a possible Wari administrative center in the middle Ingenio valley of the Nasca drainage (Silverman 2002:273–74), further supporting the notion that Wari had direct investment in this region. In sum, Wari presence in the Nasca drainage contributed to shifts in local settlement patterns and alterations in material culture and mortuary practices (Schreiber 1999, 2001; Silverman and Proulx 2002). Also, as discussed in subsequent chapters, the shift from pre-Wari to Wari eras saw Nasca populations undergo changes in health status (Drusini 2001; Kellner 2002; Tomasto 2009) and experience an increase in dietary breadth that was coupled with larger dietary differences between people; maize, however, continued to be a common resource in both temporal periods even though its pattern of consumption was more heterogeneous (Kellner and Schoeninger 2008).

In line with the southward Wari expansion, the site of Cerro Baúl in the Moquegua valley marks the southernmost Wari site in the empire (Moseley et al. 1991; Williams 2001). This large site represents a Wari intrusion into the Tiwanaku cultural sphere, thus representing the only known area where major Wari and Tiwanaku settlements coexisted (Moseley et al. 1991; Williams 2001; Williams and Nash 2005). Cerro Baúl was an administrative, residential, and ceremonial site located atop a prominent mesa with commanding views of the valley and mountain deities (Williams 2001; Williams and Nash 2006). Its residential compound was occupied as early as AD 600–650, indicating that Wari expansion was quite rapid after its rise in the imperial heartland circa AD 600. In the ninth to tenth centuries, Cerro Baúl underwent a reconstruction phase that coincided with general reorganization of the Wari administrative infrastructure (Williams 2001). Alas, there are few human remains from Cerro Baúl, so demographic profiles and health status information for those who lived in the southernmost sphere of the Wari Empire are unknown. Nevertheless, this site is of great importance, as it marks the southern extent of Wari control and demonstrates the expansive nature of the Wari.

Wari in the Majes Valley of Southern Peru

Wari presence has also been documented in this project's hinterland study area—the Majes valley (discussed below)—which has a Pacific outlet located about halfway between Pacheco in the Nasca valley and Cerro Baúl in the Moquegua valley (figure 3.1). Wari influence is clearly documented throughout much of southern Peru, but it would not have been equal in all valleys or sections of valleys. Instead, it probably resembled "a mosaic of strategies of control" (Schreiber 1992:69); particular valleys would have been heavily administered by the Wari state, while some would have been only partially integrated, and yet others would have remained marginal.

The Wari Empire expanded into the Majes valley, the location of two of the three sites in this study: Beringa and La Real. Lumbreras (1974) identified Wari ceramics of the Viñaque style in Majes, suggesting Wari influence circa AD 700–900. Later, small-scale excavations by students from the Universidad Católica de Santa María (Ratti de Luchi Lomellini and Zegarra Arenas 1987) and by de la Vera Cruz Chávez (1989) from the Universidad de San Agustín de Arequipa documented Wari ceramics at Beringa and other Majes valley sites. A reconnaissance in the middle Majes valley in the 1980s also recovered numerous Wari ceramics, particularly from Beringa (Garcia Márquez and Bustamante Montoro 1990), and excavations at La Real uncovered a plethora of Wari ceramics and textiles, including finewares that could be imports from the imperial heartland (de la Vera Cruz Chávez and Yépez Alvarez 1995). Finally, local museum collections include elaborate Wari ceramic finewares, including oversized face-neck jars in imperial styles, reportedly collected from the middle Majes valley. Unfortunately, no provenience is available for museum collections, and until this study, no radiocarbon dates were available to establish the timing and tempo of Wari expansion into this region.

The coastal stretch of the Majes drainage, known as Camaná, is about 70 aerial kilometers from this project's study area, and survey and excavation projects have documented Wari presence in that coastal zone (Malpass 2001; Manrique and Cornejo 1990). Based on orthogonal architecture layout—a Wari hallmark—at the site of Sonay, Malpass (2001) has suggested that it was a Wari administrative compound. Two radiocarbon assays indicate that it was built around AD 900 and abandoned about a century later (Malpass 2001). Thus, Wari administrative presence in the coastal area of Majes appeared late in the Middle Horizon and ended quickly.

Wari sites also have been identified in higher altitudes of this river drainage, but ambiguity persists regarding these claims. Numero 8, a site in the Chuquibamba valley, a highland tributary of the Majes, has been described as a Wari center (Sciscento 1989). Directly upriver from the middle Majes valley where Beringa and La Real are located, in the section known as the Colca valley, the site of Achachiwa has been identified as a "Wari administrative unit that included the entire Majes River drainage" (Sciscento 1989:268). And although de la Vera Cruz (1989) originally described it as a local site, he later agreed with Sciscento's interpretation (de la Vera Cruz Chávez 1996). Schreiber, in contrast, doubts that Achachiwa was a Wari provincial site (Schreiber 1992:104). More recently, Wari-influenced ceramics were recovered at Achachiwa, but no architectural details reminiscent of Wari were observed (Doutriaux 2004).

Wari influence diminishes above 3,300 meters in the Colca valley. Detailed archaeological survey of the middle Colca valley did not reveal Wari sites, and the few Wari-influenced sherds were only broadly derivative of regional Wari styles (Wernke 2003). This region may be the limit of Wari influence in the southern highlands, as it appears to constitute an overlapping boundary between Wari and Tiwanaku (Wernke 2003). Although no Tiwanaku ceramics or sites have been documented (Wernke 2003), the bulk of obsidian at the Tiwanaku capital was derived from the Chivay source in the central Colca valley, suggesting intensive trade with the Tiwanaku sphere (Burger et al. 1998; Burger et al. 2000). In short, mild Wari influence is present in the local ceramic tradition, particularly in the lower stretches of the Colca valley, but strong economic ties to Tiwanaku are apparent based on intensive trade of obsidian.

Finally, in the high-altitude Cotahuasi valley, located one valley north of

Majes, Jennings (2002:191) suggests that two sites (Collota and Netahaha) display evidence for Wari influence in their architectural designs, but he concludes they were administered by local elites, not Wari agents. In subsequent studies, Jennings (2007) documents Wari-style ceramics in tombs and notes that Collota was also an Inka site.

The Environmental and Archaeological Context of the Three Sites

Conchopata

Conchopata is located in the southern end of the Ayacucho valley, in the central highland Andes (figures 3.1 and 3.2). The site is approximately 2,700 m.a.s.l. and covers at least 20 hectares atop a large north–south-running mesa sided by the Quebrada de Huatatas on the east and the Quebrada de la Totorilla on the west (Isbell and Cook 2002; Pozzi-Escot B. 1991). Surrounding valleys and slopes are intensively cultivated today just as they were in the past.

Recent excavations by the Conchopata Archaeological Project, directed by William Isbell and Anita Cook, and the Proyecto de Excavaciones en un Poblado Alfarero de la Epoca Huari, directed by José Ochatoma and Martha Cabrera, have provided much information about this important Wari site. Conchopata includes large patio groups, mortuary areas, and D-shaped and circular ritual structures (figure 3.3), similar to those at the Wari capital (Isbell and Cook 2002; Tung and Cook 2006). Those civic-ceremonial buildings so common at Conchopata appear to be part of a sacred landscape that represents Wari imperial ideology and state-sanctioned belief systems repeatedly found at Wari sites (Anders 1989; Cook 2001; Schreiber and Gibson 2002). The large patios likely served as public spaces for state-sponsored feasting ceremonies (Cook and Glowacki 2003), and the ritual structures were used for ceremonies involving the intentional destruction of beautifully decorated, oversized ceramic urns (Cook and Benco 2002; Cook and Glowacki 2003; Ochatoma and Cabrera 2002; Tung and Cook 2006). This study investigates other activities that occurred in those ritual spaces, particularly those that involved human corpses and body parts, to understand more fully the function and meanings associated with those apparently sacred spaces.

In addition to ceremonial activities, Conchopata was a locus of ceramic production, leading Pozzi-Escot (1991) to term the site a "community of potters." Studies by Cook and Benco (2002) further demonstrate this and add more nuanced details, noting that pottery production may have had dual organizational schemes. Based on the ubiquity of pottery production tools and open firing areas throughout the site, some ceramic production may have been linked

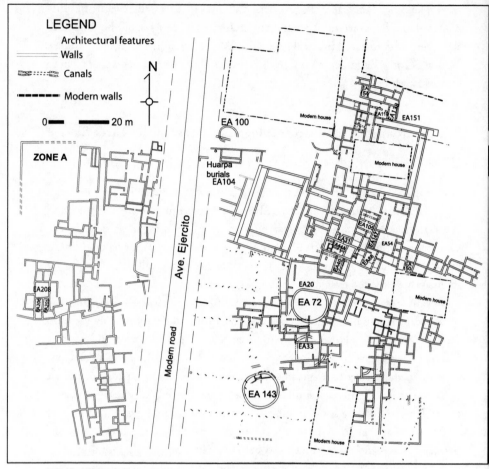

Figure 3.3. Map of Conchopata. (Based on site map by Juan Carlos Blacker.)

to individual households, while ceramic fineware production in firing kilns may have been administered by elites (Cook and Benco 2002). Leoni (2001) has argued that the latter production system was more likely because the firing kilns were near structures that have been interpreted as palaces (Isbell 2001b), so these areas may have housed attached pottery specialists producing for resident elites. Nevertheless, Cook and Benco (2002) have argued that Conchopata pottery production did not obey the rules of any single, popular production model, and new frameworks for understanding this aspect of politico-economic organization are needed (also see Janusek 1999).

Conchopata has also been interpreted as a palace compound that housed a "royal" male (Isbell 2001b; Isbell and Cook 2002) or lord, and perhaps even "a succession of three lords [who] ruled from" one of the palace compounds in the northern part of the site (Isbell 2007). However, this has been difficult to test, because the area identified as the royal tomb (EA110) (Isbell 2001b) was severely looted and relatively few diagnostic human bones or high-status goods have been recovered from this area. Instead, Tung and Cook (2006) suggest that the data point to the presence of large, intermediate elite households and extended families that engaged in ancestor veneration practices, elaborate rituals, and mortuary activities that, in general, were shared by those at the capital. The similarities between Conchopata and Huari mortuary practices, however, exclude funerary contexts reserved for the highest elites interred in monolithic stone slab tombs like those observed at Cheqo Wasi at Huari. Nothing resembling those "royal" tombs has ever been documented at Conchopata.

Previous Radiocarbon Dates from Conchopata

Given the complexity and multicomponent occupation at Conchopata, radiocarbon dates have been an important data set for reconstructing the timing and tempo of Wari imperial activities. Ketteman's overview of radiocarbon dates from Conchopata demonstrates that it was occupied from Huarpa (AD 425–550/600) to Wari (AD 600–1000) times, and possibly into the first part of the Late Intermediate Period (AD 1100). Of particular interest for this study are the dates associated with the burials; according to radiocarbon data presented by Ketteman (2002), a majority of the Wari mortuary spaces postdate AD 800.

New Radiocarbon Dates from Conchopata

While radiometric dates suggest that many human burials date to the second half of the Middle Horizon (Ketteman 2002), two radiocarbon samples processed for this study exhibit earlier dates. They derive from an undisturbed tomb in EA105 (figure 3.3). A wooden board that had been a burial litter for a young male at the bottom of the rock-cut tomb yielded a date of AD 714–953 (calibrated 2 sigma; Sample AA45796). A human rib fragment from the individual buried at the opening of the tomb yielded a radiocarbon date of AD 343–645 (calibrated 2 sigma; Sample AA45795) (table 3.2). The early date is unexpected; according to the law of superposition, the top of the tomb should yield dates later than the base of the tomb.

The odd radiocarbon dates may be a result of the organic material tested. Research with burial samples from the Moquegua valley has shown that human bone consistently provides dates that are from zero to nearly 350 years older than other nonhuman organic materials from the same context (mean=100 years, s.d.=~110 years) (Owen 2002). Owen (2002) suggests that the older age from human bone may be related to the marine diet of the individuals sampled. However, given the dearth of marine foods in this highland population's diet (Finucane et al. 2006), this explanation seems unlikely.

Table 3.2. Radiocarbon (AMS) dates from the three sites in this study

Site	Lab code	Unit and locus	Description of material	δ13C	14C age (years BP)	1 sigma (AD)	2 sigma (AD)
Cnchp	AA45795[a]	EA105L2095	Human rib (Ind. 1) from adult female at top of tomb	-15.9	1614+75	421–574	343–645
Cnchp	AA45796[a]	EA105L2095	Small wood platform under adult male at base of tomb	-28.2	1245+32	780–885	714–953
Cnchp	GX31863[a]	EA143T3L2985	Carbon from inside trophy head #19	-17.8	1560+50	445–631	433–643
Cnchp	Beta133539[b]	EA100	Organic sediment from skeleton	-19.3	1450+40	436–555	425–601
Cnchp	Beta133541[b]	EA33	Wood charcoal; from end of use of D-shaped EA33; it thus dates EA72	-25.0 (estimated)	1180+60	777–945	691–983
Cnchp	Beta133542[b]	EA33	Wood charcoal; from end of use of D-shaped EA33; it thus dates EA72	-25.0 (estimated)	1210+60	720–892	685–975
Cnchp	Beta133547[b]	EA38	Vegetal cord from a cist tomb, probably once wrapped a burial	-25.0 (estimated)	1040+60	898–1147	886–1159
Cnchp	Beta133548[b]	EA31	Plant material from an intact tomb beneath floor of EA31	-25.0 (estimated)	980+50	784–997	779–1018
Cnchp	Beta146400[b]	EA6	Wood charcoal; sample predates construction of room EA6 and the tomb in NE corner of EA6; reed-boat-warrior sherds found in deposits beneath the floor	-21.2	1320+40	623–684	599–765
Cnchp	Beta146401[b]	EA106	Wood charcoal from possible ceramic firing location w/in EA106; sample taken from ash deposit beneath floor of room EA106B	-23.2	1270+40	671–769	654–848

		EA93		δ13C			
Cnchp	Beta146403[b]	EA93	Charcoal (EA93 is next to EA105)	-25.0 (estimated)	1300±70	657–798	620–890
Brng	AA45791[c]	U14L1050	Wood from wall fill north of tomb	-28.2	1406±53	600–674	540–762
Brng	AA45790[c]	U14L1095	Wood from wall post west of tomb	-22.4	1353±32	651–688	622–767
Brng	AA45789[c]	U21L1075	Carbon from ceramic vessel near east tomb in room	-24.4	1330±31	659–711	651–771
Brng	AA45793[c]	U01L1001	Textile wrap around mummy	-23.3	1243±33	692–858	689–879
Brng	AA45794[c]	U11L1011	Textile wrap around mummy	-24.1	930±32	1037–1158	1024–1187
Brng	AA45792[c]	U16L1025	Cord wrapped around mummy	-8.5	840±42	1163–1256	1044–1278
LR	Beta191644[c]	C1-L929[e]	Textile wrap around mummy	-17.9	1350±40	650–690	640–760
LR	Beta191642[c]	Est5-L633[e]	Textile wrap around mummy	-15.3	1250±40	700–790	680–880
LR	Beta191643[c]	Est5-L782	Carbon from mummy filling	-25.4	1220±40	770–880	690–900
LR	AA86622[d]	Est5-L644	Beans	-24.3	1028±37	1020–1137	993–1150
LR	AA86618[d]	Est5-L331	Peanuts in a textile bag	-25.8	1055±37	989–1105	980–1149
LR	AA86621[d]	Est5-L488	Peanuts	-24.4	1112±31	906–1020	896–1026
LR	AA86615[d]	C1-L929	Cactus spine	-10.4	1199±37	785–976	779–984
LR	AA86619[d]	C1-L742	Seeds from a ceramic vessel	-25.7	1280±37	722–872	687–888
LR	AA86614[d]	C1-L899	Cotton and vegetal string	-26.8	1309±37	684–805	673–872
LR	AA86617[d]	C1-L929	Textile threads	-16.2	1318±38	680–778	667–868
LR	AA86616[d]	C1-L761	Textile threads	-17.1	1319±37	682–777	667–867
LR	AA86623[d]	C1-L347	Cotton seeds from a mummy bundle	-25.2	1335±35	680–771	659–859
LR	AA86620[d]	C1-L714	Carbon (burned wood)	-25	1427±38	624–681	597–767

[a] This study.
[b] Ketteman 2002.
[c] Tung 2007.
[d] Yépez Álvarez and Jennings 2010 and Jennings n.d. (in press).
[e] C1=*Camara* 1 (the mortuary cave) and Est5=*Estructura* 5 (the ritual structure in front of the mortuary cave). L=*Lote*, a discrete area within an excavation unit.

If these radiocarbon dates are accurate, then the top burial—a middle-aged pregnant female—may represent an ancestral mummy that was saved for veneration rituals until final interment several centuries after her death. Her reproductive status should not go unnoticed. She may have embodied ideals of fertility that were highly valued in ancient Andean society (Frame 2001; Meddens 1994). She also could have been a high-status individual and matriarch of an extended family; perhaps the 13 other individuals in the tomb were her descendants.

Beringa

Beringa is in the middle Majes valley (part of the Colca-Majes-Camaná drainage) in the District of Aplao, Province of Castilla, within the Department of Arequipa (figure 3.1). The middle portion of the valley is situated at 700 m.a.s.l. and receives a negligible amount of rainfall each year. Therefore, all agricultural fields must be irrigated by the Majes River, which derives its plentiful water supply from rainfall and snowmelt from the Andean peaks. The middle valley is a yungas zone: a subtropical region ideal for growing a variety of crops and harvesting river shrimp (*Cryphiops caementarius*).

The middle Majes valley is located between the arid Majes-Ocoña pampa to the west and the Majes-Siguas pampa to the east, essentially boxing in the valley with dry, desert landscapes (figure 3.4). The valley is sided by steep cliffs that rise approximately 800 to 1,000 meters above the valley floor, and *quebradas* (ravines) are common around the site, creating treacherous terrain as one descends from the settlement to the river and agricultural fields below. The site itself is made up of a two-tiered alluvial terrace approximately 50 meters above the Majes River, along the left river margin (figure 3.5).

Based on earlier surveys by Peruvian archaeologists, Beringa was identified as a domestic and mortuary site, occupied sometime during the Middle Horizon (AD 600–1000) and Late Intermediate Period (AD 1000–1450) (Garcia Márquez and Bustamante Montoro 1990; Ratti de Luchi Lomellini and Zegarra Arenas 1987). The lower, smaller tier of the site, closest to the river, has terraces, small rectangular buildings and Chuquibamba ceramics: a local Late Intermediate Period ceramic style (Garcia Márquez and Bustamante Montoro 1990).[1] On the upper, main plateau of the site, there are quadrangular domestic structures, collective tombs, and a predominance of Wari-influenced ceramics known as Q'osqopa (Garcia Márquez and Bustamante Montoro 1990).[2] Given the preliminary evidence for human burials with Wari ceramics at Beringa, this site was selected for study to elucidate the health status and lifeways of a hinterland community in the Wari Empire.

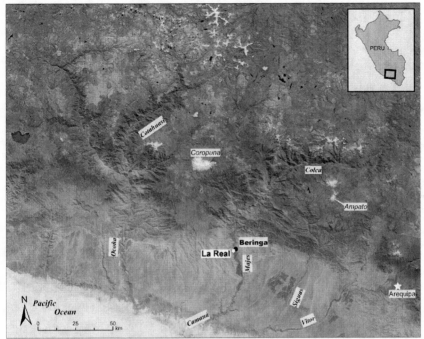

Figure 3.4. Satellite image of Majes and surrounding valleys. (Courtesy of NASA/ GSFC/LaRC/JPL, MISR Team.)

Figure 3.5. Aerial photo of Beringa in the Majes valley. Excavations directed by Tung focused on Sector A. (Courtesy of Servicio Aerofotográfico Nacional de Perú.)

New Archaeological Insights from Beringa

I directed excavations at Beringa in 2001, mapping the three sectors: Sectors A, B, and C (figure 3.6). Sector A includes dozens of domestic rooms, a few ritual spaces, tombs, and an open plaza; this area is 3.21 hectares (figure 3.7). Sectors B and C are domestic areas, and they are 1.46 hectares and 0.33 hectares, respectively. All human burials were derived from Sector A, an area that had been badly looted, leaving hundreds of human skeletal remains scattered on the surface. Those areas were superficially collected to obtain human remains and associated artifacts before they further decomposed, and additional areas were excavated to recover in situ human remains and artifacts.

Archaeological materials recovered from Beringa clearly demonstrate Wari influence at this village site (Owen 2007; Tung 2007c). Wari tie-dye textiles and Wari ceramics were recovered, indicating that several subgroups in the community had plentiful access to exotic Wari goods (figure 3.8). Additionally, XRF analysis by Nico Tripcevich of four obsidian pieces from Beringa demonstrates that they were from Wari obsidian sources. One was sourced to Alca in the Cotahuasi valley, two were from Quispisisa, and one may have been from Anillo. The latter two sources are in the Department of Ayacucho, within the Wari imperial heartland, and Alca is a well-known obsidian source used by the Wari. Although it is unclear whether Wari traders themselves brought these obsidian pieces to Beringa or if other middlemen traded in these pieces, their presence at the site further demonstrates how people at Beringa were more closely tied into the Wari trade network. Furthermore, although the Beringa obsidian sample that has undergone analysis is small, all four are linked to Wari obsidian sources, not Tiwanaku ones. For example, the common Tiwanaku obsidian source located in Chivay in the Colca valley, directly upriver from Beringa, has not yet been identified as an obsidian source at Beringa.

Several objects recovered from Beringa were weapons, suggesting that inhabitants may have been involved in violent conflicts, some of which could have caused skeletal trauma. A couple of wood machetes, wood sticks/clubs, slings for throwing stones (*hondas*), and isolated sling stones were recovered from both disturbed and intact contexts (see figure 5.13).

Beringa was occupied by individuals who engaged in a variety of occupational activities, including textile weaving, farming, fishing (Tung 2007c), and some low-level ceramic production (Owen 2007). Textile production implements, including spindle whorls, unspun wool and cotton, balls of spun string, and wood battens were ubiquitous at the site, but ceramic production tools were rare. Fishing implements, such as nets and river baskets, along with fish bones, marine shell, and river shrimp exoskeletons were present in several contexts. These food items from the river and sea would have been good sources of protein but also of parasites.

The Beringa Menu: Meat, Veggies, Seafood, and Beer (Chicha)

The plethora of plant domesticates and the site's proximity to agricultural fields indicate that residents engaged in farming. Botanical remains were plentiful; our team recovered nearly 90 kilograms. About 60 of those 90 kilograms were potential food resources: maize (*Zea mays*), molle (small, hard berries that grow on trees) (*Schinus molle*), peanuts (*Arachis hypogea*), pacay (*Inga feullei*), yucca (*Manihot esculenta*), lucuma (*Pouteria lucuma*), camote (*Ipomoea batatas*), coca (*Erythroxylum coca*), and several species of squash (*Cucurbita* sp.) and beans (*Phaseolus* sp.). Of these plant foods, maize and molle were the most common, representing approximately half of the plant food sample based on weight (Tung 2007c). If the botanic sample is representative of the menu at Beringa, then maize and molle were certainly staples in the Beringa diet. The deep deposits of molle seeds and the large ceramic vessels indicate that molle was likely consumed as *chicha* (a fermented beverage, like beer). Modern inhabitants (and archaeologists) of the valley and surrounding regions still drink this beverage today. Chicha de molle was produced at Beringa as well. Peduncles from *S. molle* were common at the site, suggesting that the villagers did not individually pick the berries from the tree but brought them back in bunches (like grapes on a vine) to be processed later (Tung 2007c). This is similar to harvesting and production patterns of molle at the Wari site of Cerro Baúl in the Moquegua valley (Goldstein et al. 2009), where a chicha de molle "brewery" has been identified (Moseley et al. 2005). As I have suggested elsewhere, the similarities in production and consumption patterns of chicha de molle at these two Wari sites suggest that this fermented drink was "an integral and integrating" element of Wari imperialism in the southern hinterland (Tung 2007c:260).

Faunal analysis shows that there were at least 15 different genera of animals at the site, represented by 13,893 animal bones, shell, and feathers (Gladwell 2003). While the vast majority of the animal remains would have been dietary items, a few animal remains may have had other functions (pets, sacrifices, feathers and wool for textile production and decoration). There was one intact (and partially mummified) parrot from the Amazon (Gladwell 2003); the colorful feathers from this (and other Amazonian birds) were used to decorate the elaborate Wari-inspired textiles.

The NISP (number of individual specimens present) indicates that half of the nonplant menu derived from the Majes River and Pacific Ocean: 10 percent freshwater shrimp (*Cryphiops caementarius*), 8 percent marine/river fish (class Osteichthyes), and 32 percent marine shell (class Bivalvia and class Gastropoda);

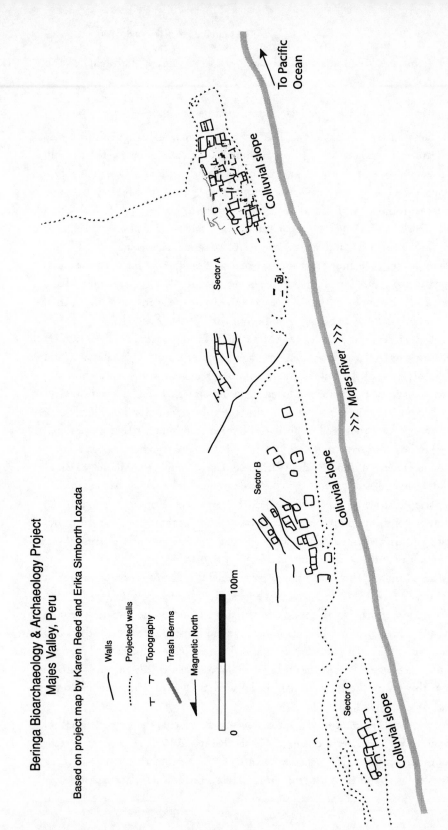

Beringa Bioarchaeology & Archaeology Project
Majes Valley, Peru

Based on project map by Karen Reed and Erika Simborth Lozada

Walls
Projected walls
Topography
Trash Berms
Magnetic North

0   100m

Sector A

Sector B

Sector C

Colluvial slope

Colluvial slope

Colluvial slope

Majes River >>>

To Pacific
Ocean

Figure 3.6. Map of Beringa, all sectors.

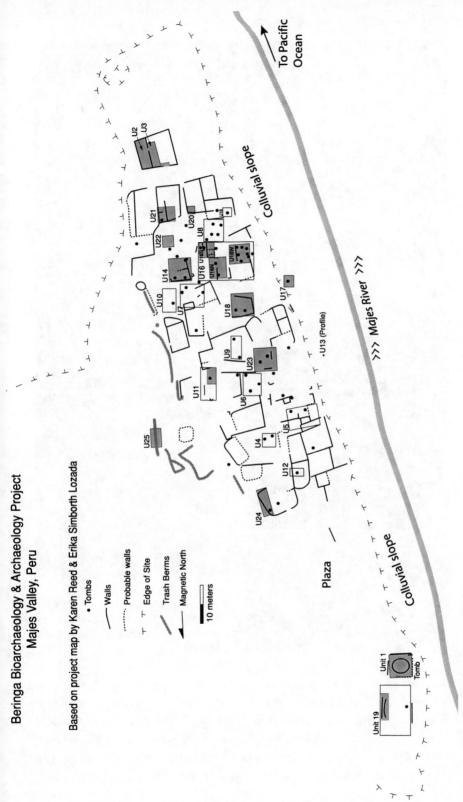

Beringa Bioarchaeology & Archaeology Project
Majes Valley, Peru

Based on project map by Karen Reed & Erika Simborth Lozada

• Tombs
——— Walls
········· Probable walls
┬ ┬ Edge of Site
〰 Trash Berms
Magnetic North

10 meters

To Pacific Ocean

Colluvial slope

Majes River >>>

Plaza

Colluvial slope

U2 U3
U21
U20
U22
U8
U16
U14
U10
U7
U18
U17
U9
U23
U11
U6
U25
U4 U5
U12
U24
U13 (Profile)

Unit 19
Unit 1
Tomb

Figure 3.7. Map of Sector A at Beringa.

Figure 3.8. Photos of Wari-influenced ceramics and textiles recovered from Beringa. (Center four photos by Bruce Owen.)

the other 50 percent was derived mainly from guinea pig (8 percent) and llama (42 percent) (Gladwell 2003). The faunal and botanical remains suggest that the Beringa inhabitants enjoyed a diverse diet, even if much of their diet included iron-inhibiting food, such as maize, and potentially parasite-loaded foods from the river and ocean. These resources likely contributed to the high prevalence of iron-deficiency anemia and other vitamin deficiencies (as gleaned from rates of cribra orbitalia and porotic hyperostosis) among juveniles and adults at Beringa (Tung and Del Castillo 2005).

Radiocarbon Dates from Beringa

Radiocarbon dates collected from in situ contexts confirm that Beringa was occupied in the Middle Horizon and Late Intermediate Period. Based on seven AMS radiocarbon measurements, Beringa was occupied circa AD 600–850 (the first half of the Middle Horizon) and again circa AD 1040–1250 (the first half of the Late Intermediate Period) (Tung 2007c). Based on these dates, I have suggested that Beringa was depopulated or abandoned in the latter half of the Middle Horizon, an action that corresponds with other major construction or renovation projects at other Wari sites; these events might hint at imperial reorganization during this time (Tung 2007c). Granted, it is possible that sampling strategies at Beringa missed the later Middle Horizon components; thus, additional radiocarbon samples are needed to evaluate this further. (All radiocarbon dates are summarized in table 3.2.)

La Real

The third site in this study, La Real, is a mortuary site located about eight kilometers downstream from Beringa, on the right (west) side of the river margin. It has two main sectors: a rectangular semisubterranean structure that likely housed ceremonial activities, and a separate mortuary cave. The site is located within the modern town of La Real and was discovered when workers for the local municipality began to clear the area to construct a soccer field. Archaeologists Pablo de la Vera, Marco López, and Willy Yepez, among others, performed a salvage excavation in 1995 under the auspices of the National Institute of Culture and the local municipality. The site is now covered by concrete.

La Real Site Description

The semisubterranean structure was constructed of a double coursing of stone, measuring 10 by 9 meters. There was an internal dividing wall with a doorway that divided the building into two unequal sections. Excavations within the structure recovered thousands of disturbed human and animal bones, many of which were burned. The burning was done at low temperature, as evidenced by the black color and absence of vitrification. Artifacts included textiles, ceramics, and wood and metal objects. A few textiles were decorated with colorful feathers, and some metal objects were embossed. Other artifacts included a figurine of a person holding a human trophy head (de la Vera Cruz Chávez and Yépez Alvarez 1995) as well as a carved wooden snuff tablet (Garcia Márquez and Bustamante Montoro 1990). These artifacts appear to be items associated with ceremonial activities and probably belonged to high-status individuals. Unfortunately, several of these items, textiles in particular, were stolen from the local museum in Aplao, so other than viewing photos of them, I was never able to observe these artifacts.

The mortuary cave was a few meters from the semisubterranean structure, and although its opening was small, the internal portion was approximately two meters high in some areas. The cave yielded similar items as the structure but included more human remains, many of which were burned. Several individuals were placed in *fardos* (reed bags used for wrapping mummy bundles), but because of looting, the preponderance of human skeletal remains and mummies were commingled.

The site layout, architecture, and artifacts from La Real indicate that it was solely used as a ceremonial and mortuary complex (de la Vera Cruz Chávez and Yépez Alvarez 1995; Garcia Márquez and Bustamante Montoro 1990). There appears to be an associated domestic component located on the alluvial and rocky slopes far above the mortuary cave. However, it is unclear whether the burial catchment for the La Real burial cave includes this one habitation site only or several Middle Horizon settlements in the middle Majes valley. That is, the La Real burial cave and associated structure could have been the final resting place for a select group of high-status individuals from one or more sites. In short, the uniqueness of the mortuary cave, the ceremonial structure, and the rare, high-status goods indicate that this burial ground was likely used by an exclusive, high-status group who had access to exotic goods from the Wari trade network, the Nasca cultural sphere, and the Amazon. Obsidian in particular derives from the Wari sphere of trade, similar to the sources for the obsidian recovered from Beringa. According to recent analyses by Yépez Álvarez and Jennings (2010), among the seven obsidian pieces analyzed through XRF analysis, six are from Wari sources (five from Alca and one from Quispisisa) and one is from the Chivay source, which is typically identified as the obsidian source for the Tiwanaku sphere.

Radiocarbon Dates from La Real

La Real was used as a mortuary site during the first and second parts of the Middle Horizon, spanning approximately AD 600 to AD 1150 (Tung 2007b; Yépez Álvarez and Jennings 2010) (table 3.2). The mortuary cave where the majority of the human remains were recovered appears to predate the use of the ceremonial structure that was in front of the cave (Yépez Álvarez and Jennings 2010). The cave component yielded calibrated dates primarily within the AD 600 to AD 890 range, while the structure yielded calibrated dates between AD 700 and AD 1150 (Yépez Álvarez and Jennings 2010).

Synthesis of Wari Studies in the Majes Valley

The archaeological data suggest possible Wari administrative control of a short duration in coastal Majes (Camaná) (Malpass 2001) and limited indirect influence in the Colca highlands (Wernke 2003). In the middle Majes valley, current evidence suggests that local groups were not under direct Wari administrative control, as no Wari administrative center has yet been documented there. Nonetheless, Wari influence was dominant in the region. The obsidian is linked to Wari sources, and the quantity of Wari ceramics and textiles exceeds a few eccentric pieces, so Wari influence surpassed isolated incidences of trade. Indeed, the vast assemblages of Wari artifacts and high-status goods at several Majes sites suggest that Wari wielded influence through local elites in the Majes valley. High-status goods, such as Wari ceramic finewares, Wari feathered textiles, tie-dyed textiles, and gold and silver embossed plaques indicate that the relationship between Wari agents and local elites may have been based on a new exchange system of prestige goods.

Additionally, Wari imperial strategies may have included oversight of the mundane, whereby they targeted low-lying yungas regions where a variety of semitropical plant foods could easily grow, including socially valued plant foods, such as maize and molle. Thus, this novel politico-economic arrangement between Majes and Wari groups likely altered local political and social networks, which in turn may have differentially affected the health status of members within each community. Clearly, a bioarchaeology of imperialism is needed to elucidate how imperial-local interactions affect community organization, health status, and rituals involving the body, and not just for subject groups but for both sides of imperial-local interactions.

Wari Community Organization

Demography, Migration, and Mortuary Treatment

Imperial policies can affect the population composition of subject communities in a variety of ways. The imperial power may relocate populations and aggregate them, similar to that imposed on native populations during the time of *congregación* (or *reducción*) in early colonial Spanish Florida (Worth 2001) and early colonial Peru (Gade and Escobar 1982; Málaga Medina 1974). Imperial leaders may also dictate the temporary relocation of individuals for labor projects, particularly young, unmarried males, as was done in the Spanish colonial *repartimiento* system throughout the Americas (Premo 2000; Worth 2001:18).[1] Notably, studies of the Inka Empire show that they too relocated whole and parts of populations for state labor projects, for military campaigns, and to prevent or quell rebellions (D'Altroy 1992). Given that many aspects of Inka statecraft likely derived from the preceding Wari, Wari imperial policies may have stipulated the relocation of individuals and communities to meet state goals. Wari policies and practices also could have contributed to population movement more generally, thus affecting the population composition of heartland and hinterland communities.

The process of peopling a settlement and the resultant demographic profile can reveal much about community organization. For example, urban sites like Conchopata may be populated by people from diverse areas, such as descendants of those who long lived in the region and by migrants from neighboring or distant areas. Identifying locals versus migrants from other zones is possible with strontium isotope analysis, a data set in this study that is combined with the age-at-death and sex profiles and ancient mtDNA data to evaluate the population composition of the Conchopata community. This is done not just for demographic analysis but also as a means to reconstruct the social identities of community members. These combined data sets can then aid in clarifying the various ways that inhabitants may have interacted with each other, either cooperatively or antagonistically. The presence of foreign migrants at a settlement may suggest that it was a cosmopolitan center with expansive trade and marriage networks where individuals settled in pursuit of greater social, economic, or other opportunities (Arutinov 2002). Nonlocal individuals at a site may also reveal that there were state-managed resettlement programs—and attendant tensions—as when the Inka resettled people to new, distant lands (D'Altroy 2002; Rowe 1946), or it may indicate that military agents engaged in abductions of people from other villages, taking them back to their home settlement as captives. Conversely, a community constituted solely of local people may suggest an exclusive settlement designed to keep foreigners out, or it might reflect migrants' disinterest in settling there.

The site of Tiwanaku is an example of a cosmopolitan center with diverse groups of people living there or at least being buried there. The various cranial modification forms observed at Tiwanaku suggest that people from diverse regions settled there (Blom 2005), as do the wide range of strontium isotope ratios observed in the Tiwanaku skeletons (Knudson and Blom 2009). Whether the capital city—Huari—was similarly cosmopolitan is unknown, as no Middle Horizon skeletons have yet been analyzed from this important site (Tung 2008b). We can, however, examine the population composition of the secondary Wari site in the heartland—Conchopata—to evaluate whether foreigners were absent or present at the site. If present, we can further query whether they voluntarily settled there or were brought there against their will (that is, as captives).

Indirect Effects of Imperialism on Population Compositions

Empires can also impact population profiles in a less direct manner than forced resettlement. For example, imperial practices may prejudicially affect mortality rates among a particular subgroup in one community or contribute to increased mortality among an entire population. On the one hand, excessive demands on males to participate in risky activities, either for state labor projects or warfare, for example, can lead to increased male mortality and a decrease in the mean age-at-death among males. On the other hand, imperial policies can contribute to better health among community members by limiting dangerous activities or provisioning them with adequate resources or the means for resource production (Costin et al. 1989; D'Altroy 1992). Additionally, sex-based differential access to resources can lead to poorer nutritional status among one sex relative to the other, and because inadequate nutrition is linked to increased morbidity and mortality (Armelagos 1994; Huss-Ashmore et al. 1982; Larsen 1997), differences in age-at-death profiles between males and females may develop.

These imperial effects on the demographic composition of communities can be evaluated through bioarchaeological analysis. By determining the sex and age-at-death of skeletons, the demographic profile of a once-living population can be reconstructed with some degree of accuracy (Hoppa and Vaupel 2002; Jackes 1992; Milner et al. 2000; but see Bocquet-Appel and Masset 1982). As a result, population profiles of archaeological communities can be compared to each other, or mortuary populations can be compared to expected population distributions because ancient demographic patterns should not deviate too greatly from nonindustrialized modern human groups (Milner et al. 2000). Additionally, demographic compositions can be reconstructed to document changes through time. As a case in point, among a historic ossuary population from a church in Quito, Ecuador, adult longevity increased for males and females from the prehistoric to historic period, and female age-at-death was, on average, higher than that of males (Ubelaker and Ripley 1999:31). In the Nasca region of south-central Peru, a detailed paleodemographic study of pre-Wari- and Wari-era skeletons showed that mean age-at-death declined from pre-Wari to Wari times, leading Drusini to conclude that Wari-period populations in Nasca were under more physiological stress than their predecessors (Drusini 2001:167).[2]

Why Reconstruct Demographic Profiles?

Estimating the age-at-death and sex profiles of a skeletal population is an essential part of bioarchaeological inquiry and serves as an important foundation for anthropological studies of community organization. Demographic reconstructions should be carefully undertaken, however, as there are many variables that can affect the outcome, ranging from inter- and intraobserver error in aging and sexing accuracy to differential skeletal preservation, incomplete excavations, and biased skeletal recovery and long-term curation (see Hoppa and Vaupel 2002; Milner et al. 2000). However, if a large mortuary area has been excavated, the skeletal sample is sufficiently preserved, and nothing about the burial patterns suggests that a particular subgroup (for example, children) was interred in a special zone, then the mortuary sample may represent the once-living population. If so, these data can be used to describe possible forms of ancient community organization. For example, the investigator can estimate whether the demographic profile matches that of a village comprising extended families with adults (parents and other consanguines) and children, a community that practices polygyny or polyandry, a place for sequestered women, or a temporary settlement for a predominantly male work group. In this way, skeletal data on demography can be taken to the next level of anthropological interpretation and be used to investigate the social organization of ancient communities.

The estimation of skeletal age and sex also enables an investigation into sex-based differences in health and changing health profiles through the life course. When skeletons are sorted into sex and general age categories, demographic subgroups, such as men or children, can be aggregated with observations on pathological lesions, skeletal fractures, and metrics to chart sex- and age-based distributions of disease, trauma, and general health and nutritional status. Observations on individual skeletons can also be used to describe individual identities and individual life experiences as a way to provide more nuanced and detailed insights into the life conditions of past peoples.

Documenting skeletal age and sex also provides insights into how these aspects of identity may have structured one's health status during the time of Wari rule. That is, because age and sex are such salient characteristics of one's identity, often playing a significant role in opportunities and actions afforded to particular peoples—and in turn their health status—these empirical data provide a more concrete way to evaluate how social structures shaped people's lives in Wari society. How did one's sex (or socially performed gender) structure his or her access to food acquisition, production, and preparation capacities? In some societies, hunting is an activity reserved for males, which can lead to sex-based differences in protein consumption (Hill and Hurtado 1996). In this way, we can see how one's sex structures access to nutrients. Similarly, gender-based social roles—for example, whether one becomes a warrior or not—can structure the likelihood that a person will engage in violence and suffer life-threatening injuries.

Age and sex should also be evaluated in terms of how these inherent characteristics factored into structural constraints on other aspects of livelihood, not just health (Featherstone et al. 1998). In the same way that age cohort or sex designation often structures social interactions for peoples today—think of classrooms, career paths, sports, or living arrangements—these traits also would have been critical aspects to one's identity and place in society in the past. Although we don't know how the Wari would have marked the passage of time or assigned "age" to a particular person, some social categories were likely linked to maturation rates. As such, an individual's age and sex could enhance or inhibit the ability to participate in particular facets of family and community life or gain social and political status. For example, boys and girls could not directly participate in biologically reproducing their community until after puberty, and even then, there may have been cultural factors that stipulated appropriate reproductive partners. Another example that shows how age structures social action can be seen in the authority afforded to elders in some communities. Elders may be viewed as more knowledgeable about community history and traditions, so their insights may be favored in decisions affecting the group. As a result, older adults may more readily access higher social and political status by virtue of their age, combined with other inherent and acquired qualities. In short, analyzing the skeleton to identify age-at-death and sex provides a glimpse into how ancient societies were organized, while providing more-focused views of individual gendered and aged experiences.

The ways in which age and sex can structure a person's actions in society differ between cultural groups and vary through time. Anthropological bioarchaeology must therefore use age-at-death and sex data to evaluate how structures enhanced and inhibited the agency of particular persons in particular facets of their lives (Bourdieu 1977; Bourdieu 1994; Dobres and Robb 2000). How did personal characteristics, such as age and sex, aid and limit people as they maneuvered through societal structures? Bioarchaeology, although rarely associated with this kind of inquiry (but see Dobres and Robb 2000), is ideally suited to address this because of its inherently careful consideration of the individual agent (represented by the skeleton) in his or her cultural and ecological contexts. If, for example, females are more commonly buried with exotic grave goods, then this may indicate that they (or their mourners) more freely accessed long-distance trade networks. By extension, this may suggest that women, or those who cared for their corpses, had less-fettered access to these exotic goods. In turn, as women and their caretakers accrued these items, they continued to create and reproduce the social norms and social structure that allowed them relatively greater access to these exotic goods.

Other factors that are built upon and tethered to age and sex also play a role: social class, family status, spiritual identity, or political rank can greatly affect how one engages with society. This is not to say that age and sex are primary determinants and these other traits are secondary. To the contrary, age, sex, and a variety of other attributes work in tandem to situate individuals within a social structure that their aged, gendered, and socialized behaviors tend to reproduce (Bourdieu 1977). Using skeletal analysis to document age and sex is thus an important first step in documenting how these traits related to one's health status and lifeways, while also providing the foundation for documenting the form of social organization for the community under study.

Reconstructing the Demographic Profile

Age-at-death and sex estimates were based on methods presented by Buikstra and Ubelaker (1994), though the age categories in this study were slightly altered from the ones presented in "Standards" (Buikstra and Ubelaker 1994) (see list below). The age-at-death profiles are based on general age cohorts, not specific age designations, because commingled bones prevented determination of specific ages for all individuals. The age-at-death categories include the following:

F=Fetus (in utero)
I=Infant (birth–3 years)
C=Child (4–14 years)
T=Teen (15–19 years)
YA=Young adult (20–34 years)
MA=Middle adult (35–49 years)
OA=Old adult (50+ years)
A=Adult (20+ years)

After age-at-death and sex profiles are reconstructed, they must be evaluated to determine how closely they represent the once-living population. Factors such as differential skeletal preservation (Gordon and Buikstra 1981; Walker et al. 1988), mortuary practices that may include separate burial areas for children and adults, and decisions about where to excavate (Milner et al. 2000) greatly impact the resulting demographic profile (Hoppa and Vaupel 2002). Thus, all of these factors are considered in the analysis of the three skeletal populations in this study. (See Tung 2003 for a detailed discussion on factors that can affect the reconstruction of skeletal demographic profiles.)

Following Walker and Cook (1998) and Sofaer (2006), I make a distinction between skeletal sex and socially performed gender. The osteological methods used in this study are suited only for identifying skeletal sex. In contrast, gender is best identified based on burial treatment and grave good associations, at least in archaeological contexts in the Andes. Certainly, one should never base skeletal sex on artifact association. However, in the Andes, archaeological and historical evidence have demonstrated that *tupus* (bone or metal pins used to pin clothing together) were primarily—but not always—worn by women, indicating that this particular object was most commonly associated with female identity. More importantly, a previous study on burials and grave goods from Conchopata demonstrates that tupus are found only with female burials (Tung and Cook 2006). In short, when skeletal sex cannot be determined but a tupu is present with an individual, I note that the social gender of the person is likely female but that skeletal sex is unknown. Although third or more genders (Fausto-Sterling 1993), akin to the berdache among Navajo society, may have been socially recognized in the ancient Andes, there is currently no archaeological evidence for this during the Wari era.

Population Profiles and Mortuary Treatment at Conchopata

The MNI at Conchopata

My previous research has shown that the minimum number of individuals (MNI) at Conchopata was 300 (Tung 2003). Since that study, additional human skeletal remains have been excavated, which represent at least another 17 individuals and hundreds of skeletal fragments that could be assigned to preexisting individuals. Thus, in total, the minimum number of individuals (MNI) at Conchopata is 317: 27 Huarpa (pre-Wari) burials, 259 Wari-era burials, and 31 Wari-era trophy heads (table 4.1).

Huarpa Age-at-Death and Sex Distributions at Conchopata

Twenty-seven individuals come from three architectural spaces dating to the pre-Wari component (EA100, EA104-T5, and the burial pit excavated in 1977). The age distribution reveals that one-third are infants and children (<15 years old) and two-thirds are adolescents and adults (≥15 years old). In particular, adolescents constitute the largest cohort at 22 percent (6 out of 27), which is remarkable given that it includes only those between ages 15 and 19 years old. The frequencies of all age cohorts for the Huarpa era are shown in figure 4.1. No fetuses were recovered from the Huarpa tombs.

Females far outnumber males in the Huarpa-era burial population. Of the 16 adults whose sex could be determined, women ($n=14$) and men ($n=2$) constitute 87.5 percent and 12.5 percent, respectively. The Huarpa sex profile does

Table 4.1. Minimum number of individuals (MNI) at the three sites evaluated in this study

Site	MNI for pre-Wari (Huarpa)	MNI for Wari	Wari-era trophy heads[a]	MNI for Wari/post-Wari[b]	Totals
Conchopata	27	259	31	0	317
Beringa	0	151	1	85	237
La Real	0	145	7	0	152
Totals	27	555	39	85	706

[a] Trophy heads are not counted with the individuals from the formal mortuary areas; they constitute a separate group at each site.

[b] There are 85 partial skeletons from Beringa that could not be specifically assigned to one time period, so they are included only in the initial description of the Beringa demographic profile and are excluded from subsequent data presentations. Those excluded individuals do not correspond solely to the Middle Horizon but instead date to Middle Horizon/Late Intermediate Period (Wari/post-Wari).

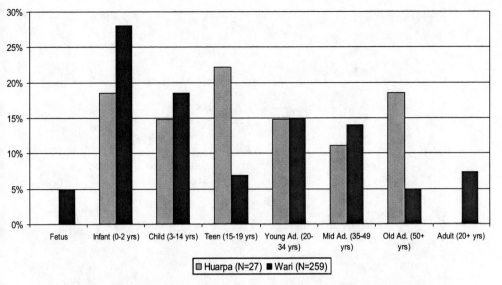

Figure 4.1. Age-at-death distribution for Huarpa (*N*=27) and Wari (*N*=259) individuals at Conchopata.

not conform to the sex distribution of a normal human population. Instead of the expected 1:1 ratio of males to females, the male-to-female ratio is 1:7. The difference between the observed sex distribution and a symmetrical distribution is statistically significant (Fisher's exact, $p=0.027$).

That so many of the Huarpa burials are female is intriguing, yet given the small sample size and abnormal distribution of age cohorts, this burial group probably does not reflect the once-living Huarpa-era population. That is, based on current data, I do not suggest that Huarpa-era inhabitants at Conchopata were primarily adolescent and adult females. Rather, the observed demographic profile may reflect unique mortuary practices in which groups of women were interred together.

Huarpa Burial Treatment

The spaces where the Huarpa-era bodies were interred are located in the northwest area of Sector B, near the modern road (see figure 3.3). The burials were either in a seated, flexed position; placed upon or alongside stone slabs (for example, Locus 2107); or in a reclined, flexed position with a Huarpa vessel on top of the body (for example, Locus 2099) (figure 4.2). This sector with the Huarpa burials remains an enigma because the "Pink Plaza" under which 15 Huarpa skeletons were recovered (EA104-T5) has been variably interpreted as ceremonial (Isbell and Cook 2002) and as a space for large-scale ceramic production (Wolff n.d.).

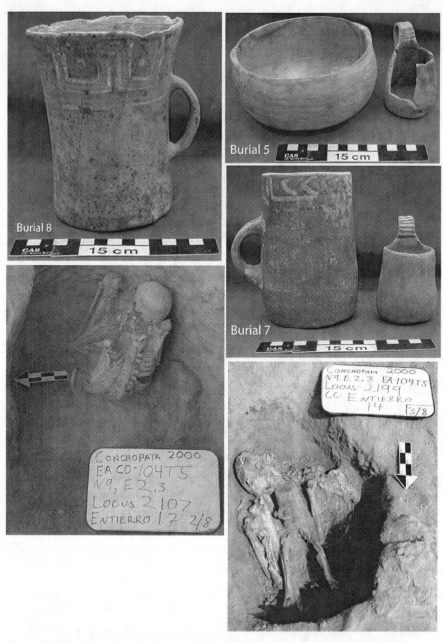

Figure 4.2. *Top*: Huarpa ceramic vessels that were interred with Huarpa-era burials in EA100. Burial 8 (*top left*) was a 3–4-year-old child; Burials 5 and 7 (*top and middle right*) were old adult females. *Bottom*: In situ burials from the Huarpa era (EA104T5). *Bottom left*: Older adult female (50+ years) buried on top of stone slab. *Bottom right*: Old adult male (45–50 years) buried with a Huarpa cup on his chest. (Locus number on the board should read 2099, not 2199.) (Ceramic photos by T. Tung, with permission from William Isbell and Anita Cook; burial photos courtesy of William Isbell and Anita Cook.)

Isbell and Cook suggest that this Huarpa-era "little cemetery became a public ceremonial area, with the addition of thick layers of reddish sand" (that is, the Pink Plaza) where offering jars and urns were deposited in pits (Isbell and Cook 2002:290), and a sacrificed camelid was interred atop a large obsidian axe. The reddish sand does not naturally occur at the site and was carried in from neighboring ravines, perhaps to demarcate this particular space in a highly visible manner.

Wolff (n.d.), in contrast, suggests that the Pink Plaza may have been a ceramic production center placed on top of earlier Huarpa burials. The reddish sand could have been used as temper, and the canal running through the plaza may have brought in water necessary for producing ceramics (Wolff n.d.). Importantly, Wolff's analysis has also shown that 15 percent of all ceramic production implements came from EA104, the Pink Plaza.

To the north of EA104, a large quadrangular area was denoted as EA100 (see dotted lines around EA100 in figure 3.3). It contains a circular ritual structure in which large quantities of oversize urn fragments and "regular sized pottery" were found, likely representing an offering smash (Isbell and Cook 2002:264). Three individual human burials were recovered from stratigraphically lower levels than the Wari-style ceramic offerings. One of the burials, a child of 3–4 years, was interred with an intact Huarpa cup (Burial 8, Locus 1339) similar to the one interred with the old adult male from Locus 2099, shown in figure 4.2. The other two Huarpa burials were old adult females, each of which was associated with two Huarpa ceramic vessels (Burial 7, Locus 1319 and Burial 5, Locus 1288) (figure 4.2).

The third group of pre-Wari burials is immediately west-northwest of the Pink Plaza and was uncovered in 1977 by William Isbell and colleagues during a salvage excavation. The stratigraphy, burial goods, and radiocarbon dates from neighboring rooms suggest that it is transitional Huarpa/Wari (Ketteman 2002). Archaeologists in the 1970s designated five tombs in this space, which yielded a total of nine females. Specifically, Tombs 1 through 4 each contained a partially complete female skeleton, ranging in age from adolescence to old adulthood. Tomb 5 contained five complete burials: three adolescent females and two young adult females. These five women were flexed and lying on their sides next to one another. Four of them were associated with a total of three worked bone pins, a spindle whorl, and eleven large and small copper pins (*tupus* and *t'ipkis*) used for fastening clothing (Tung and Cook 2006). In particular, the worked bone pins were found near the skull of one female and suggest that she was wearing a *ñañaca* (head scarf) (Tung and Cook 2006), which was reserved for women of high status in later Inka times (Cobo 1990 [1653]:185–89). The clothing adornments suggest that these were women of relatively high status who could afford items of prestige or were perceived by their mourners as women deserving of these ornamentations.

Wari Period Age-at-Death and Sex Distributions at Conchopata

Of the 290 individuals that date to the Wari era, 259 were occupants of tombs in 51 different architectural spaces. The remaining 31 individuals are trophy heads from two ritual structures, and because of their unique treatment, they are not considered as part of the formal mortuary sample from Conchopata. Data on the trophy heads are presented separately in chapter 6.

The age-at-death distribution of the 259 individuals shows that fetus, infant, and child deaths constitute more than half of the mortuary population; 51 percent (133/259) are individuals under 15 years of age and 49 percent (126/259) are 15 years old or older (figure 4.1). Specifically, fetuses and infants make up 32 percent of the burial sample. This calculation includes 12 fetuses that were disassociated from the pregnant women (that is, not in the womb of a female). (The one fetus in the womb of a pregnant female, discussed in chapter 3, is not calculated in the MNI, nor is it factored into the age-at-death distribution.)

Among the 93 individuals whose sex could be determined, 59 were female (63%) and 34 were male (37%). This represents an asymmetrical sex ratio; the male-to-female ratio is 1:1.74. The difference between the observed and expected sex distributions is statistically significant (Fisher's exact, $p=0.044$), suggesting that there may have been significantly more women at Conchopata than expected for a normal human population distribution.

Wari Burial Treatment

Single burials were uncommon at Conchopata during the Wari era; only 11 of the 52 architectural spaces had single interments. Multi-individual tombs were the apparent norm; 41 of the 52 mortuary rooms contained multiple burials ranging from two to as many as 30 individuals, where men, women, children, and fetuses were buried together. They could be interred together in large, underground bedrock pits (for example, EA105) (Isbell 2004; Tung and Cook 2006) or in a cist tomb (for example, EA151). In some cases, several cist tombs were grouped together in a room or group of adjoining rooms and multiple burials were placed within each cist tomb (for example, EA37/38B/44A and EA39/39A/39B/39C/39D) (see figure 3.3).

All intact burials whose body position could be observed were buried in a flexed position, and while body positioning was uniform, tomb design was not. Isbell (2004) and Tung and Cook (2006) have described in detail the various mortuary styles at Conchopata, showing that there were at least eight tomb types. These include tomb forms such as stone-lined or stone-capped cist tombs, pits cut into bedrock or soil, and mortuary rooms with several stone-lined cist

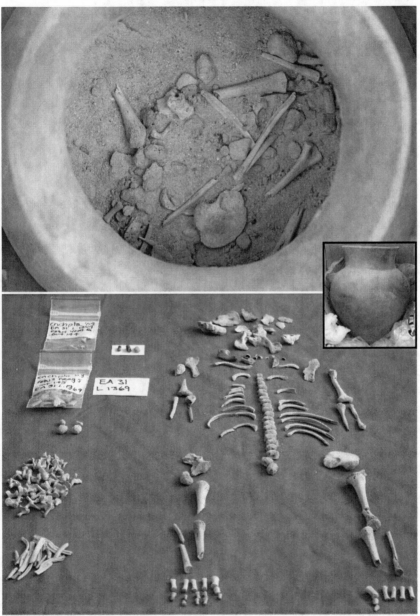

Figure 4.3. *Top*: Ceramic vessel with fetus (EA31, Locus 1369, HE536, Conchopata, Wari era). *Bottom*: Fetus bones from vessel. *Inset*: Profile view of ceramic vessel (height=26.20 cm).

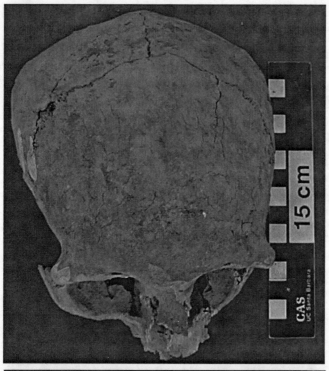

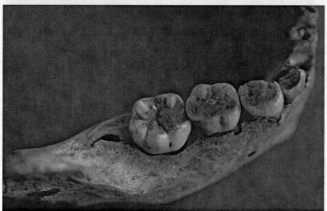

Figure 4.4. *Top*: Cinnabar on the surface of an old adult female cranium (EA150). *Bottom*: Cinnabar on the mandible and dentition from a child (EA179).

tombs surrounded by rectangular stone enclosures. Fetuses were often placed in ceramic jars filled with white ash and capped with an upside-down bowl (figure 4.3). Cinnabar was also observed on the surface of bones of several individuals, demonstrating that corpses were covered with this bright red mineral as part of the mortuary treatment (figure 4.4).

Genetic Structure of the Conchopata Community

In collaboration with molecular anthropologist Brian Kemp and geneticist Marshall Summar, we attempted to extract mtDNA from 49 Conchopata samples: 16 out of 49 (33%) of the samples contained analyzable mtDNA. All 16 samples that contained mtDNA could be assigned to one of the Native American haplogroups documented in South America: either A, B, C, or D. Three samples taken from one individual (1998.01, excavated by José Ochatoma and Martha Cabrera's team) all yielded the same results: sample numbers 2, 9, and 27 resulted in the designation of haplogroup D. (Kemp was unaware that these three samples were from the same skeleton, so these results help to confirm the reliability of the techniques. For a detailed discussion of methods, see Kemp et al. 2009.)

The 16 samples represented 14 individuals, and haplogroup B was by far the most common (table 4.2). Results show the following: 4 out of 14 (28.6%) are haplogroup A; 7 out of 14 (50%) are haplogroup B; 2 out of 14 (14.3%) are haplogroup C; and 1 out of 14 (7.1%) is haplogroup D (Kemp et al. 2009). (The one female that belongs to haplogroup D may slightly postdate the other burials [Ochatoma, pers. comm. 2007], but because there are no radiocarbon dates from her, the temporal separation is unknown.) The high frequency of haplogroup B, followed by haplogroup A, coincides with what has been observed for other central and south-central Andean populations, both ancient and modern (Forgey 2005; Kemp et al. 2009; Lewis et al. 2007; Lewis et al. 2005 Schurr 2004; Shimada et al. 2004; Shinoda et al. 2006). Thus, at the regional level, the Conchopata population is clearly closely related to other Andean groups and in no way represents any kind of population isolate.

At the site level, the distribution of haplogroups reveals no clustering of maternal groups (figure 4.5). Because mtDNA is maternally inherited, a clustering of one haplogroup in a particular patio-tomb group might suggest that households were organized based on shared maternal relationships. However, given the small sample of haplogroup data currently available, this does not appear to be the pattern.

A focused examination of individuals' age, sex, and haplogroup (Hg) within a particular room, however, is quite revealing. For example, in EA208 there were four incomplete burials in the southeast corner of the space: a middle-aged female, a middle-aged male, an adolescent (13–15 years old), and a fetus-infant. These burials had been disturbed, but it was easy to extract a tooth from the crania of the female, male, and teenager to ensure no overlap. (The fetal-infant remains were too poorly preserved to justify an attempt at mtDNA extraction.) EA208 was likely an open patio that was next to an important room (EA205)

Table 4.2. Haplogroup (Hg) and strontium isotope ratios ($^{87}Sr/^{86}Sr$) from Conchopata

Lab ID[a]	EA[b]	Locus	Burial code[c]	Osteology code	Bone/tooth[d]	Sex	Age	Hg[e]	$^{87}Sr/^{86}Sr$
Conch35/ F1228	**6**	**2004**		**2004.01**	**Rib**	**?**	**1–2 y**	**?**	**0.70673**
Conch25/ ACL0749	**20**	**1371**		**1371.01.05**	**L Md C**	**F**	**17–22 y**	**B**	**0.71058**
Conch22/ ACL0747	88	3032	54.03	3032–54.03.06	R Md C		11–14 y	C	0.70579
ACL0779	89A	2052	09	2052–09.01.01	R Mx M2	F	45+ y	N/A	0.70552
ACL0786	104T5	2107	17	2107–17.01T	L Md P3	F	45+ y	N/A	0.70571
ACL0787	104T5	2107	17	2107–17.02T	R Mx M1	F	45+ y	N/A	0.70571
ACL0788	104T5	2107	17	2107–17.03B	R humerus	F	45+ y	N/A	0.70572
2095.01T/F1219	105	2095		2095.01T	L Md M2	F	30–39 y	?	0.70560
F1218	105	2095		2095.01B	R fibula	F	30–39 y	N/A	0.70610
2095.01B	105	2095		2095.01B	Rib	F	30–39 y	?	N/A
2095.02B	105	2095		2095.02B	Rib	F	21–29 y	?	N/A
F1220	105	2095		2095.02B	R fibula	F	21–29 y	N/A	0.70574
F1221	105	2095		2095.02T	R Md M2	F	21–29 y	N/A	0.70563
F1222	105	2095		2095.03B	R fibula	F	7–53 y	N/A	0.70586
F1223	105	2095		2095.03T	Md M	F	47–53 y	N/A	0.70565
Conch37	105	2095		2095.03B	Rib	F	47–53 y	?	N/A
F1224	105	2095		2095.04B	L fibula	F	31–37 y	N/A	0.70566
2095.04T/F1225	105	2095		2095.04T	L Md M2	F	31–37 y	?	0.70565
2095.04B	105	2095		2095.04B	Rib	F	31–37 y	?	N/A
2095.06B/F1226	105	2095		2095.06B	Rib	M	23–27 y	?	0.70574
2095.06T/F1227	105	2095		2095.06T	R Md M2	M	23–27 y	?	0.70548

Conch31/ACL0767	110	1993		1993.02	R Md M1	?	Adult	A	0.70584
1993.01	110	1993		1993.01	L Md M1	?	Adult	B	N/A
2112.01	110	2112		2112.01	L Md M1		Adult	?	N/A
Conch28	110	2112		2112.02	L Md M		Adult	?	N/A
ACL0780	147	2884	42	2884–42.01.01T	r decid md m2	?	6–7 y	N/A	0.70570
ACL0781	147	2884	42	2884–42.01.02T	R Md M2	?	6–7 y	N/A	0.70571
Conch10/ACL0782	150	2981	94.01	2981–94.01	L femur	F	50+ y	?	0.70576
Conch04/ACL0783	150	2981	94.02	2981–94.02	R ulna	F	18–22 y	?	0.70589
ACL0784	150	2981	94.03	2981–94.03	R ulna	F	14–17 y	N/A	0.70569
Conch01/ACL0785	150	2981	94.04	2981–94.04	Metacarpal	?	3–6 y	?	0.70569
Conch26/ACL0795	151	2858	51.01	2858–51.01	R Mx P4 & L Md M2	F	30–35 y	A	0.70571
Conch12/ACL0745	187	3335		3335.155	R Mx C	?	Adult	B	0.70565
Conch05/ACL0764	205	3521	104.01	3521–104.01.64	L fibula	?	12–18 m	?	0.70570
Conch08/ACL0765	205	3521	105.02	3521–105.02.55	L rib	?	12–18 m	C	0.70572
Conch06/ACL0743	205	3521	107.03	3521–107.03.66B	R hand phalanx	F	35–50 y	?	0.70565
Conch20/ACL0766	205	3521	107.03	3521–107.03.18T	R Md P3	F	35–50 y	?	0.70560
Conch07/ACL0744	205	3554	106	3554–106.01.44	R fibula	?	9–12 m	?	0.70572
Conch23/ACL0750	208	3547	108.01	3547–108.01.13	L Mx M2	M	35–50 y	A	0.70558
Conch21/ACL0746	208	3547	108.03	3547–108.03.05	L Mx I2	F	35–50 y	B	0.70556
Conch24/ACL0748	208	3577	108.05	3577–108.05.01	R Md M1	?	13–16 y	?	0.70558
Conch33	N/A	2200		2200.01	Mx M	?	Adult	?	N/A

continued

Table 4.2. —continued

Lab ID[a]	EA[b]	Locus	Burial code[c]	Osteology code	Bone/tooth[d]	Sex	Age	Hg[e]	$^{87}Sr/^{86}Sr$
Conch36	N/A	2400		2400.54	Md M3	?	Adult	B	N/A
Conch29	39A	1728		1728.01	L Md P3	M?	Adult	A	N/A
ACL0776	39A	1728		1728.01	L Md M3	M?	Adult	N/A	0.70571
ACL0775	39A	1728		1728.01	Md frag.	M?	Adult	N/A	0.70573
Conch14	39A	1818		1818.01	Md M1	?	20–35 y	?	N/A
ACL0778	39A	1818		1818.01	L Mx M1	?	20–35 y	N/A	0.70561
Conch13	39A	1818		1818.01	Mx frag.	?	20–35 y	N/A	0.70573
Conch16	39A	1818		1818.03	Cran. frag.		Adult	?	N/A
Conch17	39A	1818		1818.04	Md M1		Adult	?	N/A
Conch30	39D	2026		2026.01	Md M		Adult	B	N/A
Conch34	39D	2045		2045.01	Md M		Adult	B	N/A
950.01	44A	950		950.01	M3	M	35–50 y	?	N/A
ACL0773	44A	950		950.01	R Mx M2	M	35–50 y	N/A	0.70575
Conch03/ ACL0774	44A	950		950.01	R humerus frag.	M	35–50 y	?	0.70574
ACL0772	44A	950		950.01	Atlas frag.	M	35–50 y	N/A	0.70577
Conch15	Tower			Airport tower	Md M3	M	30–45 y	?	N/A
ACL0792	Tower			Airport tower	R Md I2	M	30–45 y	N/A	0.70587
ACL0793	Tower			Airport tower	L femur frag.	M	30–45 y	N/A	0.70591
Conch32	N/A	1799		1799.01	Md M	?	Adult	?	N/A
Eb3–5.01		Tomb 5		5.01	Rib	F	Adult	?	N/A

Eb3-5.03		Tomb 5		5.03	R Mx P4	F	Adult	?	N/A
Conch27			1998.01	Ochatoma1	Md M3	F	48–55 y	D	N/A
Conch02			1998.01	Ochatoma1	L metacarpal	F	48–55 y	D	N/A
Conch09/ ACL0791			1998.01	Ochatoma1	L metatarsal	F	48–55 y	D	0.70580
ACL0790			1998.01	Ochatoma1	R Mx C1	F	48–55 y	N/A	0.70583
ACL0789			1998.02	Ochatoma2	L radius frag.	M	46–55 y	N/A	0.70576
Conch11	143T3	2985	21	2985.21.01	Trophy head frag.	?	Adult	?	N/A
Conch18	72	N/A		EA72 trophy head D	Md M1	M	20–35 y	?	N/A
Conch19	72	N/A		EA72 trophy head C	Md M2	M	25–45 y	?	N/A

Note: Samples in boldface type denote the possible nonlocals as identified through strontium isotope ratios.

[a] Conch# are mtDNA samples processed by Brian Kemp in Dr. Marshall Summar's ancient DNA lab, Vanderbilt University Medical Center. Lab codes that match the osteology codes are mtDNA samples processed by Brian Kemp in David Glenn Smith's ancient DNA lab at UC–Davis. F# are strontium isotope samples processed by Kelly Knudson and Paul Fullagar in Paul Fullagar's Isotope Geochemistry Lab at UNC–Chapel Hill. ACL# are strontium isotope samples processed by Knudson at the Archaeological Chemistry Lab and W. M. Keck Foundation for Environmental Biogeochemistry at Arizona State University.

[b] EA=Espacio Arquitectronico (architectural space) at Conchopata.

[c] Burial codes were only sometimes assigned to burials excavated at Conchopata, and the coding system differs among the three different teams that excavated there. Osteology codes (see next column) were added to the burial codes where appropriate, because the excavation teams started the burial code at 1 each year, leading to a duplication in burial codes over the multiyear excavations.

[d] L=left; R=right; Md=mandible; Mx=maxilla; I=incisor; C=canine; P=premolar; M=molar; frag.=fragment.

[e] Hg=haplogroup. If a sample was processed for mtDNA, then it is designated as either haplogroup A, B, C, D, or ? (?=haplogroup unknown). N/A=not applicable because the sample was not tested for mtDNA.

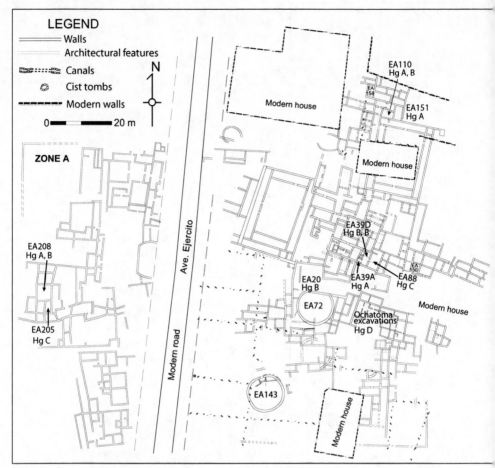

Figure 4.5. Map of Conchopata showing the burial locations of individuals with a known haplogroup.

where a "venerated woman" and three infants had been interred with ritually smashed oversized ceramic vessels (Isbell and Groleau 2010). However, the relationship between rooms EA208 and EA205 is unclear because wall preservation was so poor (Isbell and Groleau 2010). Although the goal was to examine the genetic relationships between those interred in these two rooms, analyzable mtDNA was obtained only for the man and woman in EA208 and one infant from EA205. Nonetheless, it is notable that the man (Hg A) and woman (Hg B) did not belong to the same haplogroup, eliminating the possibility that they shared the same mother or were maternally related in some other way. If they represent, for example, a spousal pairing, then these genetic data indicate that the marriage partner was not someone who was related along the maternal line. Because no mtDNA was present in the adolescent tooth, precisely how this teenager was related to the adults is unknown.

The infant in the neighboring room (EA205) belonged to haplogroup C, but because no mtDNA was obtained from the adult female in the same room ("the venerated woman") or the other infants, whether the woman was the mother (or some other maternal relative) to the three infants remains unknown. Moreover, these mtDNA data indicate that the infant in EA205 was not maternally related to the man or woman in the neighboring room (EA208).

Finally, there was one elderly female who belonged to haplogroup D. She was the only one who belonged to this unique maternal line, suggesting that perhaps she was a nonlocal individual or was born at Conchopata to a nonlocal mother. (She is further discussed in chapter 5 after the data on her skeletal injuries are presented.)

Strontium Isotope Analysis at Conchopata

Methods for Detecting Nonlocals

Forty-six dental and/or bone samples were taken for strontium isotope analysis from 32 individuals interred in tombs at Conchopata. (Samples were also taken from the human trophy heads, but those are presented in a later chapter.) Strontium isotope analysis is an ideal method for determining whether individuals from distant geological zones migrated to Conchopata, because strontium isotopes are incorporated into the teeth and bones of humans from the foods that the person consumes (Grupe et al. 1997; Price et al. 1994). Thus, if a person eats calcium-rich plants grown in local soils (and animals that eat local plants), then their teeth and bones will reflect the strontium isotope ratio of that geological region (Bentley et al. 2004; Grupe et al. 1997; Price et al. 1994).

Although there are a variety of geologic formations in the central Andean highlands, the likely Wari agricultural fields have been documented in the river valleys immediately east and west of Conchopata and near the capital site of Huari (Isbell et al. 1991; Pozzi-Escot B. 1991; Schreiber 1992). These areas are in the Ayacucho Formation, which is composed of late Cenozoic andesites, felsic lavas and ash-flow tuffs, and lesser lacustrine and fluvial sandstone, siltstone, and mudstone (Wise 2004). These would have been the most probable sources of dietary strontium for Conchopata inhabitants. However, because we should not assume an isomorphic relationship between local geological formations and human strontium isotope values, particularly where various geologic formations abound (Wright 2005), local small animals (Knudson and Tung 2007) were also tested in an attempt to establish the range of the local bioavailable strontium isotope ratio. The strontium isotope ratio from six guinea pigs purchased at the local Ayacucho market indicate that the local $^{87}Sr/^{86}Sr$ equals 0.705672 to 0.711766 (Knudson and Tung 2007), a fairly wide range that may indicate that two of the modern guinea pigs consumed food produced elsewhere or that imported fertilizers were used on the local plant foods. Two of the six guinea pigs had higher than expected strontium isotope ratios relative to what was expected based on the local geological formations (Wise 2004); the other four exhibited strontium isotope ratios expected for this geological region: the values ranged from 0.705672 to 0.706306 (Knudson and Tung 2007).

Another method for determining whether any of the burials represent nonlocal persons is to examine the descriptive statistics of the sample and evaluate whether there are outliers in the sample (Wright 2005). That is, because a local population that shares a similar diet should exhibit a normal distribution of strontium isotope ratios, those that fall outside that range may be identified as nonlocals.

An additional technique that I propose for identifying nonlocals based on strontium isotope ratios consists of listing all of the values in ascending order and calculating the difference between each succeeding sample. The sample that shows the largest break in value may indicate that the sample and all subsequent samples derive from nonlocal persons. For example, consider the following hypothetical data set:

Sample 1 $^{87}Sr/^{86}Sr=0.70700$
Sample 2 $^{87}Sr/^{86}Sr=0.70701$
Sample 3 $^{87}Sr/^{86}Sr=0.70705$
Sample 4 $^{87}Sr/^{86}Sr=0.70723$

The difference between Samples 1 and 2 is only 0.00001 and the difference between Samples 2 and 3 is 0.00004, while Samples 3 and 4 differ by 0.00018. The difference between Samples 3 and 4 is much greater and could represent a break in the population, suggesting that Sample 4 is nonlocal. Large data sets, as used in this study, and additional data on burial location at the site, burial treatment, cranial modification styles, and so forth should also be examined to determine whether the distinct strontium isotope ratio indeed represents a nonlocal. This method should not be used in isolation.

Strontium Isotope Ratios from Conchopata Burials

The strontium isotope ratios from the 46 samples are presented in table 4.2 and figure 4.6. They exhibit a mean $^{87}Sr/^{86}Sr$ of 0.70584 ± 0.00074, and the median $^{87}Sr/^{86}Sr$ is 0.70571 (table 4.3). Two burial samples, from EA6 and EA20, have the greatest difference from the mean and the median (table 4.3). When they are excluded, the "trimmed" burial data ($n=44$) exhibit a normal distribution with samples clustered around the mean (figure 4.7). The mean $^{87}Sr/^{86}Sr$ of the trimmed burial data set is 0.70572 ± 0.00011, and the median $^{87}Sr/^{86}Sr$ is 0.70571 (table 4.3). In the trimmed burial data set, the mean and median are nearly identical, suggesting a normal distribution of the data. Wright (2005) has suggested that this should be expected for a local population that consumes a similar diet. Thus, the individuals from EA6 and EA20 may be nonlocals.

When the strontium isotope values are listed in ascending order and the difference is calculated between each succeeding sample (table 4.4), the same two individuals are identified as outliers: those from EA6 and EA20. Specifically, the sample from EA6 differs from the preceding sample by 0.00064, suggesting a break in the population and marking the last two samples, the same that were identified with Wright's method (2005), as possible nonlocals. That the third to last sample is nonlocal ($^{87}Sr/^{86}Sr$=0.70610, a difference of .00019 from the preceding sample) is also possible, but this remains unclear based solely on the strontium isotope ratios. This individual from EA105 is a unique case: she was the pregnant female from whom an AMS date indicated that she was some two hundred years older than the others in the tomb (see chapter 3). Her geographical status is further evaluated in chapter 6, when all strontium isotope data from the site (burials and trophy heads) and a few other Andean regions are compared.

The two individuals identified as outliers by both methods are an infant from EA6 (bone $^{87}Sr/^{86}Sr$=0.70673) and an adolescent female from EA20 (mandibular canine $^{87}Sr/^{86}Sr$=0.71058). The relatively high radiogenic strontium isotope ratio from the infant suggests that s/he was not natal to the Ayacucho Basin, and although this juvenile was initially identified as a possible local (Knudson

Table 4.3. Descriptive statistics for the strontium isotope ratios from the Conchopata burials

Statistic	Burials	Trimmed burial data
Mean	0.70584	0.70572
St. dev.	0.00074	0.00011
Median	0.70571	0.70571
Min.	0.70548	0.70548
Max.	0.71058	0.7061
Range	0.00510	0.00062
Skewness (std. error)	6.181 (.350)	0.778 (.357)
Kurtosis (std. error)	40.062 (.688)	2.317 (.702)
# of samples	46	44
# of individuals represented by the samples	31	29

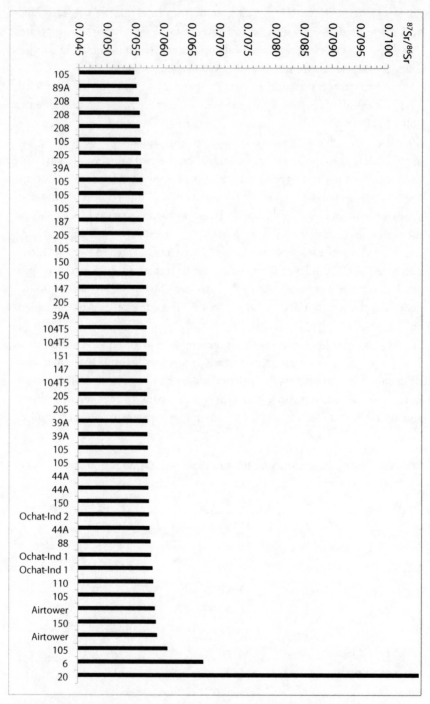

Figure 4.6. Strontium isotope ratios from Conchopata burials. The *x* axis is labeled with architectural room numbers from which the burials came.

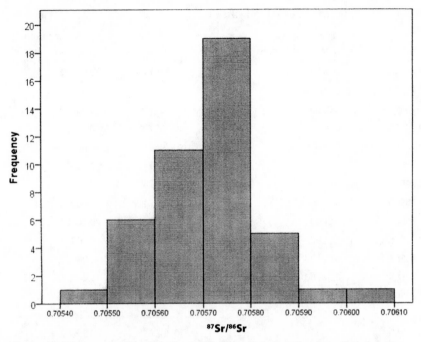

Figure 4.7. Histogram of the "trimmed" strontium isotope ratios from Conchopata burials (*N*=44), which exhibit a normal distribution (see Wright 2005 for description of this method).

and Tung 2007; Tung and Knudson 2008), this larger data set gives refinement to the local strontium isotope ratio of those who resided at Conchopata.

The second outlier is a female between 17 and 22 years old. She received mortuary treatment distinct from all others at the site; she was deposited in a small pit prominently placed directly in front of a D-shaped ritual structure (EA72), where 10 human trophy heads had been deposited (see chapter 6). She was apparently buried in clothing or a shroud, as there were four small copper tupus (pins) with her that still had textile fragments adhering to them (Anita Cook, pers. comm. 2010). There was mild periostitis on a tibial midshaft fragment and left ulna, but whether the periostitis was bilateral on the leg and arm is unknown, because the other tibia fragments and right ulna were too poorly preserved. Thus, no determination could be made about whether she suffered localized trauma on the shin and lower arm or a mild systemic infection. Her cranium and cervical vertebrae were too poorly preserved to examine for trauma, so whether violence-related trauma to the head or neck was the mechanism of death could not be determined. (The nonlocal infant and adolescent female are discussed in more detail below.)

The elderly female who belonged to haplogroup D (described above) exhib-

Table 4.4. Strontium isotope ratios in ascending order, showing differences in value

$^{87}Sr/^{86}Sr$	Difference from preceding sample	$^{87}Sr/^{86}Sr$	Difference from preceding sample
0.70548	N/A	0.70572	0.00001
0.70552	0.00004	0.70572	0.00000
0.70556	0.00004	0.70572	0.00000
0.70558	0.00002	0.70573	0.00001
0.70558	0.00000	0.70573	0.00000
0.70560	0.00002	0.70574	0.00001
0.70560	0.00000	0.70574	0.00000
0.70561	0.00001	0.70574	0.00000
0.70563	0.00002	0.70575	0.00001
0.70565	0.00002	0.70576	0.00001
0.70565	0.00000	0.70576	0.00000
0.70565	0.00000	0.70577	0.00001
0.70565	0.00000	0.70579	0.00002
0.70566	0.00001	0.70580	0.00001
0.70569	0.00003	0.70583	0.00003
0.70569	0.00000	0.70584	0.00001
0.70570	0.00001	0.70586	0.00002
0.70570	0.00000	0.70587	0.00001
0.70571	0.00001	0.70589	0.00002
0.70571	0.00000	0.70591	0.00002
0.70571	0.00000	0.70610	0.00019
0.70571	0.00000	**0.70673**	**0.00064**
0.70571	0.00000	**0.71058**	**0.00385**

Note: The last two samples (in boldface) exhibit the most significant increase in value; they represent the infant from EA6 and the adolescent female from EA20, respectively.

ited enamel and bone strontium isotope ratios expected for the local Ayacucho Basin (canine $^{87}Sr/^{86}Sr=0.70583$ and bone $^{87}Sr/^{86}Sr=0.70580$). This suggests that she spent her childhood and adulthood in the local region.

Synthesis and Discussion of Conchopata Demographic Data

Early Intermediate Period (Huarpa)

The Huarpa-era burials at Conchopata show a sex distribution in which women are seven times more common than men and an age-at-death distribution in which adolescents constitute the greatest percentage of deaths. It is possible that Huarpa males and other age groups were buried elsewhere at Conchopata and have not yet been recovered. But given that much of the site has been excavated (and exposed by construction for the airport), it is more likely that adolescent and young adult females, particularly those of high status, were preferentially selected for burial in those Huarpa tombs, particularly the one excavated in 1977: nine of the 14 Huarpa females come from this one tomb group. Simply put, the Huarpa demographic profile does not match expectations for a normal human population distribution (Hoppa and Vaupel 2002; Howell and Kintigh 1996; Milner et al. 2000; Sattenspiel and Harpending 1983). Rather, Huarpa mortuary practices appear to have disproportionately selected females for burial at the site.

The differences in the Huarpa- and Wari-era age-at-death profiles at Conchopata are statistically significant ($\chi^2=17.77$; $p=0.007$; df=6; $N=286$). While this could reflect a major shift in population structure from pre-Wari to Wari times, the data cannot uphold this interpretation because the small sample size of Huarpa burials does not likely reflect the once-living Huarpa-era population. Thus, demographic shifts in the Ayacucho Basin that accompanied the rise of the Wari state have yet to be identified.

Middle Horizon (Wari Era)

A focus on the Wari-period demographic profile at Conchopata, in contrast, yields interesting insights into the population structure. The observed sex distribution significantly deviates from a symmetrical sex distribution, such that women outnumber men nearly two to one. This leads to one of two questions: Where are the men? Or why are there so many women? This is not a result of differential preservation, for the fragile bones of elderly females usually degrade more easily than male skeletal elements (Walker et al. 1988). While it is possible that Wari mortuary practices included different burial areas for males and females, and excavations have yet to discover a male mortuary sector, this seems improbable because many parts of the site have been excavated (Isbell and Cook 2002; Ochatoma and Cabrera 2000). Also, both males and females have been uncovered together in Wari-era tombs. Moreover, there is only one sex-specific tomb, EA150, which included three females and two children. Tombs within EA37/38B/44A were originally described as a sex-specific mortuary space with only three males (Tung 2003), but the expanded analysis presented here shows that two females and a child were also interred there.

Although there are significantly more women than men, these women do not appear to be like *acllacunas* (virgins of the Sun God), known as such from Spanish chroniclers who describe that in Inka times, a select group of celibate women were cloistered away to weave cloth, brew chicha, or make other goods for the Inka state. At Conchopata, the numerous fetuses, infants, and children at the site belie the notion that Conchopata was a settlement where celibate women were cloistered away; these women, however, may have produced chicha, pottery, and other goods for themselves, their families, and/or Wari state leaders.

Was Conchopata a Polygynous Community?

In light of the large-scale excavations that have uncovered more than three hundred burials, I suggest that the reconstructed sex distribution likely reflects the proportion of males and females who died at the site. Test pits and trenches in several other areas of the site (that is, outside the main architectural limits of the site) revealed only two other burials: one in a boot-shaped tomb (Lumbreras 2000b) and another in a pit underneath the modern airport tower (José Ochatoma, pers. comm. 2009). Thus, the high female-to-male ratio may accurately reflect the once-living adult sex ratio at the site, providing a foundation to begin reconstructing how the Conchopata community was organized. Earlier studies presented the asymmetrical sex distribution at Conchopata (Tung 2001), prompting Isbell (2007) to suggest that the higher frequency of females represented polygyny at the settlement. The demographic profile of one of the tomb groups (EA105) was crucial to the interpretation. The tomb included five adult females, one male, and one unsexed adult, but the identified male was only 23–27 years old. He was likely much too young to have acquired multiple wives. Moreover, the young male and an old female in the tomb both exhibit a vastus notch on the patella, a genetic trait that may be indicative of genetic relatedness (Finnegan 1978). Therefore, perhaps the young male and this female who died late in life were related through biology, not marriage.[3] Additionally, an AMS date from the pregnant female skeleton at the top of the tomb was two hundred years older than the AMS date obtained from the base of the tomb where the male was buried. This time difference indicates that he was not her sexual partner. Thus, based on the youthfulness of the male, shared skeletal traits indicating genetic relatedness, and a time difference that indicates the pregnant female was not a consort of the male, this tomb group is unlikely to house an elite male with his numerous wives. This conclusion is in contrast to Isbell's suggestion that "Conchopata's social context does not seem to have been independent families of middle-class artisans but, rather, elite palace complexes, within which wives and concubines appear to have labored in crafts and services to create social events of aggrandizement for lords sponsoring competitive and status-building feasts, parties, and drinking bouts" (Isbell 2007:73).

While Conchopata certainly was a locale for status-building events (for example, ceremonies, feasts, and religious rituals), the demographic data do not support the notion that it was a palace complex constituted solely of polygynous men with their wives and concubines. The high female fertility at Conchopata belies this. That is, cross-cultural studies of marriage have shown that polygyny leads to lower female fertility in comparison to monogamy (Bowers 1971; Garenne and van de Waller 1989; Hern 1992). Among polygynous groups, the lower fertility rate is likely due to postpartum sexual abstinence, a practice that is better adhered to by polygynous groups than monogamous ones (Caldwell and Caldwell 1977; Garenne and van de Waller 1989; Hern 1992). In effect, the more sustained postpartum abstinence leads to longer birth intervals, which leads to fewer average births per woman in polygynous societies (Bowers 1971). If this is correct, then the Conchopata age-at-death distribution is in contrast to that expected for a polygynous community; there are numerous fetus/infant deaths (32 percent of the burial sample), suggesting high female fertility (see Milner et al. 2000; Paine and Harpending 1996; Sattenspiel and Harpending 1983). (Although common sense might suggest that numerous infants in a burial sample, and the concomitant reduction in mean age-at-death, indicate high infant mortality, several scholars have convincingly argued that a decrease in mean age-at-death actually reflects an increase in fertility [see Milner et al. 2000; Paine and Harpending 1996; Sattenspiel and Harpending 1983].)

While there may have been a few elite males who practiced polygyny, these data indicate that it was not the dominant form of social organization at Conchopata. Extended families made up of biologically related kin and affines (for example, grandparents, parents, offspring, and siblings of the older generations), living in a patio group compound, may have been the more common form of social organization.

Mobile Men on Military and Administrative Campaigns

How then might we explain the demographic profile with fewer men than women? I suggest that this may be related to Wari imperial policies that sent males away for state projects, including such things as administrative tasks or formal military campaigns, as the subsequent Inka Empire did (D'Altroy 2002). Wari iconography on state-produced ceramics shows warriors brandishing weapons and military elites wearing uniforms that may have signaled rank (Isbell and Cook 2002; Ochatoma and Cabrera 2002). On the external surface of large ceramic urns, there are also images of warriors kneeling on reed boats as they carry weapons and shields (see figure 5.5). Given that reed boats would have been unnecessary in the Ayacucho Basin, the depiction of Wari warriors on this kind of watercraft may suggest a military subclass affiliated with mobility and expansion into distant lands, such as the Pacific coast and the Lake Titicaca Basin.

This is compelling evidence that the Wari state had a class of military elites or at least the goal of establishing one. As discussed in later chapters, cranial trauma frequencies among Wari-affiliated populations and the presence of human trophy heads in ritual buildings at Conchopata support the notion that Wari imperial policies included military campaigns and raids, activities that would have taken men away from Conchopata and, in effect, out of the local mortuary population if they died while away from home. Although men may have left Conchopata for reasons unaffiliated with imperial agendas, the Wari military iconography and knowledge that the later Inka Empire relocated military, administrative, and labor personnel make it more likely that males traveled under the auspices of the Wari state. At the least, these individual agents could have benefited from trade opportunities created by the Wari-built roads and political networks, while simultaneously enhancing Wari standing and the desire for Wari goods in various Andean communities.

While many of the Conchopata men may have traveled to distant locales, Conchopata women were less mobile, residing at the site and apparently engaging in specialized tasks for the community and the state. These activities may have included production of ceramics, textiles, jewelry, and food, as well as caring for infants and young children, processing human trophy heads, and overseeing rituals.

Locals and Foreigners at Conchopata

Among the 46 strontium isotope ratios from the 32 burials, 30 burials ($n=44$ samples) exhibit nearly identical values. This indicates that those 30 individuals lived their lifetimes at Conchopata and the immediately surrounding area (or a region with similar strontium isotope ratios). People at Conchopata were not migrants from distinct geological locales, suggesting that it was not a cosmopolitan center to which people migrated to resettle there. Rather, it was a settlement comprising individuals from the local area.

The remaining two samples are outliers with much higher strontium isotope ratios, suggesting that they derived from a region other than the Ayacucho Basin. These two samples represent an infant and an adolescent female, both of whom were buried in a manner distinct from others at Conchopata.

A Nonlocal Infant at Conchopata

The infant in EA6 (locus 2004) with the nonlocal strontium isotope ratio received distinct burial treatment relative to other infants at the site. There was no inverted ceramic bowl on the infant's head, which is a typical funerary treatment for Conchopata infants (and children and adult females) (Tung and Cook 2006) (figure 4.8). The infant was, however, associated with several ceramic sherds. One came from a fancy Pacheco-like vessel with a black background and depictions of plants (for example, maize and perhaps cotton), and another fragment from an oversized Conchopata-style urn shows the hand of what is probably the Front Face Deity holding a staff (Anita Cook, pers. comm. 2010). The infant was deposited in a room that also yielded a complete llama offering, five guinea pigs, and sherds from oversized ceramic urns, several of which depict the "Wari boat warriors." A burned piece of wood associated with the boat-warrior ceramics yielded an AMS date of Cal AD 620 to 690 (2 sigma) (Sample number Beta-146400; 1320+40 BP) (Ketteman 2002). Although the dated wood was not in direct association with the infant, it suggests that this room was used for ritual (and mortuary) activities in the early part of the Middle Horizon. Thus, the foreign infant in the upper-level strata was likely placed there during that time or later.

The boat-warrior ceramics are identified as Type 3 ceramic offerings (that is, oversized ceramic urns about one meter in diameter, as opposed to oversized face-neck jars [Isbell and Cook 2002]). The "boat warriors" wear military attire

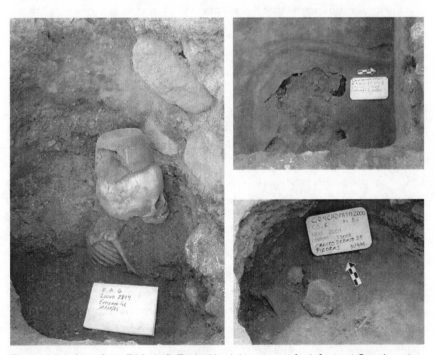

Figure 4.8. Infants from EA6. *Left*: Typical burial treatment for infants at Conchopata with inverted ceramic bowl on head (locus 2819). *Right top*: Tomb of the nonlocal infant (locus 2004). *Right bottom*: Rock above infant's head. (Photos courtesy of William Isbell and Anita Cook.)

and carry weapons, and they kneel on reed boats, a form of transport unnecessary in the Ayacucho Basin. As such, their depictions might tell a tale of journeys to distant lands, such as the coast or Lake Titicaca (Isbell 2000; Ochatoma et al. 2008; Tung 2008a).

The strontium isotope value from the infant also reflects its mother's strontium isotope ratio because this infant was likely still breastfeeding. The strontium isotope ratio ($^{87}Sr/^{86}Sr$) of a mother's breast milk is not significantly altered as it goes to the next trophic level (that is, as the infant consumes it) (Carr et al. 1962; Comar et al. 1957; Hodges et al. 1950; Kulp and Schulert 1962; Mays 2003; Rehnberg et al. 1969; Schroeder et al. 1972). Thus, the infant's mother may be a nonlocal; she could have voluntarily migrated to Conchopata, or she could have been taken captive and forcibly brought to the settlement, perhaps by mobile Wari warriors like those shown on the ceramic urns from the same room (EA6). It is also possible that only the infant was taken from the foreign location. As I discuss in a later chapter, although there is compelling evidence that the human trophy heads from Conchopata are individuals abducted by Wari warriors, it is unknown how this infant (and apparently his or her mother) came to Conchopata. Nevertheless, the distinct mortuary treatment and strontium isotope ratio suggest that the infant came from some locale other than the Ayacucho Basin.

The Sacrifice of a Nonlocal Adolescent Girl

The adolescent female from EA20 (locus 1371) exhibits an extremely high strontium isotope ratio unlike anyone else at the site, suggesting that she was a foreigner. Because her mandibular canine was analyzed, which completes enamel formation around age five, she would have arrived to Conchopata sometime after that age or as recently as a few days before her death. (If she had arrived to Conchopata in her infancy, she would have incorporated local strontium into her canine dental enamel during development and would thus have appeared as a local.)

Further evidence of her nonlocal status can be seen in her unusual burial treatment. Rather than being interred under a house floor with several other kin, as was the usual funerary custom (Isbell 2004; Tung and Cook 2006), she was deposited alone directly in front of the D-shaped ritual structure (EA72). Although she could have died a natural death after voluntarily migrating to Conchopata, her unique burial location and premature death in late adolescence require consideration of other explanations.

This adolescent girl may have been taken captive from a distant location, similar to the trophy head victims found inside the ritual building (discussed in chapter 6). If she was indeed taken captive, then the context in which she was abducted was likely not a battlefield, where teenage/young adult women are unlikely to be encountered. Rather, she may have been taken in a village raid.

The abduction event was eventually followed by her probable sacrifice. That her body was prominently deposited in front of the D-shaped ritual building suggests that she may have been involved in the rituals within, perhaps as a sacrifice to sanctify the ritual space and the ceremonies that occurred within it.

Those elaborate rituals included the sacrifice of camelids, one of which was placed above the human trophy heads (Ochatoma and Cabrera 2002), a group of individuals who were also likely sacrificed (Tung 2008a). The rituals also included the intentional destruction of oversized ceramic urns that had images of Wari warriors brandishing weapons and some wearing trophy heads around their necks (Ochatoma and Cabrera 2002). Clearly, this was a major ritual space, and the placement of her body near the building's entrance suggests that she may have had an exceptional life and/or exceptional death, making her ideal as a sacrificial offering. Given that she is currently the only female to exhibit a nonlocal strontium isotope ratio, it appears unlikely that Conchopata men abducted women from distant locales to force them into new social roles as servants or wives. This further supports the notion that the asymmetrical sex distribution likely resulted from men leaving the settlement, rather than additional women being brought in.

Population Profiles and Mortuary Treatment at Beringa

The MNI at Beringa

The MNI at Beringa for both time periods combined (Middle Horizon and mixed Middle Horizon/Late Intermediate Period) equals 237 individuals: 236 individuals and one trophy head. The total MNI for the site was calculated by summing the MNI for each excavation unit, with the exception of Unit 1 and Unit 19, which were combined because looters mixed materials between the two spaces. (One exception is Locus 1030 within Unit 19; it was not collapsed with Unit 1, because it was clearly a discrete space with one mummy bundle.) Units 13, 20, and 25 were excluded from the total MNI because bones from those areas could have derived from nearby spaces. Excluding them prevented an overestimation of the MNI.

Age-at-Death and Sex Distributions at Beringa

Of the total individuals from Beringa, only a portion derive from the Middle Horizon period, the time of Wari presence in the Majes valley. All following discussions focus on human remains attributable to that time period only.

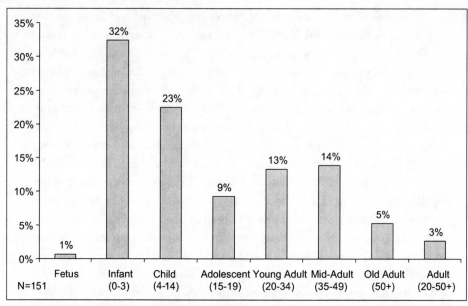

Figure 4.9. Age-at-death distribution for Beringa individuals associated with the Middle Horizon temporal component only (*N*=151).

There are at least 151 individuals associated with the Wari era. Fifty-six percent of the mortuary population is under 15 years old. Specifically, the age-at-death distribution shows that one-third are fetuses and infants and 23 percent are children. The complete age-at-death profile is presented in figure 4.9. The sex profile for human remains dated to the Middle Horizon exhibits a nearly equal distribution among the 42 sexed adults: 22 are females (48%) and 20 are males (52%).

Beringa Burial Treatment

All burials were interred in a seated position with knees to the chest, and all were wrapped in a layer or layers of textiles and bound with vegetal cord. Those who prepared the bodies for burial sometimes tucked cotton or leather bags with plant offerings into the mummy bundle. Mourners often placed grave offerings such as ceramics, weapons, and *placas pintadas* (painted stone tablets) in and around the tomb (Tung 2007c).

Five tomb types are identified at Beringa based on differences in size and construction. These include the following: (I) a circular, stone-lined tomb, 4.5 meters in diameter and 1.4 meters deep, with several dozen mummy bundles inside; (II) small circular tombs built with stone from rim to near the base; (III) small circular tombs adorned with a stone-lined opening; (IV) semicircular tombs

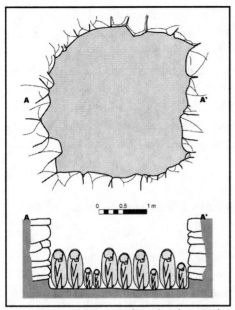

Tomb Type I. Drawing of Tomb 1 from Unit 1.

Tomb Types II and III. Type II is stone lined to a greater depth, while Type III is stone lined at the opening only.

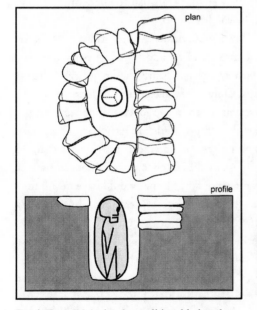

Tomb Type IV. A circular wall is added to the wall of a building to create a tomb.

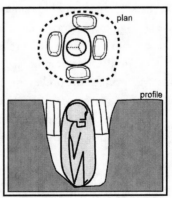

Tomb Type V. A mummy bundle is placed in a pit tomb and rocks are placed around the head.

Figure 4.10. Beringa Tomb Types I–V, with II and III combined. (From Tung 2007c.)

built by adding a half circle of rocks to a straight stone wall; and (V) simple pits that usually contained an infant or child with rectangular rocks placed upright on two or four sides of the skull (figure 4.10) (Tung 2007c). Types II—V are smaller and more variable in size, measuring from 70 to 110 centimeters deep and 50 to 100 centimeters in diameter. Although no intact burials were found in Tomb Type IV, one or more mummy bundles are presumed to have been buried in them, because human bone was found near these (looted) tombs. These circular spaces did not appear to be storage pits, because they did not contain any plant remains.

Beringa Synthesis: Village and Family Life in the Periphery of the Wari Empire

The demographic profile of the Beringa Wari-era burial population parallels that expected for ancient societies (Hoppa and Vaupel 2002; Howell and Kintigh 1996; Milner et al. 2000; Paine and Boldsen 2002; Paine and Harpending 1996; Sattenspiel and Harpending 1983). The sex distribution is symmetrical, suggesting that sex-specific subgroups were not transplanted here or sent away on labor projects, as was practiced by the Inka state.[4]

The Beringa population suffered many infant deaths: one-third of the skeletal sample died before the age of three, and an additional 23 percent of the population passed away before reaching age 15. Clearly, the majority of deaths occurred in the younger age groups. Only five percent lived beyond the age of 50 years. Looters could have inadvertently removed more adult bones from the skeletal sample, as grave robbers tend to target adult mummy bundles because those are in easy-to-locate tombs and often include more grave goods than do infant burials. However, because looters deliberately and systematically target the artifacts, not the bodies, the removal of adult bones would have been minimal. Based on these considerations, the Beringa age-at-death distribution likely reflects the once-living population.

Because there is no Early Intermediate Period (pre-Wari) skeletal sample from Beringa, no determination can be made of whether the percentage of infant deaths during the Middle Horizon represents an increase or decrease from the preceding period. Nevertheless, the high percentage of fetus and infant deaths (33%) suggests high fertility rates (Milner et al. 2000; Paine and Harpending 1996; Sattenspiel and Harpending 1983), a pattern that mirrors that of Conchopata, where 32 percent of the deaths were also of fetus and infants.

The Beringa demographic profile closely matches expectations for an ancient population comprising family groups; thus, Beringa appears to have been a village of families whose overall population configuration was little altered by Wari imperialism. That is, no specific subgroups (such as all male laborers) were relocated there for state or other projects. This interpretation is generally corroborated by the archaeological evidence, which shows that Beringa was a village community engaged in domestic activities, the production and consumption of foods, and minor production of textiles. Detailed analysis of cooking vessels, however, shows that they came in sizes suitable for serving meals to two to three people or for groups as large as 12 to 24 people (Owen 2007). It is notable that there is a gap in vessel size that would have been ideal for serving a midsize group of a few adults and children, especially because the midsized vessels that are missing at Beringa are common in the Wari heartland (Owen 2007). The absence of family-size serving vessels seems in contrast to what the demographic profile implies in terms of community organization, in which Beringa appears to have been a village community comprising family groups. However, this gap in vessel size may be an artifact of excavation strategy; a major portion of the domestic areas at Beringa (Sectors B and C) have not yet been excavated, so midrange vessel sizes may yet be uncovered in those sectors. In conclusion, the Beringa demographic data suggest that the settlement was not home to single-sex work groups, all-male military personnel, or polygamous households. Rather, Beringa was a village of extended families, likely comprising parents, their children, other consanguines, and affines.

Population Profiles and Mortuary Treatment at La Real

The MNI at La Real

At the Middle Horizon ceremonial and mortuary site of La Real, the MNI is 145. (The seven La Real trophy heads are excluded from this part of the analysis.) The MNI is based on 109 crania from adults and adolescents over 15 years of age, 19 crania from children, and 14 crania from infants, plus three mandibulae from young children whose ages clearly differed from the others (that is, these mandibulae did not belong to the other crania). The next section divides these age groups into smaller categories.

Age-at-Death and Sex Distributions at La Real

Of 145 individuals, most were over age 15 at the time of death. Three-fourths of the skeletal sample (109/145) consists of adults and older teenagers. The remaining one-fourth (36/145) includes infants and children (<15 years old). No fetuses are in this sample. The age-at-death profile for the La Real mortuary samples is presented in figure 4.11.

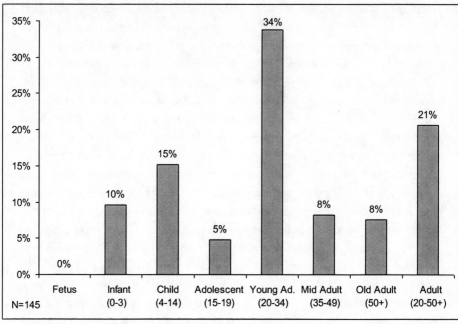

Figure 4.11. The La Real age-at-death distribution (*N*=145).

Among the 67 individuals whose sex could be determined, 26 were female (39%) and 41 were male (61%), a female to male ratio that equals 1:1.58. However, the difference between the expected and observed sex distributions is not statistically significant (Fisher's exact, p=0.128).

La Real Burial Treatment

Based on the few intact mummy bundles and associated textiles and cordage, the La Real burials were similarly prepared as those from Beringa—flexed burials wrapped in textiles and cords—except that the La Real textiles were of much higher quality. They included polychrome textiles and textiles with feather adornments from exotic jungle birds. Feathered textiles are a typical high-status Wari item (Stone-Miller et al. 1992), further demonstrating ties between La Real and Wari.

La Real Synthesis: A Mortuary Cave for Elites

The composition of this cave burial population shows many more men than women, but the difference is not statistically significant. This suggests that the La Real cave was not primarily reserved for the interment of elite men; women were sometimes buried here too, just not in equal numbers.

Much more notable, however, is the age composition of the La Real burial group. There are far fewer infants and children than adults: the former constitute only one-quarter of the burial sample. A low percentage of infants and children is common among archaeological skeletal samples, especially when soil conditions lead to a higher loss of fragile infant bones (Gordon and Buikstra 1981; Walker et al. 1988). But given the arid environment of the Majes valley, where textiles, soft tissue, and hair are well preserved, the infant and children bones at La Real are unlikely to have degraded at a significantly greater rate than sturdy adult bones.

Instead, I suggest that the observed demographic profile reflects the mortuary population, not the once-living population of a village. In other words, mourners opted to bury only certain individuals in the La Real mortuary cave, and the observed age-at-death and sex profiles are a reflection of those cultural decisions. Adult men, particularly those of high status, appear to be the preferred category of persons interred in this location. This mortuary custom of burying infants and adults in separate areas is not unheard of in the Andes (Carmichael 1988), and it is somewhat common in other world regions, such as the Hellenistic Mediterranean (Angel 1947; Moyer 1989).

It is unknown if the individuals interred at La Real are a subset of individuals from one settlement or several different settlements. The excavated area of La Real includes only the ritual and funerary areas. Although the burial catchment for this mortuary site is unknown, the skeletal and archaeological data indicate that high-status males from either one or a variety of settlements were interred there more frequently than juveniles. In a subsequent chapter, I explore aspects of these men's social identities and roles in society, evaluating whether they were perhaps warriors, ritual specialists, or something else altogether.

The demographic profile of the La Real burial group is useful for reconstructing mortuary behaviors, as described above. But because the La Real demographic profile probably does not reflect a once-living settlement population, these data cannot be used to reconstruct fertility and mortality patterns or describe community organization. For example, the low frequency of infants at La Real does not necessarily suggest anything about birth and death rates. Rather, a more likely explanation is that the mourners opted to bury fewer infants at La Real.

Comparing the Three Wari-Era Populations

Differences in Mortuary Treatment of Fetuses

One of the most notable distinctions between the three sites is the higher ratio of fetus burials at Conchopata (12:259) relative to Beringa (1:151) and La Real (0:145), a difference that is statistically significant ($\chi^2=11.283$; $p=0.00$; df=2;

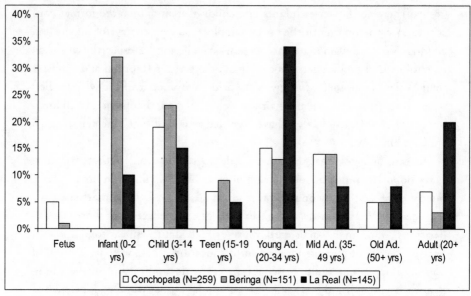

Figure 4.12. Age-at-death distributions for Conchopata, Beringa, and La Real (Middle Horizon only). Note that the last column is the unspecified adult age group (20+ years old).

N=555). The number of fetus burials relative to non-fetus burials is also significantly different when only Conchopata and Beringa are compared (Fisher's exact, p=0.037; N=410).

It is unclear if the high proportion of fetuses at Conchopata is a result of higher fertility and pregnancy loss among Conchopata women or a result of special mortuary treatment for fetuses that led to better preservation, and thus recovery, of their fragile remains. The latter is more likely, for at Conchopata, several fetuses were placed on a bed of fine ash inside ceramic vessels that were then capped by upside-down ceramic bowls. This elaborate treatment of fetal remains suggests that Conchopata women created a specific way to dispose of fetuses. Although other individuals (for example, healers or medical practitioners) could have participated in the disposal process, the women who miscarried or aborted the fetuses may have been intimately involved in preparing the fetus for deposition in the tomb. Notably, the inverted bowl on top of the ceramic vessel that held the fetus mirrors the mortuary treatment of women and children; they too had inverted bowls placed on top of their heads (Cook and Tung 2006; Tung and Cook 2006). This similar mortuary treatment for women, children, infants, and fetuses suggests that mourners were aiming to construct and reflect some shared qualities between these categories of individuals, narratives that were perhaps authored by females who were closely involved in these mortuary programs. This particular treatment of human fetal remains has not yet been documented in the southern hinterland of the Wari Empire, suggesting that this funerary custom was unique to the Wari heartland and had not been adopted by those in the southern sphere of the Wari domain.

Excluding the proportion of fetuses, which are likely underrepresented at Beringa, the general demographic profiles at Conchopata and Beringa likely approximate the once-living populations that formerly inhabited the settlements over several generations. This is supported by the observation that approximately half of each skeletal population is constituted by infants and children, a distribution expected for preindustrial populations (Howell and Kintigh 1996; Paine 1989). Moreover, extensive excavations at both sites recovered large samples, further suggesting that the skeletal sample is representative of the once-living community. This cannot be claimed for the skeletal sample from La Real (as described above). Therefore, subsequent comparisons on demographic profiles and community organization focus on Conchopata and Beringa only.

Population stationarity is not assumed for Conchopata and Beringa. That is, the living populations that resulted in the observed skeletal samples likely experienced population growth or decline; they were not stable. As Sattenspiel and Harpending (1983) have shown, if there is no population stationarity (the case in nearly all populations), then the age-at-death profiles are more reflective of birth rates than death rates. Although some scholars have thus attempted to reconstruct fertility rates among ancient groups, this study aims to make general comparisons only, exploring similarities and differences between the imperial heartland site of Conchopata and the hinterland site of Beringa.

Similar Fertility at Conchopata and Beringa

Overall, the relative number of individuals in each of the eight age-at-death categories is similar between Conchopata and Beringa ($\chi^2=10.807$; $p=0.147$; df=7; $N=410$) (figure 4.12), suggesting similar population age structures among the two communities. Although this study does not report mean age-at-death or life expectancy but instead presents percentages of deaths in each age cohort, those data can be compared to evaluate similarities and differences in population profiles. Specifically, the similar percentage of infant deaths among both groups (Conchopata, 32%; Beringa, 33%) is a good indicator, not of mortality rates but of their similar fertility rates (see above) (see Milner et al. 2000; Paine and Harpending 1996; Sattenspiel and Harpending 1983). If fertility rates were similar at the two settlements, then they are likely to have had similar reproductive patterns, limiting the likelihood that Conchopata was a palace complex with polygynous men and their "wives and concubines" (Isbell 2007:73). Again, this does not eliminate the possibility that certain males may have practiced polygyny, but it suggests that this was not the dominant marriage practice.

Sex Profile Differences at Conchopata and Beringa

Conchopata is distinct from Beringa in that the former exhibits significantly fewer males relative to a symmetrical sex distribution (Fisher's exact, $p=0.044$), while the Beringa sex ratio is nearly balanced (figure 4.13). This probably relates to differences in social organization as structured by one's sex. At Beringa, sex-based subgroups were not moved out of, or brought into, the settlement. At Conchopata, Wari imperial policies may have sent males away on military campaigns or administrative duties, leaving a community group heavily populated with women and children. Although the high ratio of females and the elaborate warrior iconography at Conchopata could be taken as evidence that males engaged in female capture, thereby increasing the proportion of females at the site, the strontium isotope ratios do not support this scenario. (Only one female had a nonlocal strontium isotope ratio, and she was likely sacrificed, not taken as a servant or wife.) If, however, Conchopata males traveled to distant regions as part of a military campaign to take enemy captives and war trophies—and then sometimes died while away on these risky sojourns—then Conchopata should yield evidence for these practices. I explore this hypothesis in chapter 6, examining the skeletal evidence for human trophies taken from other locales.

In sum, the demographic data reveal an important distinction between life in the heartland versus the southern hinterland. In the former, adult males may have been forced or encouraged or may have opted to engage in imperial programs that took them away from their natal settlement, dying elsewhere and never returning home for burial. At the site of Beringa, in contrast, community

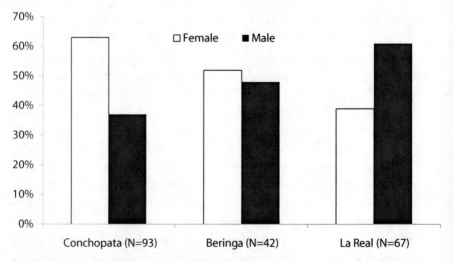

Figure 4.13. Adult sex distributions for Conchopata, Beringa, and La Real populations.

rules, regional traditions, and Wari imperial influence apparently did not require that groups of men or women leave the settlement, nor did they lead to circumstances in which groups of nonlocals moved in. Perhaps this data set is beginning to reveal that lifeways for men in the imperial heartland differed from those in the southern hinterland, inasmuch as it related to leading a more mobile lifestyle.

Finally, as the evidence from La Real shows, elaborate mortuary treatment for subgroups in the hinterland was not hindered by Wari imperial influence. To the contrary, Wari prestige items, such as Wari feathered textiles and polychrome ceramics with Wari motifs, appear to have been sought after and secured by a select group of persons in the southern hinterland. This leads to important questions about whether or not this increased access to Wari goods, and presumably other Wari social and political networks, translated into other benefits for this select group of persons: themes that are explored in subsequent chapters.

The Exclusive Community of Conchopata

The Wari heartland site of Conchopata was populated primarily by people who were natal to Conchopata and the surrounding region and who likely descended from previous Huarpa inhabitants. Based on the currently available strontium isotope and ancient mtDNA data, there is little to suggest that Conchopata was a cosmopolitan center with migrants settling there from distant areas. Rather, it appears to be a restricted settlement constituted nearly exclusively of locals.

Notably, no male burials exhibit a nonlocal radiogenic strontium isotope ratio, suggesting that men who later received normal funerary treatment (that is, men who were buried intact in tombs and not transformed into trophy heads) were not migrants from elsewhere. As such, current data suggest that Wari society—at least as represented by Conchopata—did not practice a form of matrilocality in which men from distant regions resettled at Conchopata with their marriage or reproductive partners.

The few nonlocals whose bodies were deposited at Conchopata apparently experienced tougher life conditions than the native inhabitants. They include a teenage girl who was likely taken captive, sacrificed, and deposited in front of the ritual D-shaped building and an infant who received distinct (less elaborate) burial treatment relative to other infant burials at Conchopata. A third individual, the elderly female who was haplogroup D and slightly postdates the other burials, also exhibited multiple skeletal injuries and an annular form of cranial modification (the only case at Conchopata), and she was buried alone, leading to the suspicion that she might have been a nonlocal and maltreated as a result. However, she yielded local strontium isotope ratios, suggesting that at least from her childhood years onward, she resided at Conchopata. If her mother was perceived as a foreigner (her mother also would have been the rare haplogroup D), then perhaps her poor treatment (repeated traumas and irregular burial) was related to her family's outsider status.

The strontium isotope evidence also suggests that it was rare for nonlocal women to be integrated into the Conchopata community. No adult female in a formal family tomb exhibited a nonlocal strontium isotope ratio, suggesting that abduction of foreign women was uncommon. The only female who expressed a nonlocal strontium isotope signature was the adolescent directly in front of the D-shaped structure, and her unique treatment was likely related to the ritual processing of the trophy heads in the D-shaped room next to her (see chapter 6).

Other indirect strontium isotope evidence suggests that one other nonlocal female may have relocated to Conchopata, bringing her foreign-born infant with her (the infant buried in EA6). Her infant shows a nonlocal strontium isotope ratio, suggesting that the calories ingested in utero and/or from breast milk were from a region outside the Ayacucho Basin. There is no evidence to indicate what happened to the infant's mother.

In all, the strontium isotope data from non–trophy head contexts suggest that there was one nonlocal female (or possibly two) at Conchopata, while all sampled males (non–trophy heads) were local. At first glance, this could hint that women migrated more frequently than males and that the Conchopata community practiced patrilocality. However, the likely sacrifice of the adolescent girl and the unknown life history of the nonlocal infant's mother make it difficult to conclude that this was a patrilocal society. Rather, marriage or reproductive partners at Conchopata appear to have been from the local Ayacucho Basin, thus making it difficult to use strontium isotope analysis to evaluate whether patrilocality or matrilocality was practiced there.

Instead, the data suggest that nonlocal women (and their offspring) experienced harsher life conditions and were not socially integrated into the local community. Indeed, one of these women may have been intentionally sacrificed in adolescence. This suggests that Conchopata was an exclusive Wari community that prevented the entrance and social integration of individuals from distant geological zones; it was not a cosmopolitan center to which many Andean peoples migrated, like that observed at Tiwanaku (Blom 2005). Whether the capital city of Huari, located some 10 kilometers to the north, was more cosmopolitan than Conchopata and more similar to Tiwanaku in this regard has yet to be determined.

Violence and Skeletal Trauma among Wari Communities

Wari iconography is replete with images of warriors carrying weapons, wearing trophy heads, or holding prisoners—images that hint at the value placed on militarism and belligerence. As such, it is imperative to evaluate if and how those apparent values were manifested and to what ends. Did political and military agents within the Wari Empire use violence to control both internal and external populations and use it as a strategy for expansion? An imperial strategy of this kind would not make the Wari unique in global comparison, but it would show that the Wari were novel in the ancient Andes, where the contemporary Tiwanaku state apparently did not use militarism to establish authority and control in the southern, highland Andes (Janusek 2008), at least to the extent that the Wari did. In fact, if the skeletal data show that militarism was a Wari strategy of domination and expansion, this would indicate that they were the first in the Andes to implement a military apparatus on a grand scale with the goal of dominating geographically dispersed and ethnically diverse peoples. This is also significant because it suggests that Wari military organization and modes of imperial rule may have provided many of the foundations for the imperial apparatus of the later Inka Empire.

To evaluate the degree to which militarism and violence may have been a part of Wari imperial policy and to examine the levels and kinds of violence that affected Wari-affiliated communities, this chapter presents data on antemortem and perimortem skeletal trauma. Cranial trauma is explored in particular detail, as it is an excellent proxy for violence-related incidents. The frequency and patterning of head injury at the three sites are compared to one another to evaluate how Wari imperial policies and practices may have differentially structured lifeways and risk for violence, and all are compared to other Andean populations to identify trends through time and across regions. Skeletal trauma caused by accidental injury is also presented as a means to reconstruct physical activity patterns and compare lifeways between heartland and hinterland communities.

Methodological Considerations in Studies of Violence

Given the research question regarding the role of violence in imperial expansion and maintenance of imperial authority, it is imperative to identify injuries that are likely related to violence. This can be achieved by examining the location, size, and type of skeletal trauma to determine the proximate cause in most cases (for example, a blow to the skull with a solid object or penetrating wound with a bladed weapon). At the population level (see Roberts 2000), documenting whether the trauma is healed (sublethal) or unhealed (lethal) and examining the gendered, aged, and bodily distribution of injuries, combined with information on archaeological context, can be evaluated to infer the larger social and political contexts that may have contributed to (or inhibited) the emergence of violence.

The first step to link bones to behavior is to determine whether a bone fractured before death (antemortem), around the time of death (perimortem), or after death (postmortem). Antemortem trauma exhibits evidence of healing, and if it is well healed, then the injury can be identified as sublethal. Distinguishing between ante- and perimortem skeletal trauma is crucial to determine whether a wound was lethal or not, which can provide significant insights into human intention or the efficacy of defensive apparatuses.

Bones that are scratched or broken well after death (postmortem) by, say, roots, rodents, excavators, or looters may mimic perimortem skeletal trauma (Milner et al. 1994), but the postmortem damage can often be identified by a well-trained osteologist (Walker 2001). Although that may be an overly optimistic claim, there are specific characteristics that osteologists can observe when trying to distinguish postmortem damage from actual skeletal trauma. For example, postmortem damage typically exhibits distinct colors on the unbroken bone surface versus the edge of the break, the latter of which is usually lighter in color. Postmortem breaks also tend to have straight, clean, 90-degree broken edges, and tiny bone fragments rarely stay attached to the fragmented site.

In contrast, the edges of a perimortem fracture will be the same color as the rest of the bone because both surfaces have undergone similar taphonomic changes while in the same burial environment. Perimortem fractures also tend to have adherent bone fragments or "hinging" at the margins, and the edge of the fracture is usually slanted, rather than straight at a 90-degree angle to the axis of the bone. (Think of breaking a green twig, which mimics a perimortem fracture, versus an old, dry twig, which mimics a postmortem break.) Also, perimortem breaks that occur just before a person dies show no bony evidence for healing, because rapid death stops the healing process that would otherwise be visible on bone. Perimortem fractures on a recently deceased person simply cannot heal. These characteristics aid in identifying a perimortem fracture; it does not, however, make clear whether the fracture occurred immediately before or just after death. Even so, as Walker (2001:578) has argued, the presence of injuries such as cranial fractures or arrow wounds on a skeleton "strongly suggests malevolent intent, even if some of the injuries were inflicted posthumously as a gesture of disrespect."

Skeletal Trauma: Violence or Accident?

Skeletal injuries should be identified as accidental or intentional whenever possible. Identifying trauma patterns by skeletal element is a key step in this process. Cranial wounds are a reliable proxy of violence among ancient populations, and in the context of the ancient Andes where blunt-force weapons were commonly used, well-formed (usually oval) depressed fractures are indicative of violence-related blunt-force trauma. In contrast, linear cranial fractures more often result from accidental falls (Hobbs 1984). And although the shape and size of the wound may not always correlate to the shape of the weapon (Dirkmaat et al. 2008), blunt-force trauma can generally be distinguished from injury by a bladed weapon, arrowhead, or accidental fall.

Additionally, patterns in the location of head wounds add a crucial element to understanding the nature of injuries. Wounds that repeatedly appear on the frontal bone, for example, are unlikely to result from accidental falls but probably stem from face-to-face violent encounters (Lambert 1997; Walker 1997; Walker 2001). When wounds are concentrated on the left side of the frontal bone (or left anterior parietal or temporal), most may be inferred to have been inflicted by a right-handed attacker. Wounds to the posterior of the skull are often interpreted as injuries sustained while fleeing an attacker (Walker 1997; Webb 1995), perhaps during a raid. Such a wound may also result when an individual takes a defensive position, bowing the head to protect the face. In populations in which head wounds are common and appear more frequently among a particular sex or age cohort, violence is more likely the cause than is accidental injury (Lambert 1994; Roberts 2000; Walker 1997). Of course, shared occupations can lead to similar accidental injuries, but those will typically affect the postcrania, not the skull.

Arm injuries can result from either violent encounters or accidents, but certain types of arm injuries are more likely to result from the former. Parry fractures on the shaft of the ulna are one example, resulting when an individual raises the arm above the head to protect the head from an oncoming blow (Ortner and Putschar 1981). However, Lovell (1997) cautions against identifying all parry fractures as attempts to ward off a blow to the skull; they can also result from steep falls when the ulna receives the brunt of the impact. Also, as

Judd (2008) has argued, parry fractures should have a transverse fracture line and affect the distal half of the ulna, among other criteria. However, studies of modern domestic abuse cases in Papua New Guinea show that olecranon (near the elbow) and general forearm fractures were the most common injury among abused women, sustained when they held their arms above their head in the classic defensive posture to parry a blow (Watters and Dyke 1996). In addition to the type and location of arm fractures, it is essential to evaluate whether ulna fractures coexist with cranial fractures, as their co-occurrence likely indicates violent interactions, not accidental injuries (Lambert 1994).

A Colles' fracture (broken wrist), in contrast, suggests that the wound resulted from an accident when the person flung out his/her hand to brace a fall (Ortner and Putschar 1981). Although a violent action such as shoving could lead to a Colles' fracture, there is no means to differentiate an accidental fall from an intentional shove based on this kind of bone injury. Thus, certain arm fractures can be attributed to a violent act or an accident with only some degree of certainty.

Rib and hand fractures also may relate to violent interactions. Metacarpal fractures of the hand, for example, are often caused by the "longitudinal compression impact . . . from boxing" (Lovell 1997:164) or similar physical engagements involving the fist. Conversely, hand fractures can result from accidental falls or heavy objects landing on the hand (Galloway 1999). Face-to-face combat, particularly with solid weapons, can fracture ribs, or a fall from a great height may crush them (Galloway 1999). Fractures of the lower limbs and feet are usually attributed to accidental falls and are rarely associated with violence (Lovell 1997), though foot bones might be affected in cases of torture or imprisonment when a person is hobbled (Osterholtz 2010).

Finally, embedded projectile points injury is one of the clearest examples of an intentional violent act. Although Rowe (1946) describes projectile weapons that were used by the Inka, projectile injuries are exceptionally rare in the ancient Andes. However, two unique cases are described by Tomasto (2009:153–55) in which two adults from the Nasca region had obsidian projectile points embedded either in bone or between bone spaces: a Paracas-era male had the point situated ("embedded") between the ribs (he was also missing his skull and had cut marks on his axis), and a Nasca-era male exhibited a small embedded point in the third cervical vertebrae.

Given the varied social settings in which particular injuries can occur, the complete suite of osteological and archaeological data should be taken into consideration when assessing whether skeletal injuries have resulted from accidents or intentional acts of violence.

Comparing Violence through Time and across Regions

Although bioarchaeologists have a fairly standard suite of criteria for documenting skeletal trauma, comparisons between skeletal populations are sometimes challenging. This is because some scholars report cranial trauma for *all* crania (children and adults), and because children are much less likely to have engaged in violence, the average cranial trauma frequency for entire populations tends to be lower than if only adults were included. For example, 10 adults with head trauma out of 100 individuals equals a population trauma frequency of 10 percent, but if children constitute half of the population, then the adult cranial trauma rate is actually 20 percent (10/50). Similarly, older studies sometimes failed to report percentages of violence-related trauma for each sex and distinguish between antemortem (sublethal) and perimortem (lethal) trauma, necessary distinctions if one is to re-create the possible social contexts in which violence emerged. Finally, because not all studies present "skull maps" showing the location of head injuries, evaluating and comparing the potentially different social circumstances in which violence occurred is sometimes difficult. These particular distinctions are made in this study, so other researchers can aggregate or separate the data depending on the comparisons they wish to make.

Trauma and Violence in the Wari Heartland

Huarpa Period Skeletal Trauma at Conchopata

Among the 11 observable Conchopata Huarpa period crania, one adult exhibits a head wound (1/11=9%), a healed fracture on the left zygomatic of a male at least 45 years old. The location of the wound suggests that he was hit by a right-handed attacker during a face-to-face conflict. Cranial trauma is absent among the four females and six unsexed adults, and none of the crania exhibit perimortem wounds.

A total of nine females with at least 75 percent of all long bones and 50 percent of ribs and vertebrae were observed for bone fractures. At least two of these women (possibly three) show healed fractures. One old adult female from EA104-T5 exhibits healed spondylolysis in the 11th and 12th thoracic vertebrae, and one middle-aged to old female from Tomb 1 (from the 1977 excavations) exhibits a Colles' fracture that affected the left radius and left ulna (figure 5.1). The left radius displays evidence of healing and also shows trauma-related osteoarthritis. The associated left ulna is diagnosed as a complete fracture with nonunion. That is, the marrow cavity sealed before the fractured distal end could mend to the shaft. This could be the result of insufficient blood supply to the injured region, an infection that inhibited bone healing, excessive movement of the joint during the healing process, incomplete contact between the distal end and shaft, the presence of soft tissue between the fragments, or total destruction of the styloid process (Lovell 1997). Within the same tomb (Tomb 1, which was slightly disturbed), a right radius exhibited a Colles' fracture, but whether it is from the woman with the fractured left wrist or from the other female in the tomb is unclear.[1] If it belongs to the former, then she had two broken wrists. If it belongs to the latter, then there are two women with fractured wrists within Tomb 1. Neither of these lower arm fractures was a parry fracture. Instead, they seem to have resulted when the woman (women) flung out her (their) hands to brace a fall. Overall, two out of nine (22%) or three out of nine (33%) females suffered from postcranial trauma involving the back and wrists.

The one male with a facial fracture showed no postcranial injuries. The second male was too poorly preserved to observe for postcranial fractures. Overall, Huarpa females appear more likely to have suffered postcranial trauma than

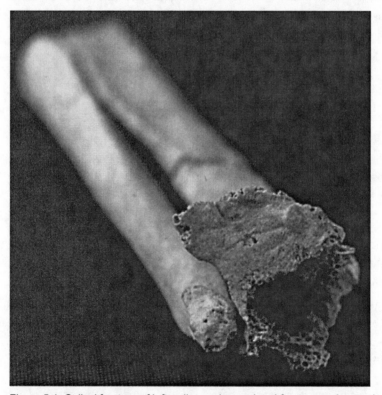

Figure 5.1. Colles' fracture of left radius and associated fracture and nonunion of left ulna. Note the trauma-related osteoarthritis on radius. Middle-aged adult female from Tomb 1, 1977 excavations, Huarpa era, Conchopata.

cranial trauma, suggesting that although they were not victims of violence that led to skull fractures, they may have engaged in activities with high risks for bodily injury.

One of the Huarpa tombs (Tomb 5, 1977 excavations) warrants additional discussion because it includes five individuals, all of whom are late adolescent females. The similarity in age and sex among them has raised much suspicion regarding human sacrifice (Isbell and Cook 1987; Isbell and Cook 2002). Although none displayed perimortem skeletal trauma indicative of this practice, the possibility of sacrifice of these five young females cannot be excluded, particularly given the uniqueness of their shared age and sex. At the site of Pachacamac near Lima, strangled females (interpreted as sacrifices) were identified by the presence of cloth ropes around their necks; none of them displayed any perimortem skeletal trauma (Uhle 1903). Thus, if archaeological evidence had been overlooked, the potential mechanism of death would have been missed. In light of this, the absence of perimortem trauma among the five young Huarpa women in Tomb 5 makes it difficult to rule out foul play or ritual sacrifice, particularly given the uniqueness of this burial group.

Wari Period Cranial Trauma at Conchopata

Among the burial population dating to the subsequent Wari period, about a quarter of the adults exhibit a head injury. An earlier study showed antemortem cranial fractures in seven out of 27 adults (26%) (Tung 2007b). New analysis of recently excavated burials shows that three out of 17 exhibit a healed cranial fracture (18%). Thus, among all 44 adult crania from Wari-era contexts observed for head trauma, 10 are affected (23%). There are no cases of perimortem cranial trauma, which suggests that no one in the burial sample died immediately after receiving a blow to the skull.

My previous research showed no statistically significant differences in head trauma frequencies between females and males (Tung 2007b). This pattern holds for the larger sample, in which six out of 25 women (24%) and four out

Table 5.1. Cranial trauma frequency among juveniles, males, females, and unsexed adults at each site

Site	Juveniles (<15 yrs)	Males	Females	Unsexed adults	Adult totals
Conchopata	0/39=0%	4/14=29%	6/25=24%	0/5=0%	10/44=23%
Beringa	1/33=3%	5/10=50%	4/13=31%	4/16=25%	13/39=33%
La Real	1/16=6%	16/39=41%	5/26=19%	11/39=28%	32/104=31%
Total	2/88=2%	25/63=40%	15/64=23%	15/60=25%	55/187=29%

of 14 men (29%) show head wounds (Fisher's exact, $p=0.519$). This suggests that both sexes similarly suffered cranial injuries, inasmuch as frequencies are concerned (table 5.1). Of the five unsexed adults, none exhibits a healed cranial fracture.

Among 39 children (<15 years old) buried in formal tombs, none exhibit any kind of cranial trauma. (Child trophy heads are excluded from this calculation, as they are clearly a distinct subgroup, described in the next chapter.)

Given that older individuals are exposed to more years of risk for violence (Glencross and Sawchuk 2003), the age-based cranial trauma differences followed an expected pattern: no skull trauma on children, and a lower frequency of trauma among young adults (14%) relative to middle-aged adults (29%) and older adults (44%) (table 5.2).

The shape of all cranial wounds was round, and the wounds on all 10 adults exhibit at least some evidence of healing, indicating that these injuries were not the immediate mechanism of death (figure 5.2). Specifically, nine of the injured adults display well-healed head wounds, and one old adult female exhibits a partially healed cranial fracture and a well-healed head wound. The incompletely healed head wound was identified as such by the presence of woven bone around the site of the fracture near bregma.

Half of the adults with head trauma exhibit only one wound, while the others exhibit two or more: four of the 10 adults (40%) exhibit two cranial fractures, and one (10%) exhibits three cranial fractures (table 5.3). The latter may have been engaged in several separate physical conflicts that led to additional head wounds. Conversely, they could have suffered several blows to the head in one incident. Among the five adults with multiple skull fractures, four of them exhibit well-healed head wounds, which precludes determining whether these were coterminous or sequential. The fifth individual, the old female with a partially healed fracture near bregma (mentioned above) and the well-healed wound on the left parietal boss, was a victim of violence on two separate occasions. She first received a nonlethal blow to the parietal boss, which healed, and later she suffered a severe wound to the superior of

Table 5.2. Cranial trauma frequencies among adult age groups at each site

Site	Late teens/ young adults	Mid-adults	Old adults	Adults	Totals
Conchopata (N=44)	2/14=14%	4/14=29%	4/9=44%	0/7=0%	10/44=23%
Beringa (N=39)	2/15=13%	6/15=40%	2/3=67%	3/6=50%	13/39=33%
La Real (N=104)	15/55=27%	2/11=18%	5/12=42%	10/26=38%	32/104=31%
Total (N=187)	19/84=23%	12/40=30%	11/24=46%	13/39=33%	55/187=29%

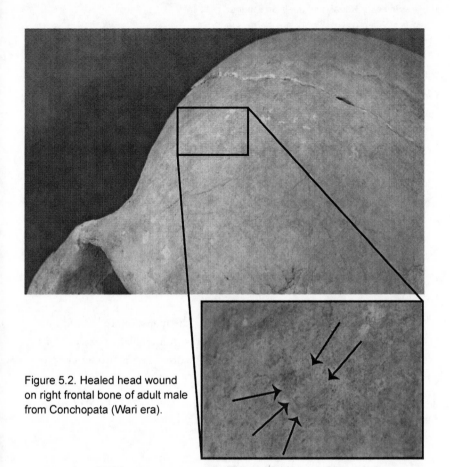

Figure 5.2. Healed head wound on right frontal bone of adult male from Conchopata (Wari era).

Table 5.3. Tally of head wounds per adult at the three sites in this study

	1 head wound	2 head wounds	3 head wounds	4 head wounds	5 head wounds	6 head wounds	Totals
Conchopata							
No. of adults	5	4	1	0	0	0	10
No. of wounds in sample	5	8	3	0	0	0	16
Beringa							
No. of adults	10	1	2	0	0	0	13
No. of wounds in sample	10	2	6	0	0	0	18
La Real							
No. of adults	22	4	3	2	0	1	32
No. of wounds in sample	22	8	9	8	0	6	53

her skull, which only partially healed before she died. Interestingly, this female belonged to haplogroup D and displayed annular cranial deformation. Both traits are uncommon among the Conchopata population, yet she exhibited enamel and bone strontium isotope ratios expected for the local Ayacucho Basin. These data suggest that she was either relocated to Conchopata as an infant or she was born in the Ayacucho Basin to a nonlocal mother (also a rare haplogroup D) who marked her nonlocal status in infancy with a unique form of cranial modification. (Cranial modification must begin in infancy, when skull bones are malleable.) Her potential outsider status, perhaps inherited from her mother, may have contributed to the likelihood of becoming a victim of violence. Her other body injuries and characteristics that mark her as an outsider are described below.

Patterning of Head Wounds among Conchopata Population (Wari Period)

Analysis of head-wound locations shows that the majority are located on the back of the skull. Of the 16 total skull fractures, 11 are on the posterior of the skull (68.75%) (occipital and parietal bosses), three are on the superior por-

Table 5.4. Head wound counts for each portion of the skull for sexed and unsexed adults at the three sites in this study

	Anterior	Posterior	Superior	Left lateral	Right lateral	Total no. of head wounds
Conchopata						
Females	0	7	2	0	0	9
Males	2	4	1	0	0	7
Sex ?	0	0	0	0	0	0
Sum of all	2	11	3	0	0	16
Beringa						
Females	1	3	0	0	2	6
Males	4	4	0	0	0	8
Sex ?	0	4	0	0	0	4
Sum of all	5	11	0	0	2	18
La Real						
Females	1	4	1	0	1	7
Males	17	6	1	3	2	29
Sex ?	9	3	1	1	2	16
Sum of all	27	13	3	4	5	52[a]

[a] One La Real head wound was not mapped; for this reason, the wound count total in table 5.3 differs from this one.

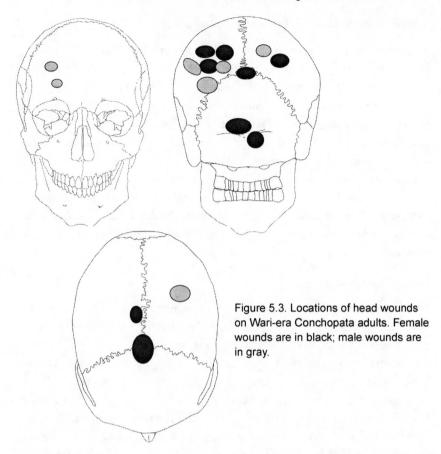

Figure 5.3. Locations of head wounds on Wari-era Conchopata adults. Female wounds are in black; male wounds are in gray.

tion (18.75%), and two are on the anterior (12.5%) (figure 5.3, table 5.4). This pattern of cranial wounds suggests specific, almost systematic, physical violence that consistently targeted the posterior of the head relative to all other cranial regions. Some of these individuals may have received blows to the back of the head while ducking to avoid an oncoming blow, or they may have been attacked from behind, as in cases of raids or abductions. Conversely, much of the trauma could have resulted in nonbattle contexts, perhaps from culturally defined punitive actions in the form of corporal punishment (see Moore 1973).

The vast majority of female head wounds are located on the posterior (7/9=78%), and none are on the anterior. In contrast, male head wounds are more evenly dispersed: 57 percent on the posterior, 29 percent on the anterior, and 14 percent on the superior (table 5.4). This sex-based patterning suggests that the social contexts in which men were engaged in fights were more variable than those for women. Moreover, when wound location is taken as a clue for bodily position and general social context, it suggests that males, not females, occasionally engaged in face-to-face conflict.

Wari Period Postcranial Trauma at Conchopata

A complete assessment of the risks of violent and accidental injury must include an overview of bodily trauma. As Lovell (1997) notes, in addition to head wounds, injuries to the hands and ribs are some of the best indicators for violence. Other bone fractures, in contrast, may provide insight into physical activities and occupational hazards. This section reports the frequencies of fractures or dislocations per bone in the Conchopata Wari-era burial population for individuals whose age at death was 15 years or older (table 5.5). For inclusion in the analysis, long bones must have had at least four of five portions present: the five portions are the proximal epiphysis, proximal third of shaft, middle third of shaft, distal third of shaft, and distal epiphysis (Buikstra and Ubelaker 1994). Ribs and vertebrae that were included in this analysis were more than half complete, and hand and foot bones were complete.

Shoulder and Arm (Conchopata)

Based on observations of the glenoid fossa and humeral head, there are no dislocations in the left or right shoulder joint. Arm fractures are generally uncommon, and parry fractures are nonexistent among the 34 left and 38 right ulnae, though one left ulna in room EA64 and two right ulnae (in rooms EA64 and EA187) exhibit bony evidence of an elbow dislocation and associated arthritis. Among the 38 adult left humeri, one adult buried in EA40A displays a healed fracture (2.9%). Of the 33 right humeri, two exhibit healed fractures (EA179 and EA64), and a third person suffered an elbow dislocation and associated arthritis (EA187). One of 38 (2.6%) right radii was fractured (healed Colles' fracture in an adult, EA179), and two of 31 left radii (6.5%) exhibit Colles' fractures; they affected adults from EA138 and EA179. (See table 5.5 for frequencies of all long-bone fractures.)

The multiple arm fractures observed in EA64 affected two adults; one adult had a fracture on the distal end of the right humerus and the proximal and distal ends of the right ulna. These elbow and wrist joints healed but show evidence for trauma-induced arthritis. The second person suffered a fracture on the left ulna. In short, fractures and dislocations of the arm are uncommon, and parry fractures are nonexistent.

Hip and Leg (Conchopata)

Bone fractures and dislocations involving the leg and acetabulum were infrequent (table 5.5). Among the two left femur fractures ($N=39$), both affected the proximal third and show incomplete healing, indicating that the individuals died shortly after sustaining the injuries, either from complications of a fractured fe-

Table 5.5. Postcranial fractures among late adolescent/adult skeletal elements at the three study sites

Bone	Side	Conchopata	Beringa	La Real
Glenoid	L	0/31=0%	0/40=0%	0/18=0%
Glenoid	R	0/28=0%	0/44=0%	0/20=0%
Humerus	L	1/38=2.6%	1/44=2.3%	1/24=4.2%
Humerus	R	3/33=9.1%	1/47=2.1%	2/24=8.3%
Radius	L	2/31=6.5%	5/44=11.4%	0/14=0%
Radius	R	1/38=2.6%	2/41=4.9%	0/17=0%
Ulna	L	1/34=2.9%	6/51=11.8%	1/23=4.3%
Ulna	R	2/38=5.3%	1/57=1.8%	0/18=0%
Acetabulum	L	1/23=4.3%	0/34=0%	0/17=0%
Acetabulum	R	0/22=0%	0/42=0%	0/16=0%
Femur	L	2/39=5.1%	0/46=0%	0/27=0%
Femur	R	0/40=0%	0/43=0%	0/24=0%
Tibia	L	0/32=0%	0/39=0%	3/25=12.0%
Tibia	R	0/33=0%	1/45=2.2%	1/21=4.8%
Fibula	L	0/28=0%	2/40=5.0%	0/8=0%
Fibula	R	0/31=0%	1/42=2.4%	0/8=0%
Cvrt		6/324=1.9%	8/392=2.0%	1/97=1.0%
Tvrt		8/577=1.4%	29/537=5.4%	5/275=1.8%
Lvrt		9/256=3.5%	5/236=2.1%	3/147=2.0%
Sacrum		3/28=10.7%	2/24=8.3%	1/10=10.0%
Clavicle	L	0/32=0%	1/38=2.6%	0/12=0%
Clavicle	R	0/34=0%	1/45=2.2%	0/11=0%
Ribs	L	9/197=4.6%	13/323=4.0%	3/124=2.4%[a]
Ribs	R	1/182=0.5%	8/343=2.3%	
Metacarpals	U	4/449=0.9%	2/435=0.5%	0/20=0%
Hand phalanges	U	4/817=0.5%	3/841=0.04%	0/40=0%
Calcaneus	L	0/36=0%	1/51=2.0%	0/17=0%
Calcaneus	R	0/38=0%	0/55=0%	0/8=0%
Talus	L	2/56=3.6%	0/53=0%	0/9=0%
Talus	R	0/56=0%	0/58=0%	0/5=0%
Metatarsals	U	1/168=0.6%	4/473=0.8%	0/30=0%
Foot phalanges	U	3/116=2.6%	3/723=0.04%	0/30=0%

[a] Adult ribs from La Real were not sided, so the percentage reported is all adult ribs combined.

mur or from some other unobserved fatal injury or illness. One of the fractured femora exhibits an incomplete union, and both exhibit woven bone around the primary fracture area, indicating associated infection at the time of death. None of the 40 right femora exhibit a fracture or dislocation.

Skeletal Thorax (Conchopata)

Based on total counts of each of the three vertebral types, lumbar vertebrae show the highest frequency of compression fractures (9/256=3.5%), followed by the cervical vertebrae (6/324=1.9%) and thoracic vertebrae (8/577=1.4%) (table 5.5). However, when calculating the percentage of adults with at least one vertebral fracture, cervical and thoracic vertebrae injuries are more common. Four out of 47 adults fractured a cervical vertebra (8.5%), and two of these individuals have two injured cervical vertebrae apiece. Four out of 49 adults (8.2%) have thoracic compression fractures; two of them have three collapsed thoracic vertebrae, and the other two adults suffered one each. Among 52 adults, four exhibit lumbar compression fractures (7.7%); one has four collapsed lumbar vertebrae, two adults have two each, and one has only one collapsed lumbar. Fractures of the sacrum affected three out of 28 adults (10.7%).

Healed and partially healed rib fractures are more common than vertebral fractures, both when calculating percentages based on number of elements and when calculating percentages based on number of individuals. Nine out of 197 left ribs are affected (4.6%). The 197 left ribs come from 35 different adults, four of whom had fractured ribs (11.4%). Six of the rib fractures are on an old female; she is the (possible outsider) female described above who also exhibits two cranial wounds. The other three left rib fractures are on three other adults. Notably, three of the four adults with rib fractures also exhibit circular cranial fractures of the kind expected from round stones or maces. The co-occurrence of head and torso injuries suggests that the rib fractures were sustained in violent encounters, not accidental falls.

Hand and Foot (Conchopata)

Four out of 449 (0.9%) unsided metacarpals exhibit a healed break known as a "boxing fracture" (Lovell 1997). These metacarpal fractures are on four out of 45 adults (8.9%). Among these four adults, one is an old female and the others are of indeterminate sex. Healed fractures are also present on four out of 817 unsided hand phalanges (0.5%). These hand phalanges derive from 30 different adults, three of whom suffered fractured fingers (10%); one adult has two hand phalanx fractures, and the two others exhibit only one finger fracture each.

Foot fractures are rare. There are no fractures on either calcaneus or the right talus, and less than one percent of complete metatarsals and three percent of complete foot phalanges exhibit healed fractures (table 5.5). The foot fractures were on four different adults, three of whom were female and one of unknown sex.

Site Distribution of Persons with Postcranial Injury

The interment locations of the injured show some interesting patterns. The elbow fractures affected two adults from room EA64, one of whom also suffered a broken wrist, while proximal femur fractures affected two adults from EA89A. Fractures were also common among adults buried in EA179, but in some cases it is difficult to assign specific bones to each individual because the bones were commingled. In EA179, there are at least two adults who suffered a collapsed sacral fracture. One, both, or a third adult also suffered fractures to the cervical, thoracic, and lumbar vertebrae and one left rib. There are also two Colles' fractures on a left and right radius from EA179, but whether one adult broke both wrists or two separate adults broke one wrist each is unclear.

Two of the four foot fractures affected a young and an elderly women in EA105; the older female also had a vertebral compression fracture and a healed cranial wound. Perhaps the arm, leg, and foot injuries were related to risky physical activities that specific burial groups shared in common, while the collapsed vertebrae were related to advanced age of the affected adults. Hand and rib fractures, in contrast, were distributed across different burial areas, suggesting that these violence-related injuries were randomly dispersed among the community.

Discussion of Trauma at Conchopata

There is an increase in the frequency of observable cranial trauma from the Huarpa to the Wari period, from nine percent to 23 percent, but these differences are not statistically significant (Fisher's exact, $p=0.292$; $N=55$). A larger sample of Huarpa-era skeletons is needed to determine whether the observed increase in cranial trauma is an artifact of preservation or signals changing social conditions that contributed to more violence.

Where Are the Wari Warriors' Bodies?

Wari iconography is replete with scenes of warriors brandishing weapons, which Ochatoma (2007) identifies as men. That, combined with the male cranial trauma rate of 29 percent, suggests that some of those injuries may have been sustained in battle-related incidents. Indeed, all head wounds are oval in shape, a characteristic that suggests they were caused by sling stones or maces. It is remarkable that only two Conchopata men exhibit injuries consistent with face-to-face combat (anterior head wounds). If there were male warriors who sustained that oft-cited combat head injury, they appear to be missing from this mortuary sample; perhaps they were interred in an area that has not yet been excavated. More likely, however, is that men with battle-related injuries died in distant military campaigns, never to return to Conchopata for burial. This is supported by the skewed sex profile showing significantly fewer men than women, as discussed in the previous chapter.

Further evidence that Wari men traveled to distant lands can be seen in the iconography (discussed below) and the human trophy head and strontium isotope data presented in the next chapter.

Wari Weapons

The excavations at Conchopata uncovered numerous items that were likely weapons used in warfare and other violent contexts. One of the most remarkable pieces is a solid copper-bronze mace from EA88 (figure 5.4), which was almost surely cast (Isbell, pers. comm. 2010). Its shape is like that of a pinecone, with a hole at the base, likely so it could be attached to a club or rope. Attached to either, a weapon of this sort—even if it was meant to be mostly symbolic—would have inflicted serious blunt-force trauma on an opponent. More-common weapon types include stone maces ("doughnut stones"), which also would have resulted in depressed cranial fractures (figure 5.4). At least 18 "doughnut stone" maces were recovered by the Conchopata Archaeology Project (Wolff, pers. comm. 2010).

Another possible weapon was recovered from EA105; it may be an archer's wooden bow, like those depicted in the iconography, discussed below (Isbell and Cook 2002). It was at the base of the burial of a young male (23–27 years old), who exhibited a healed cranial wound on the left parietal boss (posterior of the skull). The wooden object, however, could have been a weaving implement (Goldstein 2003), not an archer's bow. Poor preservation precludes definitive identification of the object. Nonetheless, the sampling of weapons from Conchopata indicates that there was an effort to create objects intended to injure and kill, perhaps even to maintain an arsenal, both for the defense of the community and for military offense that may have been part of an imperial expansionist policy.

Wari Warriors in Iconography

An evaluation of militarism and its role in imperialism should include a study of not only violence-related trauma and weapons but also artistic representations of militaristic activities. At Conchopata, the iconographic depictions of warriors

Figure 5.4. A sample of weapons from Conchopata. *Top*: Side and bottom views of a solid copper-and-bronze mace recovered from EA88. *Bottom*: Stone maces from EA132B (*left*) and EA24T1 (*right*). (Photos courtesy of the Conchopata Archaeology Project, William Isbell and Anita Cook.)

and weapons suggest state and community efforts at creating and maintaining a military class, while also presenting a general image of military supremacy (figure 5.5). There are three key groups of military personnel on Wari ceramics identified thus far (Ochatoma 2007; Ochatoma et al. 2008). Although there is need for further evaluation, the artistic representations of warriors have been identified as men (Ochatoma 2007). They are identified as men in comparison to depictions of women in figurine form (Tung and Cook 2006) and in iconography, such as the example of a woman shown breast-feeding a jaguar (Isbell and Cook 2002).

Among the three military groups identified based on iconographic details, one in particular may have been affiliated with long-distance travel (Ochatoma et al. 2008). It shows an elaborately dressed individual in profile who carries a weapon and shield and kneels on a *balsa de totora* (reed raft). The reed-boat warrior image (figure 5.5A) was first recovered at Conchopata by Ochatoma and Cabrera in 1997, and in 1999 Isbell and Cook recovered ceramics with similar iconography below the floor in EA6 (figure 5.5B,C) (see figure 30 in Isbell 2000). Thus, these depictions of reed-boat warriors have appeared in at least two Conchopata structures, on four different urns (Ochatoma, pers. comm. 2009). Evidence of the connections between Conchopata and the capital site of Huari are further illustrated by a similar image on a ceramic bottle from the Vegachayoq Moqo sector at Huari, where a warrior stands on a reed raft, facing forward, holding an axe in the right hand (figure 5.5D). The shared characteristics of these images, the most prominent of which are the reed boat and weapons, may suggest a military subclass affiliated with mobility or expansion into distant lands. Given that reed rafts would have been unnecessary in the Ayacucho Basin, their depictions may have been both a reflection of connections to distant lands and an attempt to create narratives of Wari dominance in faraway regions. That is, images of Wari warriors on watercraft could have functioned as propaganda of sorts, meant to celebrate activities that already occurred and recruit or coerce individuals into future militaristic and expansionistic activities.

The second group of warriors also carry weapons, but these warriors face forward and are not associated with reed boats, nor are they depicted with animal symbols such as those discussed next. They carry weapons in their right hands and shields in their left and wear caps with cylindrical objects protruding from the sides (Ochatoma et al. 2008). These shared traits may suggest that they shared similar military roles.

The third group of military personnel carry weapons and shields and are associated with animal symbols, perhaps reflecting the qualities of that military group (Ochatoma et al. 2008). They are portrayed on urns and large pitchers, standing upright with their torsos facing forward and heads and feet in profile. Within this third group, there are two subgroups, the most distinguishing of which is the association with either an eagle or a jaguar, animals that are often associated with warrior identities in the ancient Americas, particularly among the Aztecs (Benson 1998) (figure 5.6). The "Eagle Warrior" wields a long-handled axe and is depicted with an eagle on his shoulder, wings extended. These warriors are shown wearing block-shaped hats decorated with alternating squares and a tunic with geometric designs similar to those found on Wari textiles. Thus far, there are at least three examples of the Eagle Warrior from Conchopata ceramics (Ochatoma et al. 2008).

The other designation of "Jaguar Warrior" comes from Ochatoma and Cabrera's (2002) analysis of the spotted tunic worn by a warrior, a tunic that they identify as a jaguar pelt (figure 5.6). More convincing is the jaguar paw on the

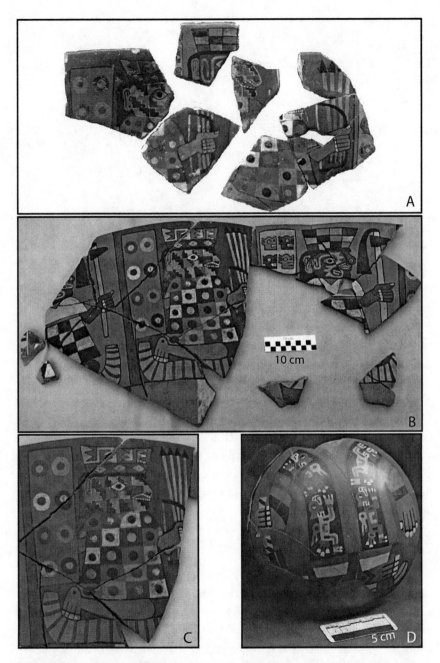

Figure 5.5. (A) Ceramic urn fragments with three Wari archers (courtesy of José Ochatoma). (B) Ceramic urn fragments with Wari warriors kneeling on reed boats (EA6) (courtesy of Conchopata Archaeology Project, originally published in Isbell 2000). (C) Detail of the Wari archer shown in figure 5.5B (courtesy of William Isbell and Anita Cook). (D) Ceramic bottle with reed-boat warrior from Vegachayoq Moqo sector at Huari (photo by T. A. Tung).

Figure 5.6. Drawing of the "Eagle Warrior" (*left*) and "Jaguar Warrior" (*right*). (Courtesy of José Ochatoma.)

left shoulder of the warrior. The Jaguar Warrior also carries a weapon and shield, and he wears a more substantive hat or helmet, at least in terms of the kind of protection it would afford. Notably, zooarchaeological analysis by Patricia Maita shows that remains from large feline predators were present at Conchopata, either jaguars, pumas, or ocelots, so these big cats were known to the Conchopata inhabitants.

Drawing from studies of Aztec warriors (Benson 1998; Hassig 1988), Ochatoma and Cabrera (2002) have elaborated an argument in which they suggest that the strength of the jaguar, its nocturnal lifestyle, and the manner in which it defleshes its victims were likely factors that led Wari warriors to identify themselves with this animal. As I discuss in the following chapter, the defleshing and dismemberment of Wari trophy heads is reminiscent of attributes associated with this feline predator.

Females as Targets of Violence at Conchopata

It is notable that one-quarter of the Conchopata females exhibit cranial trauma, most commonly on the posterior of the skull. This can be best understood by comparison to other skeletal populations exhibiting a similar pattern. In a study of Late Woodland populations (AD 1000–1300) in southeastern Michigan, many females suffered cranial trauma that likely stemmed from raiding and abduction events (Wilkinson and Van Wagenen 1993). The authors suggest that the injured women either represented natal members of the local group that enemies tried but failed to abduct, injuring them in the process, or that they were women violently abducted from other villages who were subsequently "adopted" into the local community. Because the Conchopata women could have been injured in similar circumstances, strontium isotope values were obtained from a subsample of females with head trauma ($n=3$) to evaluate whether they were abducted or migrated to Conchopata from a distant geological locale. All three women exhibit local strontium isotope ratios: $^{87}Sr/^{86}Sr=0.70552$, 0.70565, and 0.70583. That is, the values are within the expected range for individuals who consumed local foods grown near Conchopata (Tung and Knudson 2008). This suggests that they were not taken captive in a distant land, though they could have been captured or voluntarily migrated to Conchopata from regions with similar strontium isotope ratios.

Head injuries among women also could have resulted from intrahousehold violence, either male-on-female or female-on-female domestic violence. Although the preponderance of posterior wounds does not mirror the pattern for male-on-female domestic abuse in the Western world during the 19th century (that is, injury to the facial/anterior region) (Walker 1997), perhaps socially sanctioned, or at least socially common, violence targeted the back of a female's bowed head. Typically, in cases of domestic abuse, the perpetrator is the husband or some other significant male partner (Walker 1997). However, conflict between women in the same household—co-wives or mother- and daughter-in-law—may also lead to serious bodily injury. For example, among the Siriono in modern eastern Bolivia, co-wives sometimes fight, using digging sticks as weapons that can lead to serious bodily injury (Holmberg 1950). Additionally, Webb (1995:205) has documented more cranial trauma among females than males in many Australian aboriginal skeletal populations, leading him to suggest that some female wounds resulted from women fighting each other in polygynous households (also see Burbank 1994). If Isbell's (2001) assertion that Conchopata elites practiced polygyny is correct, then the cranial injuries may have been the result of co-wives fighting, which is apparently relatively common in polygynous societies (Levinson 1989:25, 32). However, as suggested in an earlier chapter, the Conchopata data do not indicate polygyny. Rather, if intrahousehold violence occurred, then it may have been male-female conflict, as described above, or female-female conflict between women of different social and generational ranks. Given rules of Andean kinship regarding parallel descent traced through the female or male line (Isbell 1997a; Zuidema 1977), higher-ranked women could have controlled and physically punished lower-ranked women.[2] Same-sex affinal relationships also may have contributed to some of the violence; higher-ranked women could have held a kinship position akin to mother-in-law, and inflicted injury on their daughters-in-law, as has been demonstrated among modern Quechua-speaking groups in the Bolivian Andes (Van Vleet 2002).

The regular, patterned locations of head wounds suggest that the cranial injuries may have been inflicted in more-controlled situations, not frenetic raiding

Figure 5.7. Images from 16th-century Murúa manuscript (2004 [1590]). *Left*: A woman is stoned as punishment for adultery, per Inka law. *Right*: The eighth Inka Captain (Apo Cama Inca) wielding a *honda* and sling stone over three victims' bodies.

events. Thus, prescribed or habitual violence against women may have occurred in other settings, such as judicial contexts. As mentioned in chapter 2, later Inka laws stipulated that particular transgressions against the community could be met with corporal punishment, such as stonings (Cobo 1892 [1653]:3: xxi, xxvii, 238, 240–41; Moore 1958; Murúa 1946 [1590]:xx, 70, 211, 213; Valera 1945 [1585]:58) (figure 5.7). This kind of Inka state-sanctioned punishment may have had its roots in the Wari state.

Although we know nothing of a Wari judicial system, the Wari state could have sanctioned corporal punishment such that individuals from Conchopata, females in particular, were punished with blows to the back of the head while kneeling or bowing. Perhaps this was part of a larger Wari imperial social and judicial system aimed at disciplining and controlling members of Wari society. The idea that women with head wounds received them in intrahousehold conflicts or judicial contexts and were indeed locals within Wari society (and not foreign women abducted from other locales) is tentatively supported by the local strontium isotope ratios from three of the injured women. However, because other Andean regions have similar geologic compositions as the Ayacucho Basin, their geographical origins are not definitive, nor are details of the social contexts in which the traumas were sustained.

Discussion of Postcranial Trauma at Conchopata

While the evidence cited above strongly suggests that cranial trauma among the Conchopata burial group was intentionally inflicted, postcranial trauma likely resulted from accidents, particularly from falls that could have occurred in the rough terrain and ravines. The prevalence and patterns of postcranial trauma differ between the Huarpa and Wari period skeletons. One-quarter to one-third of female bodies dating to the Huarpa occupation exhibit postcranial trauma, most of which were wrist fractures. In contrast, skeletons from the Wari period evince postcranial trauma in all parts of the body, in hands and arms, legs and feet, and parts of the skeletal trunk. The foot fractures that primarily afflicted women could have resulted when heavy objects (such as *batanes*, stone grinding implements) were dropped on the foot. Vertebral compression fractures in both sexes relate to the senior ages of those affected, as osteoporotic bones are more susceptible to injury. Finally, it is noteworthy that no parry fractures were observed in this sample, which, together with cranial trauma data showing only two frontal bone injuries, suggests that few injured warriors were interred at Conchopata. Rather, the majority of the observed Conchopata cranial injuries appear to have resulted in contexts other than warfare, such as injuries sustained in household disputes or as part of a larger state system that used physical punitive actions to punish and regulate behavior, particularly among women.

A Severely Injured Elderly Female: A Possible Outsider?

The old female with annular cranial deformation exhibits several skeletal fractures. All are described in the previous sections on bodily trauma, but her unique case merits examination in more detail. She exhibits two cranial fractures: one healed and the other partially healed, indicating injury recidivism (that is, they were sustained in separate incidents). She also has a healed metacarpal fracture, six compression fractures in thoracic vertebrae 10–12 and lumbar vertebrae 3–5, and fractures on six left ribs. The impact to the thorax primarily damaged the sternal portion of ribs four through seven (figure 5.8), though the second and third ribs were slightly affected as well. The rib fractures only partially healed, as evidenced by the incomplete union between normal bone and the bony callus, which suggests that the rib fractures occurred shortly before her death. Precisely how much earlier those injuries were sustained before her death is unknown; her elderly age could have inhibited swift healing of the fracture sites.

Given that she exhibits an annular form of cranial modification—rare at Conchopata—she (or her parents) may have been outsiders. (Cranial modification in the Andes is a marker of social identity that is imposed in infancy, when the cranial bones are more easily modified.) Additionally, she is the only individual who belongs to haplogroup D; the 13 others from Conchopata for

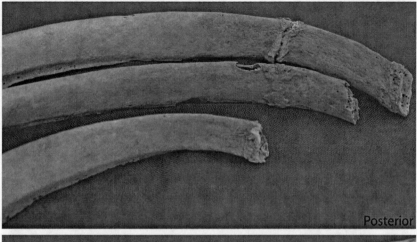

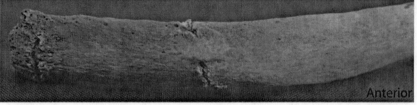

Figure 5.8. Left rib fractures (incompletely healed) on elderly female from Conchopata. Postmortem breaks are visible along the weakened location of the partially healed rib fractures.

whom mitochondrial DNA (mtDNA) was obtained belong to haplogroups A, B, or C (Kemp et al. 2009). This further marks her as unique within the Conchopata community. However, in contrast to her unique genotype and cranial modification style, the strontium isotope ratios obtained from her teeth and bones suggest that she spent her childhood and adulthood in the Ayacucho Basin or in a locale with similar geology. The strontium isotope ratios for her enamel ($^{87}Sr/^{86}Sr=0.70583$) and bone ($^{87}Sr/^{86}Sr=0.70580$) both are within the expected local range for the Ayacucho Basin (Tung and Knudson 2008). However, she could have migrated to Conchopata from another locale that is geologically similar to Ayacucho, as several other Andean regions (for example, the Moquegua valley) generate similar strontium isotope ratios (Knudson et al. 2004). Finally, the mortuary data show that she was not placed in a formally constructed tomb like others at the site. She was interred alone at Conchopata.

In sum, the mortuary, osteological, genetic, and strontium isotope data from this elderly female suggest that either she was an outsider or her mother (haplogroup derives from the maternal line) was an outsider. Her parents or other elder kin likely imposed the nonlocal form of cranial modification on her when she was an infant. In this one individual, we see an elderly woman with a rare haplogroup and a unique form of cranial modification, suggesting that she was biologically and culturally unique from the rest at Conchopata. She also had multiple skeletal injuries in various healing states, demonstrating that she was a victim of violence on at least two occasions; her corpse was also deposited in a manner different from others at the site. Perhaps her "outsider" identity positioned her in a more socially precarious position, making her more susceptible to attack and less likely to receive burial rites like others in the community.

Trauma and Violence in the Wari Hinterland: Beringa

Middle Horizon Cranial Trauma at Beringa

Four hundred kilometers to the southeast in what was the Wari Empire's southern hinterland, one-third of the 39 late teens/adults interred at Beringa during the Wari era exhibit at least one antemortem or perimortem head wound (13/39=33%) (figure 5.9). (The differences in antemortem and perimortem trauma are presented below.) Half of the males (5/10=50%) and 31 percent of females show head wounds (4/13=31%), but the difference is not statistically significant (Fisher's exact, $p=0.306$; $N=23$). Four out of 16 adult crania that could not be confidently sexed display cranial trauma (4/16=25%). Among 33 juvenile crania (<15 years), one child (8–11 years old) exhibits an antemortem head wound on the right frontal bone (table 5.1). All subsequent cranial trauma results and discussion pertain to adults only.

Of the 13 adults with head injuries, nine exhibit antemortem cranial wounds (69%), three display perimortem fractures (23%), and one shows both a healed and a perimortem fracture (8%). Thus, among the 13 adults with head trauma, 31 percent, or nearly one out of every three injured adults, suffered a violently fatal blow to the skull.

The 13 affected adults display a total of 18 antemortem and perimortem head wounds. Three individuals exhibit more than one head wound (3/13=23%); the other 10 exhibit only one cranial trauma (10/13=77%) (table 5.3). This shows that most individuals in the sample received only one blunt-force trauma to the head grave enough to cause skeletal damage. The three cases of multiple head injuries differ from each other. One male exhibits antemortem wounds on the left and right parietal bosses. Another male shows three healed injuries on the left frontal bone, right nasal, and central area of the maxilla. Because all head fractures on these two men are well healed, whether they were sustained concurrently or separately is unknown. A third individual, an old adult female, shows one healed trauma on the right parietal boss and two perimortem fractures on

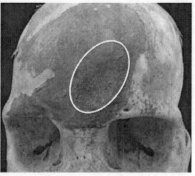

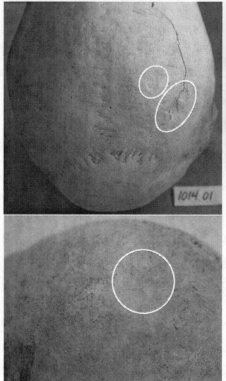

Figure 5.9. Cranial trauma on Beringa adults. *Top left*: Antemortem wound (closer to sagittal suture) and two perimortem fractures on the right parietal of an old adult female. *Bottom left*: Antemortem trauma on right parietal. *Top right*: Antemortem trauma on the frontal bone of an adult female from Unit 17. Although soft tissue adheres to the surface of the bone, the healed depression fracture is still visible.

the right lateral side. The differential healing testifies to two separate violent incidents. In the first, she received a nonlethal blow to the back of her head, and in the second, two closely placed strikes to the side of her head apparently contributed to her death (figure 5.9, top left photo).

Patterning of Head Wounds among Beringa Adults

Among the four adults with perimortem skull trauma, three exhibit wounds on the posterior and one has a wound on the right side. The sample size of perimortem wounds is small, so to provide a clearer sense of the overall wound patterning, the descriptions of the locations of antemortem and perimortem wounds are combined below.

Of the 18 total cranial wounds on adults, 11 are located on the posterior of the head (the occipital and parietal bosses) (11/18=61%), five are on the frontal/facial area (5/18=28%), and two are on the right side (2/18=11%). No adults exhibit cranial fractures on the left side or on the superior portion of the skull. (See table 5.4 for a tally of wounds and their locations.)

Eighty-nine percent of wounds are on the posterior and anterior of the skull.

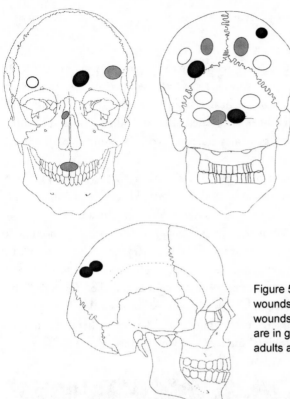

Figure 5.10. Locations of head wounds on Beringa adults. Female wounds are in black; male wounds are in gray; wounds of unsexed adults are in white.

This is not a random distribution, and it seems unlikely to be the result of accidents. These injuries probably resulted from specific violent activities in which the posterior of the head was the primary target.

The location of head wounds differs between the sexes at Beringa, suggesting that men and women sustained their injuries in different kinds of violent encounters. Among the six wounds present on female crania, three are located on the posterior of the skull, two wounds are on the right side, and one is on the anterior (figure 5.10). Males, in contrast, show half of their wounds on the anterior and half of their wounds on the posterior (figure 5.10). All of the wounds on the unsexed crania are on the back of the skull. These results suggest that women rarely engaged in face-to-face combat but were commonly in situations where they were vulnerable to other kinds of physical injury. In contrast, men more frequently engaged in face-to-face physical conflicts, as evidenced by wounds on the frontal bone and facial area. However, they also show an equal number of wounds on the posterior of the cranium, indicating that they were victims of violence in other settings, perhaps similar to those encountered by women.

Postcranial Trauma among Beringa Adults

Arm and Shoulder (Beringa)

Humeral fractures were rare (2.3%) relative to lower arm injuries (table 5.5). Of the five cases of injury to the left radius (5/44=11.4%), two are dislocations on the proximal end (elbow), two are healed Colles' fractures (figure 5.11), one of which is associated with a broken but healed ulnar styloid process, and the fifth is a midshaft fracture related to a parry fracture on the adjoining ulna (discussed below) (figure 5.12).

Of 51 left ulnae, six exhibit a fracture or dislocation (11.8%) (table 5.5). Three are antemortem fractures. The first exhibits a healed break on the distal end, and the second is a parry fracture with a nonunion at the fracture site (associated with the fractured radius mentioned above) (figure 5.12). The nonunion indicates a complete break, a characteristic of parry fractures (Lovell 1997). In this case, the distal end is completely separated from the diaphysis, as identified by callous formation and sclerosis near the medial-distal end of the shaft. (The distal end was never recovered.) The third fractured ulna is a clear example of a parry fracture with incomplete union (figure 5.12). The three other ulnar injuries are dislocations on the proximal ulna, one of which is associated with a radial dislocation mentioned above.

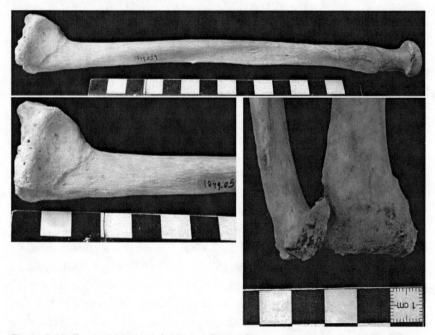

Figure 5.11. *Top and bottom left*: Healed Colles' fracture on the distal end of a left radius. *Bottom right*: Colles' fracture on the distal end of a left radius and associated fracture on the distal end, including the styloid process, of the adjacent left ulna. All bones are from Beringa.

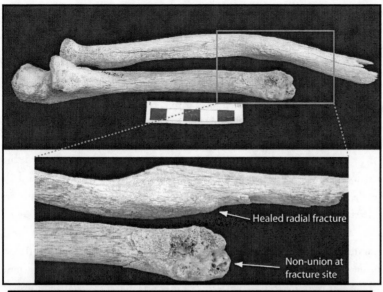

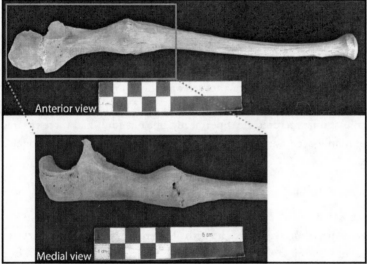

Figure 5.12. *Top and upper middle*: Probable parry fracture of left ulna and radius. *Lower middle and bottom*: Partially healed parry fracture on left ulna. All bones are from Beringa.

Hip and Leg (Beringa)

None of the well-preserved left (N=46) or right (N=43) femora show a fracture, and none evince pathological changes in the acetabulum or femoral head indicative of a hip dislocation (table 5.5). Tibial fractures are rare, and fibula fractures were observed on only two left (N=40) and one right fibula (N=42). All three fibular fractures affected the distal portion, and the two left fibulae exhibit periosteal reactions, indicating associated infections. Osteoarthritis, likely trauma induced, affected the right fractured fibula. These three adults were buried in the oversized tomb on the northern end of the site (Unit 1 at Beringa).

Skeletal Thorax (Beringa)

Among the 392 cervical vertebrae, eight exhibit evidence for traumatic injury (2.0%) (table 5.5). Specifically, three out of 69 first cervical vertebrae are affected, meaning that 4.4 percent of 69 late adolescents/adults had an injured neck; five out of 232 (2.2%) lower cervical vertebrae (cervical vertebrae 2 through 7) exhibit a compression fracture or dislocation. There were 537 thoracic vertebrae, and 29 display evidence for injury (5.4%). In particular, four of 31 individuals with an observable twelfth thoracic vertebra show compression fractures, and in one of those cases, the eleventh thoracic vertebra was also affected. Among the total number of lumbar vertebrae, five out of 236 (2.1%) exhibit compression fractures. These lumbar vertebrae represent 58 late adolescents/adults, and four of them suffered a lumbar fracture (6.9%), with one of them having two collapsed lumbar vertebrae. The sacrum and coccyx were also affected: two out of 24 individuals (8.3%) show a compression fracture or broken coccyx.

Left ribs were more commonly fractured than right ribs. Among the 343 right ribs, eight show a fracture (2.3%), and of the 323 left ribs, 13 were affected (4.0%) (table 5.5). If we examine the data another way, those 323 left ribs represent 49 adults with at least half of their left ribs present, and 10 of the 49 adults (20%) suffered at least one fractured rib. Specifically, one old adult had three rib fractures, one middle-aged adult exhibited two, and the eight others had one rib fracture each.[3]

Hand and Foot (Beringa)

Among the 435 unsided metacarpals, two were fractured (0.5%) (table 5.5). Those metacarpals represent 52 adults with at least 50 percent of their metacarpals; two adults out of 52 were affected (3.8%). The two individuals were from units situated near to each other (Unit 16W and Unit 17) (see figure 3.7). Notably, the female with the fractured metacarpal from Unit 17 also shows healed cranial trauma on the frontal bone. Three out of 841 unsided hand phalanges (0.04%), or three out of 52 adults (5.8%), exhibit a fractured hand phalanx, and they were all from Unit 1, the oversized tomb at the northern end of the site.

There are 51 (nonjuvenile) individuals with a well-preserved left calcaneous, and one shows a healed fracture with associated trauma-induced osteoarthritis (table 5.5). It likely resulted when the individual fell from a great height—off of a cliff or into a ravine, landscape features common in the Majes valley—and landed on his or her feet. Of 58 individuals with at least half of their metatarsals present, four exhibit a healed fracture (6.9%), and three out of 59 adults suffered a fractured foot phalanx (5.1%). (See table 5.5 for individual total number of skeletal elements examined.)

Discussion of Trauma at Beringa: Raiding the Village

A significant portion of the Middle Horizon population from Beringa (33%) show cranial trauma, and although a greater percentage of men than women were affected, the difference is not statistically significant, suggesting that both sexes were similarly exposed to violence. However, based on the location of wounds, the violent interactions affecting men versus women can be distinguished. The majority of female head wounds are on the posterior, suggesting that women received blows to the back of the head while fleeing during raids. Male head wounds, in contrast, are evenly divided between the anterior and posterior, indicating that they occasionally engaged in face-to-face fights, while also suffering posterior wounds in raids like their female counterparts. Violence enacted during raids is likely to be lethal in intent and consequence. Thus, it is notable that 31 percent of the head wounds were perimortem, indicating that the injury was either fatal or coincident with death from another cause.

The site of Beringa is in a defensible location above the Majes River, and weapons discovered there, such as sling stones, textile slings (hondas), and wood and stone maces, suggest that Beringa inhabitants were concerned with issues of defense (figure 5.13). Those concerns appear to have been well founded, for the data suggest that raids were a serious problem for the families living there. This does not imply, however, that they did not attempt to protect themselves and resist attack. The presence of weapons, the frontal head wounds on men, and parry fractures of the arm indicate that they endeavored to defend themselves. While these same observations could also suggest formal warfare rather than raids, the defensible site location and serious injury to both sexes—not solely men, as commonly seen in military battles—indicate that raids are the best explanation for much of the observed trauma patterns.

Identifying the perpetrators of the raids is more challenging. Were they Wari military personnel or individuals from the local area? There is no Wari administrative center in the middle Majes valley, and none has yet been identified in the surrounding valleys, suggesting that there was no overt, sustained physical presence by Wari imperial agents. The absence of settlers from the Ayacucho Basin is further supported by strontium isotope data from 52 enamel and bone samples representing 22 Beringa individuals; only two samples (from one infant and one adult male) exhibit values unexpected for the middle Majes valley (infant, $^{87}Sr/^{86}Sr=0.70960$; adult male; $^{87}Sr/^{86}Sr=0.70959$) (Knudson and Tung

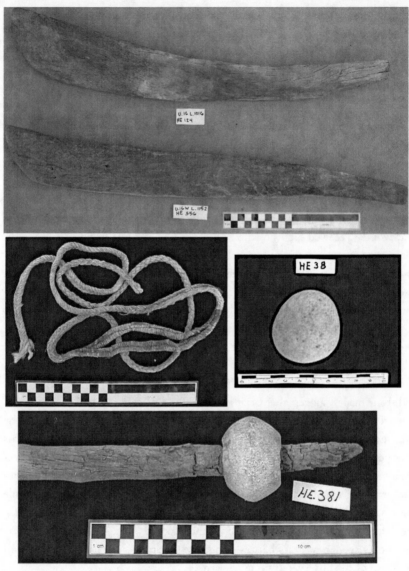

Figure 5.13. Possible weapons from Beringa: swordlike weapons or agricultural or textile tools (*top*); sling for throwing stones (*middle left*); throwing stone (*middle right*); mace with doughnut stone (*bottom*).

2011). Moreover, their strontium isotope ratios do not fall within the range expected for the Ayacucho Basin, suggesting that these nonlocals were not from the Wari imperial heartland.

Whether other sites in the Majes valley were home to Wari administrators or military personnel remains to be examined, but the current lack of evidence for overt Wari presence in Majes suggests that those who raided Beringa may have been from the Majes valley or neighboring valleys and not the Ayacucho Basin. Intraregional violence during the time of Wari rule may have been similar to intratribal conflicts that emerged on the margins of other colonial encounters. For example, European colonialism in the Caribbean and Amazonian regions contributed to local violence even where colonialists had no direct presence. Their influence spread throughout the region, altering trade alliances and political networks, spreading disease, and introducing new goods and foods to the region. This often aggravated or created new tensions between native communities (Ferguson and Whitehead 1992). Wari imperial influence in the southern hinterland may have had similar effects.

Given that trauma rates are high—33 percent—the Beringa community apparently did not experience an era absent of violence. Although there are no osteological data from pre-Wari populations in the Majes valley to use in evaluating whether cranial trauma frequencies increased or decreased, violence clearly was common among Beringa adults during the time of Wari interaction. It was more common relative to Tiwanaku-affiliated populations from the Titicaca Basin and Moquegua valley, where only six percent of adult males (4/72=5.5%) and no adult females (0/119=0%) exhibit fractures on the parietal bones of the cranium (Blom et al. 2003). While the parietal bones of Tiwanaku-affiliated adults were generally unaffected by trauma, there was one older adult female from the site of Chen Chen in the Moquegua valley with fractures to the ribs, zygomatic, and nasal bones, which Blom and colleagues (2003) interpret as evidence for domestic violence.

The percentage of cranial trauma at Beringa is also much higher than the Late Intermediate Period skeletal sample from Estuquiña, also in the Moquegua valley, where 5.4 percent exhibit cranial depression fractures (Williams 1990:191). (Whether this percentage reflects all age groups or adults only is unknown; the total number of crania observed is also unknown.) Overall, cranial trauma frequency among the Beringa inhabitants is five to six times higher than that in the Moquegua valley and Titicaca Basin samples. In sum, the presence of a foreign state in the Majes valley did little to ameliorate tensions and may have even created conflict or exacerbated native conflicts that existed prior to its arrival.

Trauma and Violence in the Wari Hinterland: La Real

At nearby La Real, 104 adult crania from the Wari period were observed for trauma. Thirty-two show at least one antemortem or perimortem head wound (32/104=31%) (figures 5.14 and 5.15). (Antemortem and perimortem wound counts are presented below.) When the sexes are compared, 16 of 39 males (41%) and five of 26 females (19%) exhibit head wounds. These differences are nearly

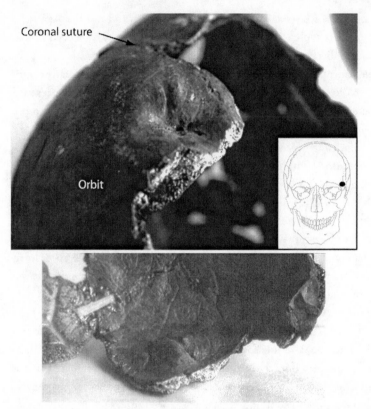

Figure 5.14. Cranial wound, La Real. *Top*: Ectocranial view of healed wound on left frontal bone, posterior to orbit. The cranium is tilted to its right, so the view is an oblique angle of the left frontal and left side. *Bottom*: Endocranial view of same wound. Note how the blunt-force trauma depressed the inner table.

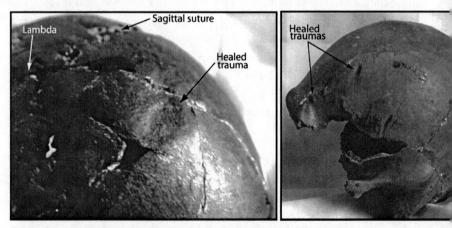

Figure 5.15. Cranial wounds, La Real. *Left*: Posterior view of healed head wound on right parietal boss. *Right*: Left lateral view of cranium with two healed wounds on left frontal bone. Note the intentional tabular-erect (fronto-occipito) cranial deformation, the common form in the coastal-yungas zones of the Andes.

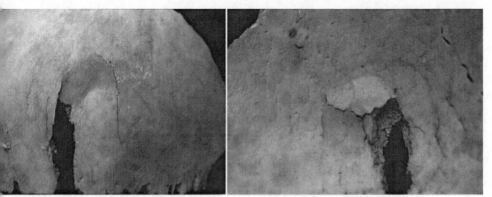

Figure 5.16. Juvenile cranium from La Real with perimortem fracture on parietal bone: ectocranial (*left*) and endocranial (*right*) views.

statistically significant (Fisher's exact, $p=0.056$; $N=65$), indicating that men were exposed to violence at a higher frequency than women. Indeed, they were violently injured more than twice as frequently as women: the ratio of female to male head trauma is 1:2.16. Of the 39 adults that could not be sexed, 11 exhibit cranial trauma (28%), and among the 16 juvenile crania (<15 years), one exhibits a perimortem fracture on the parietal (6%)(figure 5.16).

The majority of the La Real head wounds on adults are well healed. Of 32 adults with head trauma, 27 display antemortem cranial trauma (27/32=84.4%), three exhibit perimortem fractures (9.4%), and two show both antemortem and perimortem wounds (6.3%). This indicates that the preponderance of violent interactions were not fatal; rather, the intent of the assailants was to inflict injury, not death. Another interpretation is that the attackers were ineffective combatants, or the victims defended themselves well.

Because there are relatively few perimortem cranial injuries, all head wounds are combined below to present a clearer picture of injury recidivism and patterning in wound locations. Among the 32 adults with any kind of skull fracture, 22 adults exhibit only one wound (69%), and ten individuals display two or more cranial traumas (31%), including one with six healed skull fractures (table 5.3). The fact that nearly one-third of those with head trauma display two or more cranial wounds may mean that a sizeable portion of this burial group engaged in conflicts where an opponent could deliver several blows to the head in one event. Conversely, multiple head wounds could have been sustained in separate violent incidents, as in the case of the two adults who have both antemortem and perimortem head trauma (noted above). When only antemortem (well-healed) wounds are present, it is impossible to determine whether they were received in one or more violent encounters. All but one cranial wound is oval, which suggests that the vast majority were inflicted by maces, rocks, or sling stones.

Patterning of Head Wound Locations among La Real Adults

Head wounds among La Real adults are not randomly distributed but are concentrated on the anterior and posterior. Of the 32 affected persons, there are a total of 53 wounds. (Only 52 of those wounds were mapped.)[4] Twenty-seven wounds are on the anterior of the skull (27/52=52%), 13 (25%) are located on the posterior (occipital and parietal boss), and the remaining 12 wounds (23%) are dispersed across the superior and left and right lateral sides of the head (figure 5.17). The 27 anterior head wounds are not evenly distributed: 70 percent are on the left and 30 percent are on the right.

The spatial pattern of head wounds reveals much about how these injuries may have been sustained. More than three-fourths of the total wounds are

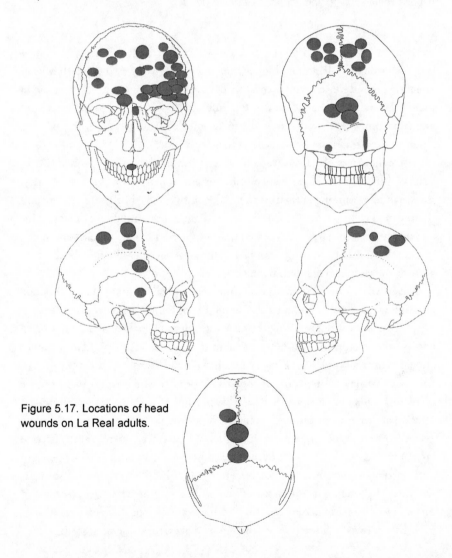

Figure 5.17. Locations of head wounds on La Real adults.

concentrated on the anterior and posterior of the head, and the high proportion of left-sided anterior wounds suggest that many were inflicted by a
right-handed attacker. This patterned wound distribution indicates that the
observed cranial traumas did not result from accidental injury or from frenetic, random violent encounters but were the outcome of intentional acts of
violence targeting particular aspects of the skull under specific rules of engagement. However, before interpretations regarding the behaviors behind
the trauma can be posited, it must be shown that the spatial distribution of
wounds is indeed patterned.

To test the null hypothesis that wounds are not associated with location but
are instead randomly (equally) distributed on the head, the observed wound locations were compared to that of an equal distribution by way of a contrast estimate,
using a log linear model to compare the distributions. The equal distribution assumes that each of the five cranial areas (anterior, superior, posterior, left lateral,
and right lateral) has an equal chance of being struck (that is, each area has a 20
percent chance of receiving a trauma). In this case, the total number of mapped
wounds equals 52, so each cranial area should have 10.2 wounds. This was not
observed. Instead, 27 wounds are on the anterior, 13 are on the posterior, three
are on the apex of the cranium, and four and five are on the left and right sides,
respectively (table 5.4). There is a significant difference between the observed and
expected wound distribution (Wald's $\chi^2=30.34$; $p<0.0001$; df=4; N=104).[5] The
null hypothesis that wounds are equally distributed on the skull is rejected.

Given that cranial wounds are not equally distributed across the surface of
the cranium, it is hypothesized that the distribution is patterned, such that
the anterior portion of the cranium exhibits significantly more wounds than
the average of the other four areas. A contrast estimate comparing the counts
of wounds on the anterior to the average of all others shows that this difference is statistically significant (Wald's $\chi^2=29.30$; $p<0.001$; df=1; N=52). The
contrast estimate value of 5.109 (table 5.6) indicates that an individual was
about five times more likely to receive a blow to the front of the head relative

Table 5.6. Contrast estimate results comparing cranial wound locations of La Real
late adolescent/adult crania

Comparison	Estimate	Lower	Upper	Chi²	P
Anterior vs. all other areas	5.109	2.8304	9.2223	29.3	<0.0001
Posterior vs. superior, left, and right	3.3208	1.5016	7.3436	8.79	0.003

Note: 95% confidence limits.

to all other areas. Clearly, this portion of the head was targeted during violent interactions.

Similarly, it is hypothesized that there are significantly more wounds on the back of the skull relative to the average of all other areas, excluding the anterior. Again, a contrast estimate compares the number of posterior wounds to the average number of wounds on the superior and left and right sides; the difference between the wound counts is statistically significant (Wald's χ^2=8.79; p=0.003; df=1; N=25), indicating that the posterior of the skull is significantly more likely to exhibit a wound relative to the superior and sides of the head. A contrast estimate value of 3.3208 indicates that the posterior of the head was three times more likely to be struck relative to all other areas, excluding the anterior. The determination that, among the La Real population, blows to the head were most likely to affect the front of the head, and next most likely to affect the posterior, suggests that rules of engagement for violent conflict influenced what sections of the head were to be struck.

Sex-based differences are also apparent in head-wound location in the La Real group. The majority of wounds on male skulls affect the anterior, while fe-

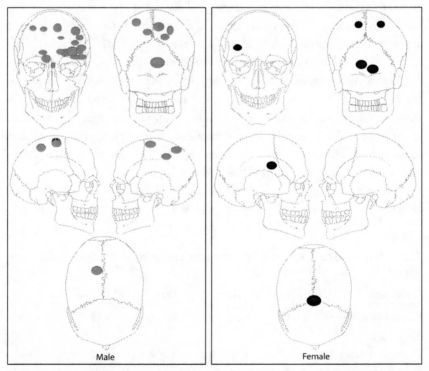

Figure 5.18. Locations of head wounds on La Real males (*left*, in gray) and females (*right*, in black). Wounds on unsexed adults are not shown.

males exhibit most wounds on the posterior (figure 5.18). Among the 29 wounds on males, 58.6 percent of wounds are on the frontal, 20.7 percent are on the posterior, and 20.7 percent are on all other areas combined. In contrast, among the seven wounds on female skulls, 57 percent are on the posterior, and the other 53 percent are on three other areas of the skull.

Postcranial Trauma at La Real

Arm and Shoulder (La Real)

Fractures or dislocations of adult arm bones were rare. Those affected include one out of 24 left humeri, two of the 24 right humeri (one fracture and one dislocation), and one left ulna (N=23) (table 5.5). The ulnar break was not a parry fracture; it affected the distal epiphysis.

Hip and Leg (La Real)

Hip and upper leg fractures were nonexistent, but left tibial fractures affected three out of 25 adults (12.0%) (table 5.5). Two were broken on the proximal third of the tibial diaphysis. The first appears to be a partial fracture, the second, a complete fracture (figure 5.19); both exhibit lesions and cloacae indicating associated infection. The third tibia exhibits a healed spiral fracture along the distal third of the shaft, resulting in a nonaligned tibia whereby the distal third of the shaft was laterally twisted away from its normal position (figure 5.19). This injury would have prevented the person from walking with a normal gait.

Skeletal Thorax (La Real)

None of the complete clavicles displays a healed fracture (N=23) (table 5.5). (There was, however, one partial left clavicle with a healed fracture near the medial aspect; an associated infection developed as a result. However, it is not included in the final tabulation, because it did not fit the criterion of being at least half complete.) Among the 124 unsided ribs, three exhibit healed fractures (2.4%). Two of the rib fractures are from one adult, and the third broken rib is from a second person.

Among 97 cervical vertebrae from 29 individuals, one exhibits a dislocation of the articular facets (that is, 1/97 individual cervical vertebrae, or 1/29 adults (3.5%), was affected); no compression fractures were observed (table 5.5). Fractures and dislocations of the thoracic region affected five out of 275 individual thoracic vertebrae (1.8%): two collapsed vertebral bodies and three dislocations of the facets. Those 275 thoracic vertebrae represented at least 33 adults, four of whom were affected (4/33=12.1%). Among the 147 individual lumbar vertebrae examined, three exhibit lumbar fractures (3/147=2.0%). The 147 lumbar verte-

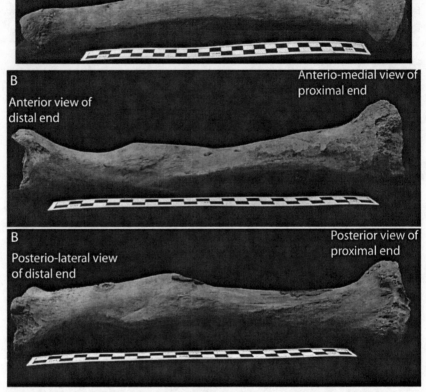

Figure 5.19. (A) Healed fracture along the proximal third of the diaphysis of a left tibia. (B) Two views of a healed spiral fracture along the distal third of a left tibia. Both bones are from La Real.

brae represent at least 37 adults, and two adults exhibit at least one lumbar fracture (2/37=5.4%): one adult exhibits spondylolysis and a compression fracture, and the other displays a dislocation/fracture on the right inferior articular facet. One of the 10 complete sacra exhibited spondylolysis.

No fractures were observed on the hands and feet of La Real adults.

Discussion of Trauma at La Real: Tinku and Physical Conflict Resolution

The patterned distribution of cranial fractures on the anterior of male skulls suggests that men often engaged in face-to-face combat that may have been governed by strict rules of conduct. Warfare has stringent prescriptions, but the nonlethality of most wounds demands that other explanations be explored. Perhaps the opponents of La Real men were ineffective war combatants, or the site of La Real was simply the main burial location for warriors who survived. Conversely, the nonlethal injuries may have been sustained in contexts other than war or raids. Indeed, the observed injury patterns are consistent with two other kinds of violent activities: ritual battles, known as *tinku* in the highland Andes, and ritualized fights, often used as a form of conflict resolution by Amazonian peoples today.

Tinku

As described in chapter 2, tinku is a ritual battle in which one of the goals is to shed blood of an opponent as an offering to the earth (Bolin 1998; Orlove 1994). Although the battles are ritual in nature, serious injuries are sustained when men (and occasionally women) hurl stones at each other with hondas or strike opponents with maces and fists (Allen 1988; Bolin 1998; Brachetti 2001; Hartmann 1972; Orlove 1994; Sallnow 1987; Schuller and Petermann 1992). The ritual battles often lead to bloody skull fractures (figure 5.20), and on rare occasions, they can be deadly (Bolin 1998; Orlove 1994; Schuller and Petermann 1992). Tinkus occur at least once a year, so tinku fighters should exhibit several head wounds. Indeed, this is observed among the La Real adults, where injury recidivism appears to characterize this group: one-third of those with head injuries exhibit more than one cranial fracture. Although determining whether multiple head wounds were sustained in one or several different violent events is difficult, those with more than one head wound leave open the possibility that violence was a recurring event, not just an isolated incident.

Recent ethnographic accounts of tinku clearly demonstrate that women are involved in these violent encounters (Allen 1988; Bolin 1998; Schuller and Petermann 1992). However, the bioarchaeological data from La Real suggest that women were only minimally involved in violent activities. They show a significantly lower trauma frequency than men, and their wounds are concentrated on the posterior of the skull, suggesting that female injuries were primarily sustained in raids or other defensive postures. Men with posterior cranial fractures also may have been wounded in raids or while protecting their face by ducking to avoid an oncoming blow. Although the male head wounds are predominantly on the anterior, the other cranial fractures suggest that they could be injured in other violent contexts too.

Physical Conflict Resolution

Physical conflict resolution in the form of ritualized club fights may also explain how some cranial injuries were sustained. The Yanomamo in the Venezuelan Amazon (Chagnon 1992) and the Oro-Warí of the southern Brazilian Amazon

Figure 5.20. *Top*: Men engaged in *tinku* (ritual fighting). *Bottom*: Man injured from stone thrown at him with a sling. (Photos courtesy of Wolfgang Schuller.)

(Conklin 2001)[6] engage in ritualized and closely watched fights to resolve tensions and disagreements. Although Tienery (2001) has asserted that Napoleon Chagnon and Timothy Ash's portrayal of Yanomamo aggression and club fighting was staged for their ethnographic film, other accounts of ritualized aggression by Amazonian groups demonstrate that conflict is often addressed through planned, ritualized fights. These are staged, performative acts of violence that are aimed at expressing and solving tensions, and though they may not be lethal, they are physically harmful, often permanently scarring the heads and faces of fighters. Among the Oro-Warí, Conklin (2001:40) notes, "serious internal conflicts may be dealt with through ritualized fights . . . [that] follow strict rules. Blows can be struck only with *temem* [wood clubs], and opponents are supposed to hit each other only on the head and shoulders. The objective is never to kill, but only to hurt and punish."

Based on Conklin's description, physical conflict resolution might thus lead to sublethal injuries on the anterior of the skull and/or clavicle and scapula. Indeed, the vast majority of La Real head wounds are on the frontal bone, and although postcranial samples are small, there was one incomplete clavicle with an antemortem fracture (it was not included in table 5.5, because it was less than half complete). Granted, whether that clavicle injury is violence related or accidental is unclear, but the high number of head wounds suggests that it could have been the former. In short, the similar injury patterns between La Real men and modern Amazonian men who engage in physical conflict resolution suggest that La Real males may have often engaged in similar conflict resolution practices.

The patterns of La Real head trauma are also similar to what Walker (1989) and Lambert (1994) have observed among prehistoric Chumash males from coastal California, leading them to suggest that Chumash men also engaged in "head clubbing" as a form of conflict resolution. Sixty-four percent ($N=94$) of Chumash males exhibited frontal bone fractures, but parry fractures were uncommon, suggesting that cultural norms for club fights meant that men should not block a hit to the head (Lambert 1994). Lambert (1994:118) further argues that if violence had occurred in less-regulated forms of lethal battles, as in warfare, there should have been more parry fractures: evidence of attempting to deflect hits to the head. The fact that they are so rare among Chumash adults makes warfare a less likely scenario. Similarly, if La Real men were in lethal military battles, there should have been some evidence of protecting oneself from potentially fatal blows, yet no parry fractures have yet been observed in the La Real population. No shields were recovered from any of the sites, so the absence of parry fractures is unlikely to be attributable to body armor.

La Real Helmets

There was, however, one hat that may have functioned as a helmet (figure 5.21). It is too large to fit the head snugly, so it may have been worn with a turban (Jennings, pers. comm. 2010), an effective layering of materials that could protect the skull from fracturing. While this hat could have been a fashion item, it more likely functioned as protective headgear given its durable design; it was constructed of layers of wood slats and reeds. (In contrast, the four-cornered textile hats found at La Real and other sites in the area were likely fashion items and markers of status or social identity, not helmets.)

Studies of head injuries when wearing lightweight (leather or plastic) ice hockey helmets from the 1950s through the modern era indicate that they are effective at dissipating blunt-force impact, resulting in lower rates of bone depression fractures (Biasca et al. 2002). (Intracranial hematomas, however, are

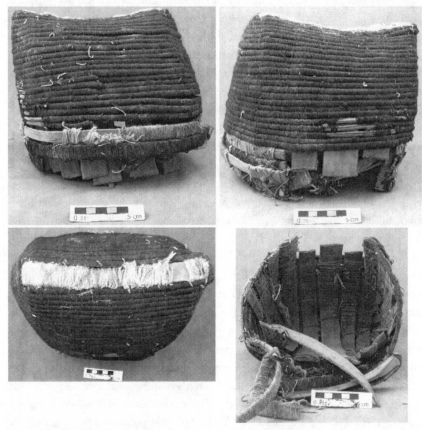

Figure 5.21. Possible helmet from the site of La Real: anterior and posterior views (*top*), though which is which has not been determined; superior view (*bottom left*); inferior/internal view (*bottom right*). (Photos courtesy of Justin Jennings and Willy Yepez.)

still sustained, though these are invisible in the skeletal record.) Data from ice hockey injuries provide a good comparison because hockey sticks and pucks are somewhat reminiscent of the weapons commonly found in the Andes (such as wood clubs, maces, and sling stones).

Andean weapons used against a person wearing a helmet like the one shown in figure 5.21 may not have resulted in focused depression fractures. That is, the helmet would have been effective at distributing the blunt-force load over a wide surface of the skull. Given this, the fact that so many adults exhibit cranial depression fractures that are well formed (that is, oval-shaped wounds with clear margins indicative of direct weapon contact on a small surface area) is curious, indicating that most individuals were not wearing helmets when they were struck on the head; the violence thus might have been spontaneous (for example, raids or household and community conflicts). It is also possible that helmets were deemed socially inappropriate during physical conflict resolution fights, when the goal was to inflict injury on the opponent. This further supports the notion that some men suffered sublethal injuries when they engaged in physical conflict resolution. That does not, however, exclude the possibility that some head injuries were sustained in warfare, raids, intrahousehold disputes, judicial stonings, or ritual battles (tinku); these contexts of violence are not mutually exclusive, for all of those social settings may have resulted in violence-related trauma. Physical conflict resolution is not the sole cause of the observed head injuries. Indeed, the one case of perimortem trauma on a child cranium could have been sustained in a raid, or it may be evidence of child abuse (intrahousehold conflict) that turned deadly. Nonetheless, the salient point is that given the current evidence, routinized forms of conflict resolution could have been a frequent occurrence causing many of the head injuries. Moreover, the high-status nature of the site suggests that participation in physically risky activities increased one's social status, providing access to this elite burial ground.

Differences in Violence and Injury among the Three Populations

In a comparison of cranial trauma frequencies between the three populations, Beringa shows the highest frequency (table 5.1), but the difference between all three populations is not statistically significant ($\chi^2=1.328$; $p=0.515$; df=2; $N=187$). Similarly, although Conchopata exhibits the lowest frequency of cranial trauma (23%), this is not statistically significantly lower than the combined frequency of the two hinterland populations (45/143=31.5%) (Fisher's exact, $p=0.178$; df=1; $N=187$). This suggests that individuals in the Wari heartland and hinterland equally experienced violent encounters.

All three populations show higher cranial trauma frequencies among males than females. However, the gender difference is nearly statistically significant at only the site of La Real ($p=0.056$). As I have suggested, these data indicate that men and women from La Real were differentially exposed to violence, not only in frequency but also in kind.

The women from La Real were the most protected from violence, as they show the lowest cranial trauma frequency of all subgroups (19%), but the percentages of female cranial trauma are statistically similar at all three sites ($\chi^2=0.65$; $p=0.723$; $df=2$; $N=64$). Moreover, women from all three populations exhibit the majority of head wounds on the posterior of the skull (figure 5.22). This suggests a broader pan-Andean behavior in which women were victims of violence involving blows to the back of the head.

In contrast, the location of head wounds among males is not uniform across the three skeletal samples. Only two Conchopata men exhibit frontal head wounds indicative of face-to-face fighting. The majority of male head wounds are on the posterior of the skull, suggesting that some Conchopata men were injured in similar ways as the women. Beringa males, in contrast, show cranial wounds that are evenly divided between the anterior and posterior, suggesting that they were involved in various kinds of violent situations, such as face-to-face combat and injury during raids. At La Real, men show a significant concentration of sublethal wounds on the anterior of the cranium, suggesting that most

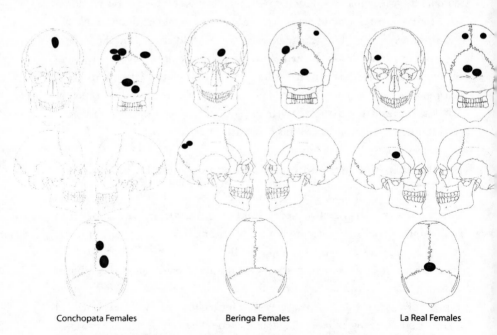

Conchopata Females   Beringa Females   La Real Females

Figure 5.22. Wound locations on female crania from the three sites in this study: Conchopata females (*left*); Beringa females (*middle*); La Real females (*right*).

were sustained in routinized physical conflict resolutions and perhaps other violent scenarios such as battles, raids, and intrahousehold disputes.

As discussed in previous chapters, the La Real mortuary population may have been organized at the suprasettlement level and may represent an exclusive category of high-status individuals drawn from several settlements. Conversely, the burial group may represent an elite subpopulation from one habitation site. In either case, this sample reflects trauma rates and patterns for a relatively higher social class than that found at Beringa. Nonetheless, while I have argued that La Real represents a different social class, the trauma frequencies are not atypical for populations from the Majes valley, suggesting that social status did not directly translate into distinct rates of violence.

What did differ is the social context of the violence. The dissimilar spatial distribution of wounds and their lethality reflect the unique circumstances of each community. Beringa—a village occupied primarily by extended families of commoners—shows a greater proportion of lethal wounds than the La Real sample, suggesting that the residents of Beringa were frequently victims of raids in which many were mortally injured. The higher-status adults buried at La Real, in contrast, sustained injuries in nondeadly conflicts, such as routinized club fights. These conflicts, though physically dangerous, were probably socially rewarding, providing participants with higher status and political clout that gave them better access to more and better nutritional resources (Tung and Del Castillo 2005) and high-quality exotic goods from the Wari Empire.

Violence in the Wari Empire's Southern Hinterland

When populations from the Majes valley are compared to other Wari-era groups in the southern hinterland, the Majes group exhibits the highest levels of violence overall. Among all Wari-era adults from Nasca (central, near-coastal Peru), 9.3 percent ($N=97$) exhibit cranial trauma (Kellner 2002), while 29 percent ($N=187$) of the Wari-era adults in this study are affected. A focused comparison of male cranial trauma shows that Middle Horizon Nasca men exhibit more trauma than the whole Wari-era Nasca population, but the frequency is still lower than that of the adult males in this study: cranial trauma among Middle Horizon Nasca males equals 19 percent ($N=36$) (Kellner 2002) compared to 40 percent ($N=63$) of the Wari-era men presented herein.

Although Nasca cranial trauma rates are generally lower than those in Majes and Conchopata, it is notable that male head trauma is at its highest in Nasca during the Wari period relative to the earlier Nasca periods (Kellner 2002:83, 110). Based on Kellner's data (2004:156, table 8.3), the rate of male cranial trauma for the entire Nasca period is 10 percent ($N=39$) and slightly rises to 19 percent

(7/36=19%) in the Middle Horizon.[7] This increase, however, is not statistically significant (Fisher's exact, p=0.213; N=75).

When additional subgroups from Wari-era Nasca are compared, Kellner's (2002) rich data set shows some interesting patterns. Adult males buried with Wari goods, known as the Nasca-Chakipampa subgroup, show the highest cranial trauma frequency (37.5%; N=8) (Kellner 2002), a percentage similar to that of the La Real males who were likewise interred with high-quality Wari goods (41%; N=39). Overall, male and female cranial trauma rates are similar among the Nasca-Chakipampa (Wari affiliated) and the La Real (Wari affiliated) samples: for Nasca-Chakipampa, 37.5 percent of men and 12.5 percent of women exhibited cranial trauma (Kellner 2002); for La Real, 41 percent of men and 19 percent of women exhibited cranial trauma. Although sample sizes are small, the similarities in terms of violent lifestyle among those buried with Wari goods in Nasca and Majes are extraordinary. Perhaps this reflects some broader experience shared by those with strong ties to the Wari state who lived in the southern hinterland. Moreover, given that men buried with Wari goods in both Majes and Nasca show the highest cranial trauma frequency of any subgroup, it appears that those with connections to Wari were more closely associated with violence. Whether or not the Wari state was promoting an ideology that valued warrior-like status or at least physical prowess remains unknown. Nonetheless, the association between Wari goods and violence-related injury is intriguing. Did men have to engage in violence to garner access to those elite Wari goods, or did that privileged access mark them as suitable targets of attack by others? One must also ask whether mourners marked the status of their (dead) belligerent men by placing exotic Wari goods in the tombs of these men. Although current data cannot yet answer these questions, future studies of trauma variations based on age, sex, and cultural affiliation can explore those issues in more detail.

Violence and Peace in the Majes Valley

Because there are currently no skeletal samples from the pre-Wari period in the Majes valley, whether the trauma frequencies presented here represent a change from the preceding period is unknown. Nevertheless, these trauma rates are high relative to other Andean skeletal populations, where the average cranial trauma frequency among the 2,357 crania from 13 regional contexts is approximately 14 percent (table 5.7) (see Andrushko 2007, n.d.; Blom et al. 2003; de la Vega et al. 2005; Kellner 2002; Kurin n.d.; MacCurdy 1923; Murphy 2004; Nystrom 2004; Standen and Arriaza 2000; Torres-Rouff and Costa Junqueira 2006; Tomasto 2009; Tung n.d.; Tung and Schreiber 2010; Verano 2003;). (The studies for which the total sample [denominator] is unknown are

Table 5.7. Cranial trauma frequencies for various Andean skeletal populations

Region	Time period	Frequency	Reference
Arica, Chile	4000 BP	24.6% (N=69 crania, all antemortem wounds)	Standen and Arriaza 2000
Atacama, Chile	Pre-AD 600	5% (N=99)	Torres-Rouff and Costa Junqueira 2006
Atacama, Chile	AD 600–950	11% (N=92)	Torres-Rouff and Costa Junqueira 2006
Atacama, Chile	AD 850–1200	36.4% (N=44)	Torres-Rouff and Costa Junqueira 2006
Atacama, Chile	AD 950–1400	30.5% (N=151)	Torres-Rouff and Costa Junqueira 2006
Nasca/Palpa, Peru	AD 1–750	5.3% (N=19)	Tomasto 2009
Nasca, Peru	AD 1–750	8.6% (N=81)	Kellner 2002
Nasca, Peru	AD 750–1000	9% (N=97)	Kellner 2002
Nasca, Peru	AD 1–1000	5.3% (N=19)	Tung and Schreiber 2010
Nasca, Peru	AD 1000–1400	8.3% (N=36)	Tung and Schreiber 2010
Titicaca Basin and Moquegua (Osmore drainage), Peru	AD 550–1000	2% (N=191 parietal vaults)	Blom et al. 2003
Lower Osmore drainage (San Geronimo, Chiribaya, Yaral)	AD 900–1350	22/545 individuals with a fracture, but not all have crania, so head trauma % is unknown (excludes verts. and perimortem trauma)	Burgess 1999
Moquegua, Osmore drainage, Peru (Estuquiña)	AD 1000–1450	"5.4% exhibited cranial trauma" (N=?) (p. 191); or 1% (2/208 cranial vaults) (p. 185)	Williams 1990
Titicaca Basin (cave burial, Molino-Chilacachi)	AD 1000–1400	14.6% (N=48)	de la Vega et al. 2005
Ayacucho Basin (Ñawinpukio and Trigo Pampa)	AD 600–1000	0% (N=5)	Tung n.d.
Andahuaylas (Turpo)	AD 600–1000	9.1% (N=22)	Kurin n.d.
Andahuaylas (4 LIP sites)	AD 1000–1400	52.7% (N=222)	Kurin n.d.
Lucre Basin, Cusco (Pikillacta)	AD 600–1000	50% (N=2)	Verano 2005
Sites in and around Cusco	AD 600–1532	15.3% (N=627); includes juveniles and adults, ante- and perimortem fractures, and 2 individuals with cranial cut marks only	Andrushko 2007

continued

Table 5.7.—*continued*

Region	Time period	Frequency	Reference
Four sites in and around Cusco[a]	AD 600–1000	8.3% (*N*=36), adults only	Andrushko n.d.
Five sites in and around Cusco[b]	AD 1000–1400	23.6% (*N*=199), adults only; ante- and perimortem fractures	Andrushko n.d.
Nine sites in and around Cusco[b]	AD 1400–1532	22.8% (*N*=219), adults only; ante- and perimortem fractures	Andrushko n.d.
Chachapoya (Laguna Hauyabamba)	AD 1000–1150	8% (*N*=25), adults only	Nystrom 2004
Chachapoya (Revash collection)	AD 1350–1470	17% (*N*=78), adults only	Nystrom 2004
Puruchuco-Huaquerones (near Lima) (Inka)	AD 1400–1532	10% (*N*=190), juveniles and adults	Murphy 2004
Machu Picchu (Inka)	AD 1400–1532	3 adults with cranial fractures (% unknown)	Verano 2003
Peruvian Highlands (8 sites combined)	Various	15.1% (*N*=225), percentage based on injured crania shown in images and described in text[c]	MacCurdy 1923

[a] The sample of 36 Wari-era burials is the adult subset of the 627 burials in Andrushko's 2007 publication, plus a few newly analyzed burials.

[b] The sample sizes of 199 and 219 are the Late Intermediate Period and Late Horizon (Inka)–era adults, respectively. They are subsets of the 627 individuals in Andrushko's 2007 publication, plus some newly analyzed burials.

[c] Those with trepanation but no mention of fractures were excluded because MacCurdy stated that he could not always identify trauma that preceded trepanation.

not calculated in the 2,357 count above.) It is important to note, however, that the cranial trauma percentages from some studies include children and adults combined, which obscures (and lowers) the frequency of trauma in the comparative groups.

A more specific and relevant comparison is the cranial trauma frequency among the adults from Wari-affiliated sites in the Department of Cusco (3/36=8.3%) (Andrushko n.d.) and those in this study: Middle Horizon Conchopata versus Middle Horizon sites in Cusco (p=0.0741, N=80) and combined frequency of Middle Horizon sites in Ayacucho (Conchopata, Ñawinpukio, and Trigo Pampa [Tung n.d.]) versus Middle Horizon sites in Cusco (p=0.109; N=88) (see table 5.7 for total counts). In comparing the Wari-era Majes valley samples to those in and around Cusco, the southern hinterland sites are significantly more affected ($p=0.003$; $N=179$). These comparisons demonstrate that adults at Conchopata suffered violent injuries nearly significantly more than their counterparts in Cusco, and those in the Majes experienced violence significantly more than Wari-era Cusco populations.

Overall, the cranial trauma rates between Middle Horizon Majes adults and those from other Andean sites show that it was greater on average in the Majes valley. On the one hand, this suggests that Wari imperial influence in the region generated conflict, perhaps by upsetting the balance of power that led to the reformulation of political alliances; this may have contributed to unrest manifested as warfare, raids, and the need for more physical conflict resolution. On the other hand, violence may already have been common in the pre-Wari era, and the trauma frequencies observed in Wari times may simply reflect a continuation of preexisting tensions. In either case, Wari rule did little to curb tensions and ease conflict in a portion of Wari's southern realm. Thus, the trauma data suggest that a *pax Wari* was not established in the Majes valley.

Violence and Empires: The Wari Heartland and Inka Heartland

Comparing adult cranial trauma frequencies between the Wari heartland and the Inka heartland (Andrushko 2007) reveals striking commonalities. Although of different time periods, the sociopolitical contexts may have been quite similar, at least in terms of how these contexts shaped levels of violence; the core areas of the Wari and Inka empires both exhibit adult cranial trauma frequencies of 23 percent (includes antemortem and perimortem cranial trauma). This is some of the most compelling evidence that imperial activities in the heartland of empires may have contributed to physical violence manifested in a variety of ways. The similarities in head trauma among the Wari and Inka may reflect social and political unrest at the local levels, imperial policies that required aggressive and physically risky activities on the part of an empire's subjects, or large-scale warfare. Although the Wari heartland skeletal samples still need larger samples of crania and more radiocarbon dates to clarify whether the majority of trauma was experienced during the rise, zenith, or fall of the empire's reign, these data offer new insights into the similarities between the Wari and Inka modes of rule. Furthermore, they coincide with other archaeological data that show some similarities between the two Andean empires: namely, similarly located road constructions, some of which were initially built by the Wari and maintained under Inka rule (Schreiber 1991a); similar masonry and architectural styles; engineering technology; and some food preferences. The studies on violence-related trauma among Wari and Inka heartland populations provide further evidence of their similarities and undergird the notion that, although the details of imperial policies and practices differed between the Wari and Inka, the parallel sociopolitical frameworks may have similarly structured people's lives. Indeed, perhaps the preceding strategies and activities of Wari proved to be foundational, such that some aspects of Inka statecraft developed from those of the Wari.

Corporeal Icons of Wari Imperialism

Human Trophy Heads and Their Representations

In light of the militaristic iconography on Wari artifacts, as well as the violence that affected Wari communities, I explore how Wari militarism was integrated into other aspects of Wari social and political life, if at all. Did the Wari state sponsor celebratory rituals of military accomplishments, as other ancient and modern states have done? If so, what were the practices in those Wari rituals? Who was involved, and to what ends were those rituals performed? This chapter explores those questions by focusing on the analysis of isolated human remains that come solely from ritual spaces at Conchopata. The remains include disembodied heads, fingers, and toes from adults and children: a grouping of bones that begs to be analyzed within the larger context of Wari militarism and ritualism. To that end, I examine those remains and inquire about the life history of those who were dismembered and deposited in Wari ritual structures, and I evaluate whether those isolated body parts and attendant rituals relate to larger Wari imperial agendas.

While human sacrifice and body mutilation have been documented in the Andes among the Nasca, Moche, and Inka, until this project nothing was known regarding whether or not Wari engaged in these activities. And if so, what were the similarities and differences in how the Wari carried out these practices relative to other Andean and precontact Native American groups. Moreover, because rituals involving human sacrifice and the mutilation of human bodies typically reflect violence and terror (Cordy-Collins 2001; Massey and Steele 1997; Milner et al. 1991; Proulx 1989; Silverman and Proulx 2002; Verano 2001), analysis of unusually modified skeletal parts recovered from ritual spaces provide insight into how Wari state agents may have used those destructive and ritualized acts to create compliance and fear in the populace, both heartland and hinterland, and marshal those to their advantage. As Dillehay notes, "[I]ntermittent mutilation and/or human sacrifice may demonstrate the power and wealth of new ruling groups and the lengths to which they would go to maintain power" (Dillehay 1995:14).

Ritual Activities at Conchopata

At Wari sites, circular and D-shaped buildings were the loci for elaborate rituals (Isbell et al. 1991; Cook 2001). This is evidenced by the size of the buildings and the architectural features themselves, which are in stark contrast to the smaller rooms at Wari sites. Artifacts recovered from circular and D-shaped structures at Conchopata similarly reveal their ritual nature, including, for example, beautifully decorated pottery that was intentionally smashed and the remains of sacrificed camelids (Ochatoma and Cabrera 2002). Prior to this study, Anita Cook (2001) suggested that the rituals in D-shaped spaces also involved the decapitation and display of human trophy heads. She based this on ceramic imagery depicting D-shaped rooms with circular features on the floor accompanied by Wari deities carrying stylized human trophy heads (figure 6.1). This is notable because, although there were numerous examples of trophy heads throughout the pre-Hispanic Andes, there had been no physical evidence of trophy heads associated with the Wari Empire. The excavations by José Ochatoma and Martha Cabrera changed that; they were the first to recover a group of isolated human skulls—later to be identified as trophy heads—from a D-shaped structure at Conchopata. Subsequent excavations at the same site by William Isbell and

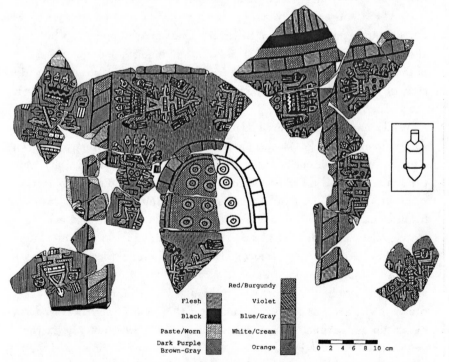

	Red/Burgundy
Flesh	Violet
Black	Blue/Gray
Paste/Worn	White/Cream
Dark Purple Brown-Gray	Orange

0 2 4 6 8 10 cm

Figure 6.1. Iconography on Wari ceramics showing D-shaped rooms, features on the floor, and Wari deities with stylized trophy heads. (Image courtesy of Anita Cook.)

Anita Cook revealed an additional cluster of human skulls from a circular building, demonstrating that the ritual deposition of decapitated heads was not a singular event. As Cook (2001) had suggested, human trophy heads were indeed an integral part of certain Wari rituals.

Rituals bind communities together, yet they also divide by highlighting the special status and authority of some and not others. Rituals, particularly those that are performed under the auspices of or in collaboration with the state, can establish and maintain state power through elaborate acts that create narratives of power and authority, bolstering state claims and those agents that support them. How then were state-sponsored rituals that involved human body parts enacted in Wari society, and to what ends may they have been directed? Answering those questions requires a detailed analysis of the heads themselves to see how they were obtained, modified, and put on display in ritual arenas at Conchopata. It also requires inquiry into the human source of the heads. Who was being decapitated and transformed into trophies: locals or foreigners? These questions are addressed by comparing strontium isotope ratios between the trophy heads and local geology, local animals, and local burials in the Ayacucho Basin.

What Is a Trophy Head?

A trophy head is an isolated skull or cranium[1] that has been intentionally modified, usually by drilling a hole somewhere on the cranial vault and threading it with a cord to display it as a trophy. In the Andes, the most numerous and best studied trophy heads come from Nasca, where they are identified by specific anthropogenic modifications, such as a hole on the frontal bone that is threaded with rope, so it can be suspended for display (Verano 1995). Among the Nasca trophy heads, the style of carrying cords varies, as does the location and size of the hole. It may be a small, perfectly drilled hole or a larger irregularly shaped perforation punched out somewhere on the frontal bone; it may be located between the orbits or much higher on the forehead (figure 6.2). The foramen magnum is also expanded or the entire occipital base is intentionally removed to extract the brain (Kellner 2002; Verano 1995). In some cases, there are cut marks on the skull vault and mandible, as on all 48 of the trophy heads from Cerro Carapo (Browne et al. 1993; Verano 1995), suggesting that the flesh was flayed and then reattached after scraping away internal layers of soft tissue (Verano 1995:212–13). It is also possible that the cut marks resulted from bloodletting rituals before or shortly after the person died (Baraybar 1987). Some Nasca trophy heads resemble facial masks, in having the posterior half of the cranium completely removed (Kellner 2002), and others have separated mandibles that

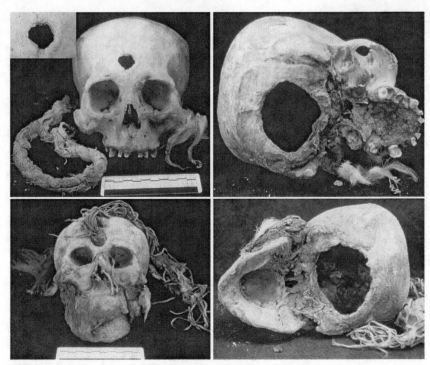

Figure 6.2. Nasca-style trophy heads. *Top*: Anterior and inferior views of the same trophy head; inset is a close-up of the irregularly shaped perforation on the frontal bone. *Bottom*: Anterior and inferior views of another trophy head.

have been tied back to the cranium (Verano 1995). Because the Nasca trophy heads are so well studied and derive from the neighboring region to the west of the Ayacucho Basin, they form a basis of comparison for the Wari trophy heads discussed herein.

Disembodied Skeletal Parts of Ancestors, Enemies, and Criminals

Identifying the kinds of people who were transformed into trophy heads will aid in understanding how they were obtained and what purposes they may have served. I review various situations in which isolated heads were used in rituals, reminding us that although disembodied human heads are potent symbols, how they are obtained, modified, decorated, displayed, and destroyed tends to be culturally specific, such that the meanings attached to them vary between societies and even for members within the same society. This is not to suggest that evidence culled from the archaeological context and the bones themselves will equally support innumerous interpretations. To the contrary, as I argue, the rich and detailed data sets point to a particularly compelling explanation regarding why human heads were used in Wari rituals. But before a case can be made, a review of the diverse social contexts in which isolated heads and body parts appear and consideration of the varied meanings associated with them are essential.

Revered Ancestors

Bodies and body parts of ancestors have long been incorporated into ancestor veneration rituals in the Andes and elsewhere. As such, it is possible that Wari trophy heads derived from valued members of the local community, being transformed into icons or relics for use in rituals. In modern Bolivia, Uru-Uru Chipaya ritual specialists use both Catholic ritual paraphernalia and human skulls in religious ceremonies (Wachtel 2001). And before the arrival of Europeans, the Inka preserved body parts and the whole corpse of Inka lords, which they venerated in public festivals and consulted in private meetings (Guaman Poma de Ayala et al. 1987 [1615]). The exuviae of the dead Inka, such as nail clippings, hair, and the afterbirth, were stored in a container and cared for by immediate kin (Salomon 1995), while the public body (the mummy itself) was carried on a litter and paraded in public spaces. Further evidence for the importance of the corpse in Andean veneration rituals is clandestine disinterment of bodies during the early colonial era. As the Spanish were attempting to squelch indigenous practices, such as ancestor veneration, native peoples sometimes removed bodies of loved ones from church cemeteries for surreptitious ceremonies. When complete bodies could not be recovered, they took individual bones and used them as stand-ins for the whole body (Gose 2003). However, the mummies and body parts of ancestors that formed such important elements in Inka rituals were not apparently modified in ways that might resemble a trophy skull.

Skeletal elements from ancestors were also modified and displayed in dramatic ways by prehistoric groups from the Great Lakes region of North America (Stothers et al. 1994). This funerary practice, known as the Younge Mortuary Complex, included public display of disembodied crania with holes drilled on the apex of the cranium and cranial plaques cut from the posterior of the skull (Speal 2006). These modified bones from dead kin may have been suspended from scaffolding during ceremonies that resembled the historically documented "Feast of the Dead," once practiced by groups such as the Iroquoian Huron (Trigger 1969) and Algonkian (Hickerson 1960).

The preservation and display of disembodied skeletal parts is, of course, not unique to the Americas. The bones of Christian saints, for example, have long been revered as religious relics in European churches and monasteries (Bynum 1991). Thus, despite our modern Western sensibilities that tend to keep corpses and body parts far from the living, displaying dismembered and modified body parts from biological or fictive kin has a temporally and geographically rich history.

Conquered Enemies

Warring factions or groups in conflict sometimes take enemy captives and violently remove body parts as trophies of war, either at the conflict site or later in sacrificial rituals (Hassig 1988). Some Wari trophy heads could have been obtained in similar ways, as was done by other groups in the pre-Hispanic Andes and other parts of the Americas (Chacon and Dye 2007). In northern coastal Peru, the Moche (AD 100–750) engaged in prisoner capture and head taking from enemy groups, as revealed by vivid iconographic details and compelling skeletal evidence (Bourget 2001; Cordy-Collins 2001; Donnan 1997; Verano 2001). In some cases, victims of the Moche were held captive for some time before being sacrificed and dismembered. This is known because many of the captives' bone fractures were partially healed, indicating that they were not immediately killed (Verano 2001). Eventually, some body parts—the skull in particular—were made into trophies (Verano 2001).

Further examples showing that trophy heads could be obtained from enemy groups can be seen at Nasca archaeology sites, where the majority of trophy heads are adult men (Verano 1995). This had led several scholars to propose that heads were taken in raids or warfare and not from ancestors (Proulx 2001; Verano 1995), especially in the later Nasca phases (Silverman 1993). This is further supported by Nasca iconography showing a person being decapitated in a battle scene (see figure 11 in Verano 1995).

The Inka (AD 1450–1532) sometimes transformed enemy leaders into war trophies, altering bones into flutes and skins into drums (Guaman Poma de Ayala et al. 1987 [1615]; Sarmiento de Gamboa 1999 [1572]). However, because pejorative characterizations of the Inka could have been used to justify the Spanish colonial agenda, the veracity of historical accounts regarding human trophy taking by the Inka must be scrutinized. Ogburn (2007) has done just that, surveying written accounts to evaluate the positions and agendas of the various historical authors. He concludes that reports of trophy taking by the Inka likely reflect real events. Thus, documentary and archaeological evidence show that the Inka displayed human body parts from both enemies and ancestors, warning us that the meanings associated with similar corporeal objects were not mutually exclusive. Context and the narratives associated with the body parts mattered.

In other parts of the Americas, some native populations also engaged in taking human heads, scalps, and postcranial parts from enemy groups. For example, scalping was practiced by Late Mississippian Tennessee groups (Smith 2003) and Northern Plains groups (Owsley 1994), and the Iroquois of eastern Canada took prisoners for sacrifice and display for several generations after "contact" (Trigger 1985). The Aztecs of Mesoamerica took prisoners for public sacrifice, sometimes using their skins as cloaks (Carrasco 1995; Hassig 1988), while the pre-Hispanic Tarascan state in Mexico may have used long bones of sacrificial victims to make *omichicahuaztli* (musical instruments) (Pereira 2005). More recently, the Jívaro in Ecuador and Peru practiced head hunting, taking heads from both adults and children during raids on enemy groups; this ended in the mid-20th century, when the state and missionary groups endeavored to end the practice (Harner 1972).

In other world regions, the Ilongot of the Philippines (Rosaldo 1980) and the Mundugumor of Papua New Guinea engaged in head hunting, and the latter group sometimes displayed skulls of enemies in their homes (McDowell 1991).

As recently as World War II and the Vietnam War, U.S. servicemen took Japanese and Vietnamese heads as war trophies but, notably, did not usually take heads of European enemies, making explicit that "Japs" and other nonwhite enemies were perceived as subhuman, and thus fair game for decapitation or skull robbing (Dower 1986; Harrison 2006).

These examples demonstrate that the abduction of enemies and the subsequent dismemberment and display of their body parts would have been effective representations of the individualized power of those who took the bodies. More broadly, these actions likely served a greater agenda that reified state or community authority in a wider network of social and political relations.

Executed Criminals

Criminals also may have been beheaded, dismembered, and transformed into trophy body parts as a form of punishment within an ancient judicial system, akin to full or partial body gibbeting—public display of a criminal's decaying corpse—in England during the 17th–19th centuries (Foucault 1977). Although we know nothing of Wari judicial practices, later Inka laws and the punishments for violating them were recorded by Spanish chroniclers; they described corporal punishment, such as public stonings, hangings, and capital punishment (Moore 1973; Murúa 2004). Also, the corpses of executed criminals sometimes remained on display so wild animals could ravage the bodies (Karsten 1949). Public display of whole or partial bodies of those deemed criminal would have been effective for communicating civic messages regarding proper decorum among state or community subjects, so it is possible that the trophy heads were tied into the Wari judicial system that served to control and discipline its subjects.

Trade Items and Heirlooms

Disembodied heads can also be traded and sold. In Papua New Guinea, for example, disembodied skulls were sometimes traded between communities, passing from village to village. In the same region, the Mundugumor collected skulls of slain enemies (mentioned above) and passed them on as heirlooms through a strict system of inheritance. When a man died, the skulls of his enemies were bequeathed to his sister's children, and when his nieces and nephews died, the heads were given back to the man's grandchildren, specifically to the children of his daughter(s) (McDowell 1991). This example shows how meanings associated with a single object can change or take on multiple meanings throughout its use-life, first as an emblem of domination over enemies and later as an heirloom that binds kin groups together.

Trophy Heads Found in Situ at Conchopata

The Conchopata trophy heads were of ritual significance, as demonstrated by their presence in uniquely shaped ritual buildings—both measuring 11 meters in diameter—that yielded large quantities of ceramics and sacrificed camelids. In the southeast quadrant of the circular ritual structure (EA143; see figure 3.3), the Conchopata Archaeology Project, directed by William Isbell and Anita Cook, recovered 21 broken trophy heads (figures 6.3 and 6.4). Although the skulls were

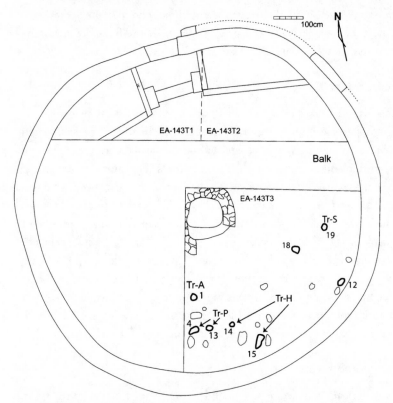

Figure 6.3. Map of EA143, the circular ritual room in the southern half of the site. Twenty-one trophy heads were excavated from the southeast quadrant. The circles in boldface represents child trophy heads, while the other circles represent adult trophy heads.

Figure 6.4. The ritual rooms at Conchopata: EA72, the D-shaped structure from which 10 trophy heads were excavated (*top*) (courtesy of José Ochatoma); EA143, the circular structure from which 21 trophy heads were excavated (*bottom*) (courtesy of William Isbell and Anita Cook).

fragmented, each was in a discrete pile on the floor, which facilitated the reconstruction of each trophy head (figure 6.5). In a few cases, cranial or mandible parts could not be associated with the rest of nearby crania, leaving some skull parts unaffiliated (table 6.1). No ceramic sherds were in direct association with the trophy heads, but some ceramics were recovered in stratigraphic levels above them. One of the child trophy heads in EA143 was associated with a juvenile camelid ulna with cut marks. No other trophy heads were in direct association with faunal remains.

Table 6.1. Trophy heads and age-at-death, sex, and basic pathological data for each

Code	Age category	Sex	Cribra orbitalia	Cranial trauma
EA143–1 (A)	Child	?	?	No
EA143–2 (B)	Old adult	M?	No	No
EA143–3 (C)	Adolescent	?	No	No
EA143–4.01 (D)	Mid-adult	F?	No	No
EA143–5 (E)	Mid-adult	M	Yes	No
EA143–6 (F)	Mid-adult	M	No	No
EA143–7.01, 16 (G)	Young adult	?	No	No
EA143–12, 14, 15 (H)	Child	?	?	?
EA143–7.02 (I)	Young adult	M	No	No
EA143–9 (J)	Mid-adult	M	No	Yes
EA143–10.01 (K)	Old adult	M	No	Yes
EA413–10.02 (L)	Mid-adult	?	?	?
EA143–17 (M)	Old adult	M	?	Yes
EA413–11 (N)	Old adult	M	?	No
EA413–12 (O)	Mid-adult	M	No	Yes
EA143–13, 4.02 (P)	Child	?	No	No
EA143–15, 8 (Q)	Young adult	M	No	No
EA143–18.01 (R)	Young adult	M	?	Yes
EA143–19 (S)	Child	?	No	?
EA143–21.01, 21.02 (T)	Adolescent	M	No	?
EA143–21.01, 21.02 (U)	Adult	?	?	?
EA143–18.02	Not separate person, unclear with whom this cranial fragment is associated			
EA143–20	Not separate person, unclear with whom this cranial fragment is associated			
EA72-C1	Child	?	?	No
EA72-C2	Child	?	No	?
EA72-C3	Mid-adult	M	No	Yes
EA72-C4	Adult	M	No	Yes
EA72-C5	Mid-adult	M	No	Yes
EA72-C6	Adolescent	?	?	No
EA72-C7	Young adult	?	No	No
EA72-C8	Late adolescent	?	No	No
EA72-C9	Young adult	?	?	No
EA72-C10	Child	?	Yes	?

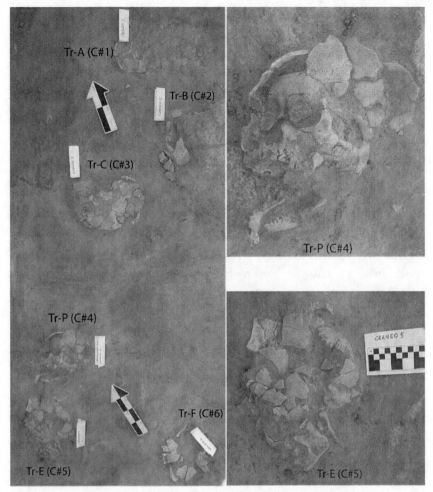

Figure 6.5. In situ trophy heads on the floor of EA143 (circular ritual structure). (Photos courtesy of William Isbell and Anita Cook; labels by Tung.)

There were ten commingled trophy heads from the southern portion of the D-shaped room (EA72; see figure 3.3) (figure 6.4), and a sacrificed camelid was deposited directly above them (Ochatoma and Cabrera 2002). These were excavated by the Proyecto de Excavaciones en un Poblado Alfarero de la Epoca Huari, directed by José Ochatoma and Martha Cabrera, who also recovered additional camelid bones and intentionally smashed ceramic urns in northern and western sections of the building. Several of those ceramics depicted disembodied heads and hands, warriors wearing trophy heads, and Wari deities dangling stylized trophy heads (Ochatoma 2007).

Trophy head remains from the D-shaped ritual structure (EA72) postdate

Huarpa occupations. Ketteman (2002) suggests that the D-shaped building was used at the same time or subsequent to the use of nearby room EA33, which yielded the following radiometric dates: AD 691–983 (2 sigma; Sample # Beta-133541) and AD 685–975 (2 sigma; Sample # Beta-133542).

The circular ritual structure (EA143) seems to prefigure the classic D-shaped structure known at Wari sites, and because it is in a stratigraphically lower level, it appears to have been constructed and used before the D-shaped ritual room. Indeed, an AMS date from wood charcoal near trophy head #19 (Tr-S) reveals the following dates: AD 433–643 (2 sigma; Sample # GX-31863-AMS). Because the human bone was severely burned (no organic matter remained), it could not be directly dated, so a piece of burned wood was used instead. Whether the sample suffers from an "old wood" problem (being felled decades or centuries before it was burned with the trophy heads) or whether it accurately dates the deposition of the skulls could not be determined. Isbell has suggested that the ritual building could have been roofed using wooden beams; if so, the wood sample could date the construction of the ritual building, not the event when trophy heads were burned and deposited on the floor. Additional AMS dating is needed to address these important chronological issues.

A third D-shaped ritual structure is located along the modern road (Ave. Ejercito) that runs through the site (see figure 3.3). Unfortunately, the road construction damaged much of the ritual building, so whether human trophy heads were deposited in that room is unknown. There is a fourth D-shaped or circular ritual building below EA33 (see figure 3.3), but it has not yet been extensively excavated.

Corporeal Transformation: Anthropogenic Modifications to the Human Heads from Conchopata

Decapitation and Defleshing

Numerous cut marks and a few chop marks on the Conchopata trophy heads indicate that soft tissue was still present when these heads were being prepared. This suggests that the processing occurred around the time of death, not years postmortem. That is, "fresh" bodies, not old skeletons, were used to produce trophy heads. (If skulls had naturally separated from the body after soft tissue decomposed, there would be no need for decapitation or soft-tissue removal.)

Two out of 22 mandibles exhibit chop marks (linear marks over two millimeters in width). These include an adolescent trophy head (EA143, Tr-T) with chop marks on the posterior edge of the ascending ramus and a child trophy head (EA143, Tr-P) with chop marks on the left and right sides of the inferior

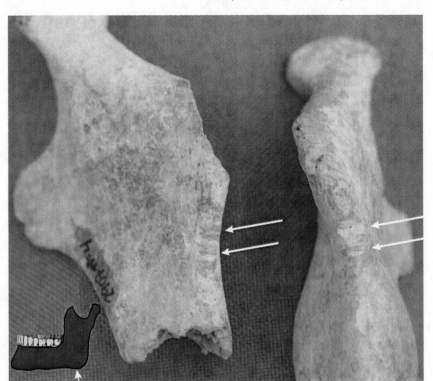

Figure 6.6. Trophy head mandible with chop marks, suggesting a decapitation blow to a bowed head.

edge of the ascending ramus (near gonion) (figure 6.6). These marks are consistent with using a heavily bladed tool for hacking or chopping (Walker and Long 1977), and their locations are consistent with beheading an individual from behind as the individual bows his/her head (Waldron 1996). Adults also may have been beheaded in this manner, but the chop marks appeared only on the younger individuals with slighter musculature. Perhaps this suggests that tools were designed for decapitating full-grown adults, not gracile children and teens. Finally, although the chop marks are indicative of beheading, whether that was the mechanism of death is unknown; these individuals could have been decapitated after death by some other means.

Cut marks (less than two millimeters in width) were observed on 50 percent of the mandibles, along the posterior border of the ascending ramus (11/22=50%) (figure 6.7), and on one-third of the zygomatic bones (3/9=33%). Because the masseter muscle originates on the zygomatic and inserts on the ramus—keeping the cranium and mandible together on an isolated head—those cut marks

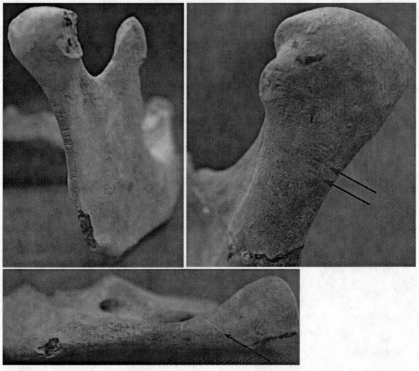

Figure 6.7. Trophy head mandibles with cut marks (indicated by arrows on the right and lower photos).

indicate that the masseter was intentionally cut to separate the two parts of the skull.

Cut marks are also present on several other skull areas, including (1) the mastoid process of EA143-I; (2) the occipital bone, lateral to the inferior nuchal lines, of trophy head EA143-N; (3) the left temporal line of EA143-K; (4) the anterior of the coronoid process of a mandible from EA72; (5) the inferior edge of the mental eminence of another mandible from EA72; and (6), not surprisingly, around the perforations on the apex of the skull, likely related to removing parts of the scalp to view the bone surface before the hole was drilled (see figure 6.8 for some examples). Bloodletting practices may also explain the cut marks on the cranium surface, similar to what Baraybar (1987) has suggested for the Nasca trophy heads. These various cut marks suggest that in some cases posterior and lateral head and neck muscles were severed. In particular, the cut marks on the coronoid process indicate that the temporalis muscle was cut; the temporalis, like the masseter, must be severed to separate the mandible from the cranium.

While cut marks were not observed on the three cervical vertebrae recovered with the EA143 trophy heads, one of them, an axis from a juvenile, had a damaged dens (Tr-P). The anterior-superior portion of the axis shows both

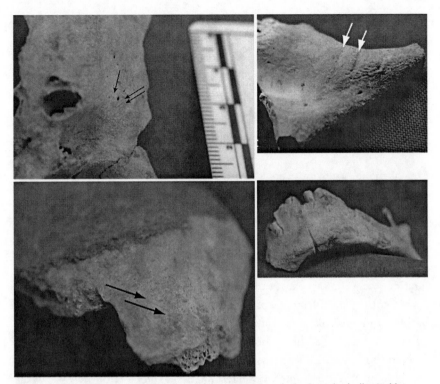

Figure 6.8. Cut marks on other areas of the trophy heads (cut marks indicated by arrows where difficult to see). *Clockwise from upper left*: Temporal bone, superior to the external auditory meatus; inferior edge of the zygomatic bone; inferior edge of the mental eminence; and occipital bone, lateral to the inferior nuchal lines.

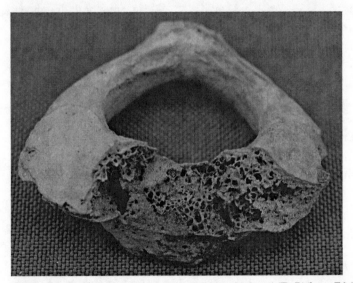

Figure 6.9. Damaged axis from a juvenile trophy head (Tr-P) from EA143. This is a superior-anterior view of the axis in which both perimortem and postmortem fracturing are evident.

perimortem and postmortem breakage; the former suggests some kind of forcible removal of the head that broke the dens off the body (figure 6.9). If the soft tissue had decomposed, reducing the head and neck to skeletal form, there would have been no need for forcible separation of the skull. There is no way to determine if decapitation was the mechanism of death or if the head was removed immediately postmortem.

Preparing Heads for Display

One of the most obvious characteristics of a trophy head is the hole drilled in the bone to facilitate a carrying cord. Among the Conchopata trophy heads, the hole was most commonly drilled on the apex of the cranium. Specifically, 20 of the 26 (77%) trophy heads with an observable calotte exhibit an intentionally drilled hole at or within one centimeter of bregma, an osteometric point where the sagittal and coronal sutures intersect (figure 6.10). Another three have a perforation along the sagittal suture on the apex of the cranium, indicating that 89 percent (23/26) of those observed were designed to ensure that the head dangled upright, looking forward. (The other five trophy heads had small bone fragments with drilled holes; however, the precise location of the perforation on each skull was unclear. Some exhibited a hole along the coronal suture, but small fragment size prevented any determination of whether the hole was at the center point of the coronal, at bregma. They were thus considered unobservable and excluded from the study of hole location.) The consistency of the design in Wari trophy heads, especially in contrast to Nasca trophy heads, for which hole placement was more variable, suggests that Wari trophy head design and production was more codified.

Holes were also drilled on the occipital bones of trophy heads. Of the eight individuals with observable occipital bones, three-quarters displayed at least one hole. In EA72, each of the two occipital bones displayed one perforation on the cruciform eminence, and in EA143, four occipital bones exhibited two holes each; they were drilled on the left and right sides, inferior to the groove for the transverse sinus (figure 6.11). Two additional occipital bone fragments exhibited one hole each on the lateral portion (inferior to the transverse sinus), and presumably if they were complete, there would have been a second hole on the opposite side, like the others. Although the placement of the perforations on the occipital bones differs in each ritual structure (single hole on cruciform eminence on those from EA72 and two symmetrical holes on those from EA143), they likely served the same purpose: they were conduits for a carrying cord. The head could have been suspended whole and intact from the posterior side, or more likely, occipital bones were worn and displayed as separate trophies,

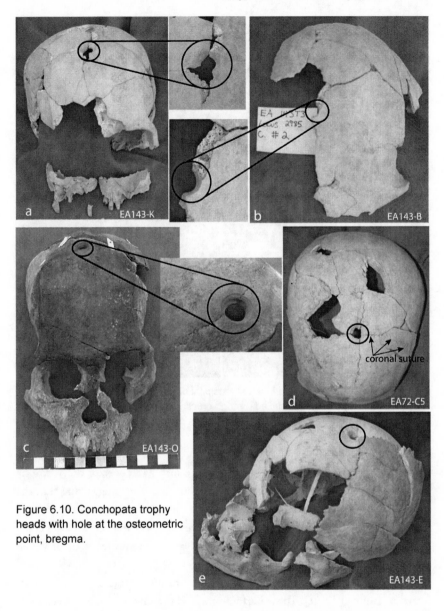

Figure 6.10. Conchopata trophy heads with hole at the osteometric point, bregma.

perhaps as a pectoral or amulet. In support of their isolated use as amulets is the presence of two occipital bones found together on the floor of the circular room (EA143), lying next to a partial cranium. Whether the cranium joins with one of the occipitals is unclear, because tiny fragments were missing and other cranial pieces were warped from burning. Even if one of those occipital bones belongs to the incomplete cranium, there remains one isolated occipital bone

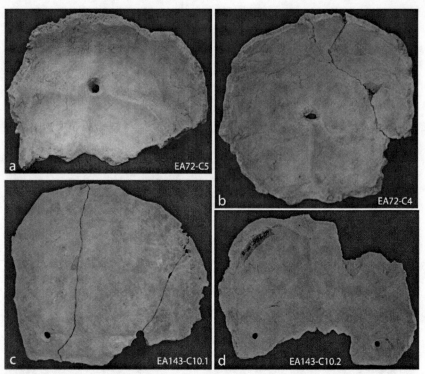

Figure 6.11. Intentionally drilled holes on occipital bones from Conchopata trophy heads: (a) and (b) single hole drilled through cruciform eminence (both from EA72); (c) and (d) two holes drilled though inferior margin of occipital bone (both from EA143).

that may have been used as an amulet of some sort. Moreover, of the 31 trophy heads, only eight complete occipital bones were recovered, suggesting that the others were separated and never rejoined with the cranium. Some also exhibit a patina, indicating that they were frequently handled, as expected for amulets.

There were 17 mandibles with at least one ascending ramus, four of which displayed a perforation (figure 6.12). Three of those (Tr-C, Tr-E, and Tr-S) exhibited holes on both sides; only the left side was observable on the fourth affected mandible (Tr-N). These perforations and the intentionally severed masseter muscle (described above) demonstrate that the mandible was separated from the cranium and occasionally tied back to it or displayed solo. Convincing evidence of the former can be seen in Tr-E, where the mandible is in anatomical position, inferior to the maxilla (see figure 6.5).

The Wari were not the only group to modify and use trophy heads in this way. There is a Moche skull bowl that similarly has holes on the ascending ramus, perhaps for tying it to the cranium (Verano 2001:fig. 8.4). Among Nasca trophy heads, the mandibles were treated somewhat differently; they were sometimes

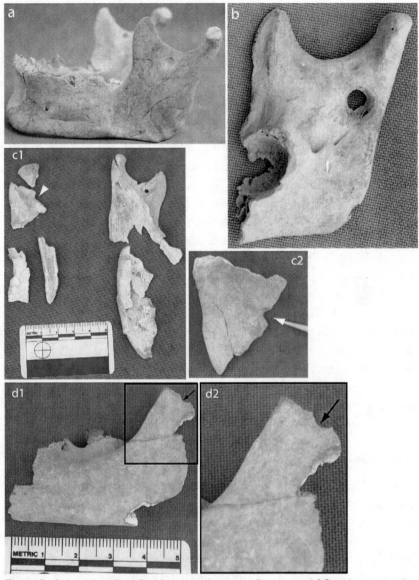

Figure 6.12. Intentionally drilled holes on the ascending ramus of Conchopata trophy heads from EA143: (a) adult mandible with hole on both sides of ascending ramus (Tr-E); (b) and (c1–2) juvenile mandibles with hole on ascending ramus (Tr-S and Tr-C, respectively); (d1) and (d2) adult mandible fragment with partial hole visible on the ascending ramus.

reattached to the cranium by wrapping cordage around the ramus and tying it to the zygomatic bone (Verano 1995). To my knowledge, the Nasca did not drill holes on the mandibles for isolated display; this is unique to the Wari and the Moche.

Finger and Toe Dismemberment

Those who were transformed into trophy heads had their fingers and toes taken as trophies too, or completely different individuals may have had hand and foot elements taken as trophies. In EA72 (D-shaped room), three hand and three foot phalanges from adults were recovered with the trophy heads; one foot phalanx (the big toe) exhibited cut marks on the dorsal side, along the proximal-medial surface. In the circular ritual room (EA143), 84 hand phalanges and 17 foot phalanges were found (from both adults and children). In four cases, the proximal hand phalanges exhibited perimortem cut marks and damage on the proximal edge of the dorsal aspect (figure 6.13). There was also one proximal thumb phalanx with cut marks on the palmar surface. Proximal, intermediate, and distal phalanges were present in EA143, while only proximal and intermediate phalanges were recovered from EA72. The location of cut marks on the hand phalanges indicates that fingers were cut off at the joint (knuckles) while soft tissue was still attached. This suggests that fingers and toes were used as trophies and incorporated into the rituals that occurred in those buildings. There is no evidence that entire hands or feet were used as trophies, as there are no metacarpals, carpals, metatarsals, or tarsals in either ritual structure. No determination could be made of whether persons were alive or recently deceased when their fingers and toes were removed. There is one hand phalanx with an apparent perforation on the proximal end and a hollowed-out shaft, suggesting that it may have been strung on a cord as some sort of amulet or trophy (figure 6.13c).

Ritual Transformation with Fire

Based on bone color, the trophy heads from EA143 were burned at a higher temperature than those from EA72, a temperature high estimated at about 800°C based on their grayish white color and vitrification (see Walker et al. 2008). In the circular room, there was one trophy head that was unburned (Tr-T) and another that was only partially burned while the temporalis muscles were still attached (Tr-O). This protected the lateral surfaces of the skull from burning (see figure 6.10c). Two others from EA72 also exhibited partial burning, suggesting that some trophy heads were sometimes displayed with flesh intact, likely leaving facial features recognizable before they were destroyed by flames. This interpretation is further buttressed by Wari iconography showing fleshed trophy heads dangling from a deity's staff and from around a warrior's neck.

It is unlikely that the burned trophy heads represent some kind of a retaliatory act at the end of the Wari reign. The deep deposits of the trophy heads, the

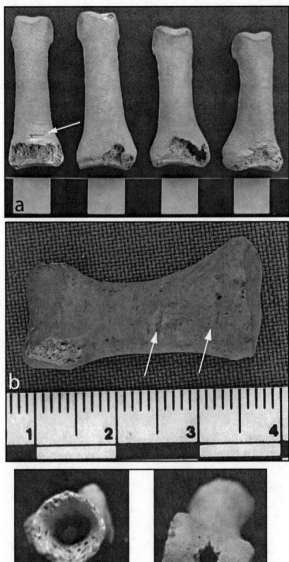

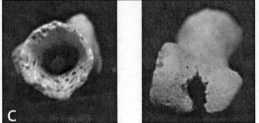

Figure 6.13. Trophy hand phalanges from Conchopata: (a) cut marks and general damage to the proximal end of the dorsal aspect of proximal hand phalanges; (b) cut marks on the palmar surface of the proximal hand phalanx 1 (thumb); (c) (*left and right*) possible hole drilled through shaft of hand phalanx.

radiocarbon dates from EA143 and rooms surrounding EA72, and the carefully placed sacrificed camelid on top of the trophy heads in the D-shaped structure belie the notion that these ritual spaces were sacked.

Instead, the ritual burning of trophy heads was likely the final act of a long ceremony, perhaps days, weeks, or months long. As suggested by Isbell and Cook (2002), the trophy heads in the D-shaped room could have been hanging from roof beams when all came crashing to the floor as the building went up in flames. This is a possible scenario, but the means by which all of the finger and toe bones would have been suspended, such that they ended up underneath trophy heads on the floor of the circular room, remains unclear. Moreover, the unburned and partially burned trophy heads, as well as the limited distribution of ash, suggest that burning occurred only in one subarea. That is, the concentration of ash and burned trophy heads in the southeast quadrant of the circular structure indicate that, rather than the entire building having burned, burning was isolated to a precise space. Similarly, ritual activities involving the burning of trophy heads in the D-shaped ritual room (EA72) were isolated to the southern section of the building.

This division of space was apparently intentional, earmarking specific areas for particular acts, and perhaps for a particular class of individuals. This is not unlike the stern division of space observed in other ritual and religious buildings (or other mundane structures), where space is used to distribute people, create or limit their authority, enable peer and self-monitoring, and generate particular kinds of behaviors (Foucault 1977). For example, churches, synagogues, and many other religious structures demarcate spaces for the separation of the congregation and the pastor/rabbi/religious leader, a division that highlights the authority of the latter and guides behaviors of each group.

The use of fire is common in many rituals in the Andes (and elsewhere), transforming sacred objects into ashes and smoke—evidence that they have been consumed by deities (Bastien 1985; Bolin 1998). In the Andes today, "ashes [that] are white like silver . . . [are] a sign that the gods have eaten with contentment" (Bolin 1998:63). While ethnographic analogy should always be used with caution, especially given that it can perpetuate false notions that Andean identity and cultural practices are essential and static, these contemporary insights add a rich lens through which to view ancient practices. The white ash and vitrified trophy heads demonstrate that the ritual space and associated objects received a good burning, perhaps signaling a satisfactory offering to Wari deities or Wari elites.

Transforming Bodies into Sacred Objects

The transformation from an individual human being—individuals who will be described below—to a sacred object marked the transition to a new kind of social entity. The dismembered body on display became a symbol of the social body, reflecting control over the bodies of subjects by ritual and political elites. However, the physical objects themselves—the disembodied heads—did not merely function as "symbols" reflecting preexisting ideals and beliefs. The process of transformation and the object it produced were also generative, constructing new ideals and naturalizing the power of ritual specialists. As these specialists transformed persons into trophy objects, they reified notions of their exotic knowledge, skills, and spiritual power. In a cyclical manner, as they created trophy heads that they and others were taught to view as symbols of authority, they simultaneously created and bolstered their positions of power. As I will argue, this intense manipulation of bodies likely translated into an effective means for controlling the body politic, both in regulating the population and in disciplining individual bodies (see Scheper-Hughes and Lock 1987). But before that case is made, I describe the individuals and their lifeways prior to their transformation into trophies.

Targeting Men and Children: The Demographic Profile of Wari Trophy Heads

Adult men were preferentially selected for transformation into trophy heads, but children were selected nearly a quarter of the time. Among the 21 trophy heads in the circular room (EA143), four were children and 17 were late adolescents/adults. In the D-shaped room (EA72), three were children and seven were late adolescents/adults (see table 6.1). When these were initially uncovered, one was identified as a "dwarf individual" (Ochatoma and Cabrera 2002:235), but my analysis shows that it was a child. The age-at-death distribution in each room was not statistically significantly different (Fisher's exact, $p=0.401$), suggesting that neither was used primarily for the display of one age group. Given that there was no significant difference, the two samples were combined to obtain a general age-at-death profile. Of the 31 total trophy heads, seven were children (23%) and 24 were late adolescents/adults (77%).

Among the 17 late adolescents/adults whose sex could be determined, males (16/17=94%) significantly outnumber females (6%) relative to an equal distribution (Fisher's exact, $p=0.018$). (Only one adult trophy head was identified as a possible female.) That so many men were targeted for trophy taking suggests that people were not randomly selected. Rather, adult men were the favored targets for abduction and/or head hunting. The Wari trophy head sex profile is similar to that of Nasca trophy heads, where the majority are also adult males (Verano 1995). Among the 151 Nasca trophy heads described in the literature, sex was reported for 98 of them: 92 percent are male (90/98) and eight percent are female (8/98) (Tung 2007a). On the basis of this male bias in Nasca trophy heads, some scholars have suggested that they were taken in warfare (Proulx 1989; Proulx 2001; Verano 1995). Some of the Wari trophy heads could have been obtained in similar militaristic settings.

However, the age-at-death distribution, in which nearly a quarter of the Wari trophy heads were children, suggests that some could have been taken, not in warfare battles, but in village raids. Only seven percent of Nasca trophy heads reported in the literature were children ($N=123$) (Tung 2007a), a distribution that is significantly lower than that of the Wari trophy heads (Fisher's exact, $p=0.021$; $N=154$). Thus, it appears that head hunting or prisoner capture occurred in situations where children were present. Village raids are one such context; battlefields are not. Perhaps the majority of Nasca heads were obtained in battles and Wari ones were obtained in raids. Of course, some of the Wari prisoners and/or trophy heads may have been taken in battles too. But given the high count of child trophy heads, the salient point is that warfare was not the exclusive source of live captives or trophies.

This demographic profile in which men were targeted as Wari trophies yet children were also taken is similar to Jívaro practices in which adult men were preferred as "shrunken heads," even though women's and children's heads were sometimes taken during raids on non-Jívaro communities (Harner 1972). Historically, part of the reason that Jívaro headhunters targeted various age groups and both sexes was related to European demands for shrunken heads; the Europeans traded one gun for one shrunken head (Ferguson 2004). Still, the important point is that head taking—among either the Jívaro or the Wari—was not solely reserved for adult male victims.

The phenomenon wherein all age and sex classes may be victimized may be explained through the notion of "social substitutability" (Kelly 2000), which states that in war or raids any individual—whether man, woman, or child—from a group may be targeted, because any one can substitute for the entire community. Any violence against one person in the community is perceived as injury to all. Kelly (2000) argues that this transition to ideas of social substitutability was a necessary step in the development of warfare. That is, prior to this, Kelly suggests, violence between groups was more of a direct tit-for-tat form of justice, in which individual killings targeted the "murderer" only, not any random person from the community.

To expand, then, the individual body under attack serves as a symbol for the humiliation and damage to the well-being of the entire social body. In turn, this likely had repercussions on the body politic, affecting behaviors, forms of social organization, and systems of rule for the communities that were victimized. That is, because of Wari raids that were likely part of the larger plan for Wari expansion, victimized communities may have reorganized themselves to improve defense or create alliances, either with Wari and Wari-affiliated communities or with other groups altogether. The manner in which potential alliance formations were carried out (and with whom) remains unclear, but the evidence for violence, head taking, and changes in settlement patterns and material culture suggests that Wari imperial practices had profound effects on the social organization of several other Andean communities during the Middle Horizon.

These aggressive acts of head and/or prisoner taking, likely by Wari warriors, also would have impacted native Wari communities from where the aggressors derived, such that state-sponsored militarism and individual warrior prowess could have been increasingly celebrated and valued. Indeed, Wari iconography from sites such as Huari and Conchopata (discussed below) indicates that this was the case.

A Violent Lifestyle

Observing for cranial trauma provides a way to reconstruct part of a person's lived experience by documenting whether they once engaged in violent behaviors. If individuals who were targeted to become trophy heads were warriors who engaged in battles or other forms of violence, then they should exhibit antemortem (healed) cranial fractures indicating a history of violence, or perimortem fractures (injuries that occurred around the time of death), suggesting a lethal battle to obtain the head. Among the 19 late adolescent/adult trophy heads observable for trauma, 42 percent were affected (8/19), suggesting that violence was common among those who were targeted to become trophy heads (see table 6.1).

Of the eight cranial wounds on the eight affected adult trophy heads, one was perimortem, indicating that the injury was sustained around the time of death (figure 6.14). The other seven wounds were well healed, indicating a nonlethal violent encounter earlier in the person's life (figure 6.14). Four wounds were on the anterior of skulls, suggesting that the men who were taken as trophies had engaged in face-to-face fighting earlier in their lives. The other four wounds were on the posterior of skulls, perhaps suggesting that these other men were injured while fleeing during raids many months or years earlier. The fact that these men ended up beheaded and on the floor of a Wari ritual structure suggests that one of the Wari raids or battles eventually led to their capture and death.

The trophy head trauma frequency (42%) is not significantly different from that of the adult mortuary sample from Conchopata's domestic spaces (10/44=23%) (Fisher's exact, $p=0.105$; $N=63$), nor is it different from the cranial trauma frequency among Wari-era Majes valley adults (45/143=31.5%). This suggests that, at least in terms of violence, trophy head and non–trophy head individuals from Conchopata and the Majes valley had somewhat similar lifestyles.

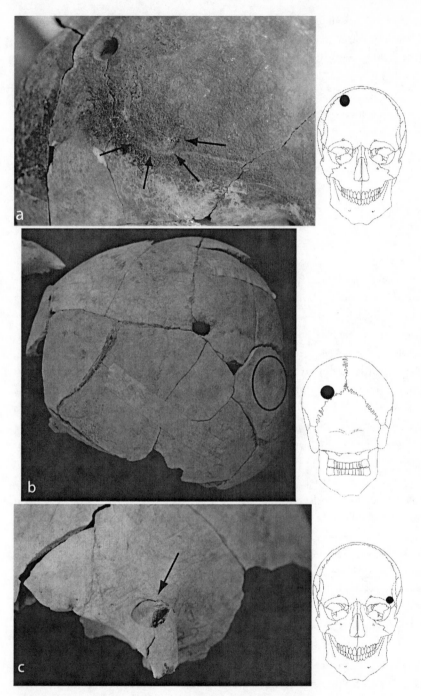

Figure 6.14. Conchopata trophy heads with trauma: (a) antemortem trauma on the right frontal bone; (b) antemortem trauma on the left parietal boss; and (c) perimortem trauma on the left orbit.

Disease Experience of Trophy Head Victims

Cribra Orbitalia

Among the 17 adolescents/adults observed, only one exhibited cribra orbitalia (6%), suggesting that childhood anemia, sinusitis, and other naso-oral infections (Walker et al. 2009; Wapler et al. 2004) were uncommon among the adolescent/adult trophy head victims (table 6.1). This cribra orbitalia frequency is similar to that among adults buried in the Wari-era mortuary spaces at Conchopata (4/46=9%) and among adults at Wari-era sites in the Nasca valley (4/77=5%) (Kellner 2002). And although the frequency is lower than that of the Majes populations in this study (19/86=22%) (Tung 2003), it is not significantly different (Fisher's exact, $p=0.108$; $N=103$) (figure 6.15).

The adult Wari trophy heads do, however, show significantly lower percentages relative to adults from the contemporaneous Tiwanaku-affiliated site of Chen Chen (60/165=36%) (Blom et al. 2004) (Fisher's exact, $p=0.007$) and the Middle Horizon/Late Intermediate Period Chiribaya sites in the Moquegua valley (126/292=43%) (Burgess 1999) (Fisher's exact, $p<0.005$) (figure 6.15).

Cribra orbitalia was present on a quarter of the child trophy heads for which a determination could be made (1/4=25%) (table 6.1), a frequency similar among children from Wari-era sites in Nasca (4/14=29%) (Kellner 2002). And while the orbital lesions on child trophy heads were more common compared to the

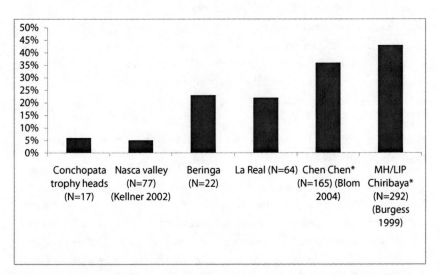

Figure 6.15. Cribra orbitalia frequencies of Middle Horizon Andean adults. Asterisk indicates a frequency that is statistically significantly different from the Conchopata trophy head frequency ($p<0.05$).

19 children from Conchopata tombs (1/19=5%) (Tung 2003), the difference was not significant (Fisher's exact, p=0.324).

In terms of the physiological stressors suggested by cribra orbitalia, the adults whose heads ended up on the floors of Conchopata's ritual structures are most similar to adults buried at Wari-affiliated sites that have been examined thus far, and they are most distinct from those at Tiwanaku-affiliated sites in southern near-coastal Peru.

Dental Disease

Of the seven adults with at least two well-preserved mandibular teeth, two adults exhibited dental caries. Among the 18 adults with at least five observable mandibular sockets, four adults exhibited an abscess (22%) and 10 experienced antemortem tooth loss (56%). These dental ailments would have been quite painful, likely interfering with day-to-day activities from time to time.

The high frequencies of dental caries and tooth loss suggest that these individuals may have consumed cariogenic foods, such as maize and other carbo-hydrates. Their dental health—and likely their diet—was similar to the Wari-affiliated commoner village at Beringa, in the Majes valley. At Beringa, eight out of 18 (44%) well-preserved adult mandibles exhibited dental caries, eight out of 27 adult mandibles (30%) had at least one dental abscess, and 15 out of 26 adult mandibles (58%) exhibited antemortem tooth loss (Tung and Del Castillo 2005). (The denominator changes because of variable preservation that some-times inhibited observations for oral pathologies.) The elite Wari-affiliated site of La Real, in contrast, had much lower frequencies of caries (2/19=11%) and abscesses (2/39=5%) (Tung and Del Castillo 2005). Although sample sizes are small, perhaps the dental data suggest that those who were selected for trophy head transformation consumed diets that were more similar to hinterland com-moners than hinterland elites.

From Whence the Trophy Heads Came: Insights from Strontium Isotope Analysis

While the data on morbidity and anthropogenic modifications of the trophy heads provide crucial insights into their biological status and treatment around the time of death and after, they do not reveal whether the trophy head indi-viduals were from the local area or from a distant geological locale. This is an important piece of information, for if some trophy heads can be shown to derive from "foreign" individuals, then they are likely to have been neither venerated ancestors nor criminals from the local community. Rather, these nonlocal per-sons (or just their heads) may have been taken as captives from distant regions, suggesting that they were perceived as enemies by Wari military personnel and others who were involved in their capture and processing.

Strontium isotope ratios were obtained from local small animals, Conchopata burials, and Conchopata trophy heads to determine if any individuals—trophy heads in particular—derive from a geological locale distinct from the Wari heartland in the Ayacucho Basin. This technique is ideal for this study because the Wari Empire expanded into diverse geological regions. Therefore, if Wari military agents took enemy heads, they were likely taken from people who lived beyond the Wari heartland, in distinct geological areas. This is in contrast to the Nasca polity, where, although they engaged in head taking, the Nasca did so from people within the same geological zone (Knudson et al. 2009). This does not mean that Nasca warriors refrained from taking enemies in raids or warfare battles ("real" or ritual); instead, because Nasca was not an imperial polity that ranged far and wide, we should not expect Nasca trophy heads to derive from people who lived far from the Nasca cultural sphere.

Seventy-two samples representing 31 Conchopata burials (see chapter 4) and 18 trophy heads (11 adults, two adolescents, and five children) were analyzed to obtain their strontium isotope ratios (see table 6.2). If a strontium isotope ratio from a trophy head does not match that of the local geology and local mammals (including humans), then the suggestion may be made that those trophy head persons did not consume a locally procured diet. By extension, this suggests that the person either consumed prodigious amounts of calcium-rich food from a foreign geological zone or, more likely, that the person lived in a foreign locale. The primary goal of strontium isotope analysis as used here is to determine whether trophy head individuals were local or foreign, not to determine their precise geographical origins. However, in light of recent studies that report strontium isotope ratios in a variety of Andean zones, a preliminary list of possible source regions may be constructed, while other areas can be eliminated.

The Trophy Heads: Locals and Nonlocals

The trophy heads exhibit a much higher average strontium isotope ratio than the burials: the trophy head mean $^{87}Sr/^{86}Sr=0.70795+0.00268$, and the median $^{87}Sr/^{86}Sr=0.70648$. In contrast, the burial mean $^{87}Sr/^{86}Sr=0.70584+0.00074$ (see chapter 4) (table 6.2). An examination of all 72 samples together shows that the Conchopata burial samples cluster together (see left side of the graph in figure 6.16). Also, the strontium isotope values of the trophy heads are much more variable than the burials. The trophy heads range from a minimum $^{87}Sr/^{86}Sr=0.70596$ to a maximum $^{87}Sr/^{86}Sr=0.71600$ (table 6.3). Finally, a comparison of box plots of the burials and trophy heads shows that the burials are

Table 6.2. Strontium isotope ratios from Conchopata burials and trophy heads

Architecture space (EA)	Bone codes[a]	Age	Sex	$^{87}Sr/^{86}Sr$	Element
44A	B-0950–01.01	MA	M	0.70575	Max RM2
44A	B-0950–01.02	MA	M	0.70577	Atlas
44A	B-0950–01.03	MA	M	0.70574	R humerus
20	**B-1371–01.01**	**Teen 17–22 yrs**	**F**	**0.71058**	**Mand LC**
39A	B-1728–01.01	A	M?	0.70571	Mand LM3
39A	B-1728–01.02	A	M?	0.70573	Mandible fragment
39A	B-1818–01.01	YA	?	0.70561	Max LM1
39A	B-1818–01.02	YA	?	0.70573	Maxilla fragment
110	B-1993–01.01	A	?	0.70584	Mand RM1
6	**B-2004–01**	**Infant**	**?**	**0.70673**	**Rib**
89A	B-2052–01.01	OA	F	0.70552	Max RM2
105	B-2095–01.01	YA-MA 30–39 yrs	F	0.70560	Mand LM2
105	B-2095–01.02	YA-MA 30–39 yrs	F	0.70610	R fibula
105	B-2095–02.01	YA 21–21 yrs	F	0.70563	Mand RM2
105	B-2095–02.01	YA 21–21 yrs	F	0.70574	R fibula
105	B-2095–03.01	OA 47–53 yrs	F	0.70565	Mand molar
105	B-2095–03.02	OA 47–53 yrs	F	0.70586	R fibula
105	B-2095–04.01	YA 31–37 yrs	F	0.70565	Mand LM2
105	B-2095–04.02	YA 31–37 yrs	F	0.70566	L fibula
105	B-2095–06.01	YA 23–27 yrs	M	0.70548	Mand RM2
105	B-2095–06.02	YA 23–27 yrs	M	0.70574	Rib
104T5	B-2107–17.01	OA	F	0.70571	Mand LP3
104T5	B-2107–17.02	OA	F	0.70571	Max RM1
104T5	B-2107–17.03	OA	F	0.70572	R humerus
151	B-2858–01.01	YA 30–35 yrs	F	0.70571	Mand LM2
147	B-2884–42–01.01	Child 6–7 yrs	?	0.70570	Mand rm2 (deciduous)
147	B-2884–42–01.02	Child 6–7 yrs	?	0.70571	Mand RM2
150	B-2981–94–01.01	OA 50+ yrs	F	0.70576	L femur
150	B-2981–94–02.01	YA 18–22 yrs	F	0.70589	R ulna
150	B-2981–94–03.01	T 14–17 yrs	F	0.70569	R ulna
150	B-2981–94–04.01	Child	?	0.70569	Metacarpal
88	B-3032–54.06	C-T 11–14 yrs	?	0.70579	Mand RC

Architecture space (EA)	Bone codes[a]	Age	Sex	$^{87}Sr/^{86}Sr$	Element
187	B-3335–00.155	A	?	0.70565	Max RC
205	B-3521–104.64	Inf 12–18 mo	?	0.70570	L fibula
205	B-3521–105.55	Inf 12–18 mo	?	0.70572	L rib
205	B-3521–107.18	MA	F	0.70560	Mand RP3
205	B-3521–107.66	MA	F	0.70565	R hand phalanx
205	B-3554–106–01.44	Inf 9–12 mo	?	0.70572	R fibula
208	B-3547–108–01.13	MA	M	0.70558	Max LM2
208	B-3547–108–03.05	MA	F	0.70556	Max LI2
208	B-3577–108–05.01	C-T 13–16 yrs	?	0.70558	Mand RM1
N/A	B-Airtower.01	YA-MA	M	0.70587	Mand R12
N/A	B-Airtower.02	YA-MA	M	0.70591	L femur
N/A	B-Ochat-Female	OA	F	0.70583	Max RC1
N/A	B-Ochat-Female	OA	F	0.70580	Metatarsal
N/A	B-Ochat-Male	OA	M	0.70576	L radius
72	Tr-EA72-MandC	YA-MA	M	0.70615	Mand RM2
72	**Tr-EA72-MandD**	**YA**	**M**	**0.70821**	**Mand LM1**
72	Tr-EA72-MandJ (Tr-C1)	Child	?	0.70616	L mand condyle
143	**Tr-2907–04–01.01 (Tr-D)**	**MA**	**F?**	**0.70719**	**Cranial fragment**
143	**Tr-2907–04–01.02 (Tr-D)**	**MA**	**F?**	**0.70881**	**Enamel fragment**
143	**Tr-2907–05.01 (Tr-E)**	**MA**	**M**	**0.70627**	**Enamel fragment**
143	**Tr-2907–05.02 (Tr-E)**	**MA**	**M**	**0.70648**	**Cranial fragment**
143	**Tr-2985–01.01 (Tr-A)**	**Child**	**?**	**0.71013**	**Cranial fragment**
143	**Tr-2985–03.01 (Tr-C)**	**Teen**	**?**	**0.70626**	**Molar**
143	**Tr-2985–03.02 (Tr-C)**	**Teen**	**?**	**0.70633**	**Cranial fragment**
143	**Tr-2985–06.01 (Tr-F)**	**MA 35–42 yrs**	**M**	**0.70762**	**Enamel fragment**
143	**Tr-2985–06.02 (Tr-F)**	**MA 35–42 yrs**	**M**	**0.70831**	**Cranial fragment**
143	**Tr-2985–09.01 (Tr-J)**	**MA**	**M**	**0.71495**	**Cranial fragment**
143	**Tr-2985–11.01 (Tr-N)**	**OA**	**M**	**0.71020**	**Enamel fragment**
143	**Tr-2985–11.02 (Tr-N)**	**OA**	**M**	**0.70923**	**Cranial fragment**
143	**Tr-2985–13.01 (Tr-P)**	**Child 6–8 yrs**	**?**	**0.70632**	**Molar**
143	Tr-2985–13.02 (Tr-P)	Child 6–8 yrs	?	0.70613	Cranial fragment
143	Tr-2985–13.03 (Tr-P)	Child 6–8 yrs	?	0.70607	Vertebra fragment
143	**Tr-2985–15.01 (Tr-Q)**	**Adult**	**?**	**0.71129**	**Molar 3**

continued

Table 6.2.—*continued*

Architecture space (EA)	Bone codes[a]	Age	Sex	$^{87}Sr/^{86}Sr$	Element
143	**Tr-2985–15.02 (Tr-H)**	**Child 3–7 yrs**	**?**	**0.71600**	**Hand phalanx**
143	**Tr-2985–18–01.01 (Tr-R)**	**YA**	**M**	**0.70626**	**Enamel fragment**
143	**Tr-2985–18–01.02 (Tr-R)**	**YA**	**M**	**0.70729**	**Cranial fragment**
143	Tr-2985–19.01 (Tr-S)	Child 5–7 yrs	?	0.70596	Max molar (deciduous)
143	Tr-2985–21–01.01 (Tr-U)	Adult	?	0.70601	Frontal fragment
143	**Tr-2985–21–02.01 (Tr-T)**	**Teen 13–16 yrs**	**M**	**0.70678**	**Cranial fragment**
143	**Tr-2985–10–01.01 (Tr-K)**	**OA**	**M**	**0.70640**	**Max RC**

Note: All strontium isotope ratios are rounded to the fifth decimal point to make them comparable to table 6.4. Samples in boldface exhibit strontium isotope ratios outside the range expected for the Ayacucho Basin.

[a] B=burial; Tr=trophy head.

more homogenous, with a limited spread in values, and that the burials and trophy heads exhibit limited overlap, further suggesting that these are distinct populations (figure 6.17).

To further evaluate whether trophy heads are from locals or nonlocals, the strontium isotope ratios of all trophy head and burial samples are listed in ascending order, and the difference between each successive sample is calculated. Using this technique, one of the largest breaks in the complete sample occurs with number 51, a trophy head that exhibits $^{87}Sr/^{86}Sr=0.70626$ (table 6.4). This suggests that this sample and all subsequent ones derive from individuals that did not consume a strontium-rich diet from the Ayacucho Basin. Thus, 14 trophy head individuals (represented by 20 samples) appear to derive from locations outside of the Ayacucho Basin. (The two burials, rank order numbers 58 and 69, are identified as nonlocals and discussed in chapter 4.)

The other (preceding) six trophy head samples exhibit local strontium isotope ratios; those samples represent five individuals. However, one of those five is a child (Tr-P; see table 6.1) who also exhibits a nonlocal strontium isotope ratio in his/her enamel ($^{87}Sr/^{86}Sr=0.70632$); this suggests that infancy/early childhood was spent outside of the Ayacucho Basin. Thus, the total number of trophy head individuals without any foreign strontium isotope signatures equals four: two children (Tr-S, Tr-C1) and two adults (Tr-U, Tr-EA72-Mand-C).

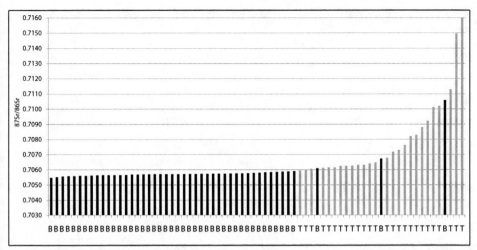

Figure 6.16. Strontium isotope ratios from Conchopata burials and Conchopata trophy heads (*N*=72).

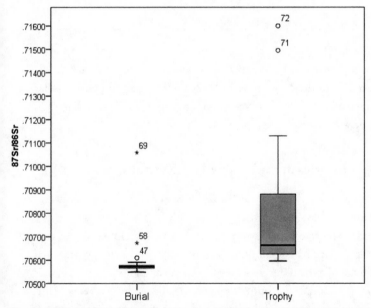

Figure 6.17. Boxplots of strontium isotope ratios for the Conchopata burials and Conchopata trophy heads, presented side by side for comparison. The numbers correspond to their rank order, as shown in table 6.4.

Given that the strontium isotope ratios of those four individuals match the local region, they likely were native to the Wari heartland or a locale with similar strontium isotope ratios, such as the Moquegua valley, where the Wari site of Cerro Baúl is located. There, the strontium isotope ratio equals 0.7059–0.7066 (Knudson and

Table 6.3. Descriptive statistics for $^{87}Sr/^{86}Sr$ of Conchopata burials and Conchopata trophy heads

Statistic	All samples	Burials	Trimmed burial data	Trophy heads
Mean	0.70661	0.70584	0.70572	0.70795
St. dev.	0.00198	0.00074	0.00011	0.00268
Median	0.70577	0.70571	0.70571	0.70648
Min.	0.70548	0.70548	0.70548	0.70596
Max.	0.71600	0.71058	0.70610	0.71600
Range	0.01052	0.00510	0.00062	0.01004
Skewness (std. error)	3.131 (.283)	6.181 (.350)	0.778 (.357)	1.924 (.456)
Kurtosis (std. error)	10.703 (.559)	40.062 (.688)	2.317 (.702)	3.419 (.887)
# of samples	72	46	44	26
# of individuals represented by the samples	49	31	29	18

Price 2007), a range that overlaps with Ayacucho. Thus, if trophy head individuals were taken from the Moquegua valley (or another region with similar strontium isotope values), then they would not appear as "foreigners" based on strontium isotope values alone.

Individual Life Histories of the Trophy Head Victims

Bone and tooth pairs from single individuals were compared in order to reconstruct the individual migration history of those who were eventually made into trophy heads. The strontium isotope ratio from enamel reveals the geological source(s) of bioavailable strontium during the developmental years when enamel is forming, while the bone, which remodels throughout adulthood, tells place of residence (or source of strontium-rich food) during the last years of life.

The intraindividual comparison of enamel and bone strontium isotope values of the trophy heads shows that four of them in particular (Tr-D, Tr-F, Tr-N, Tr-R) were quite mobile, spending their childhood in one location and adulthood in another. (It is also possible that the primary source of calcium-rich foods in their diet changed dramatically from one phase of life to the other.)

Although the exact geographical origin of the trophy heads was impossible to determine, comparing these strontium isotope values to those in other Andean regions reveals possible places of origin, while also excluding some areas (fig-

Table 6.4. Rank order of strontium isotope values from Conchopata burials and trophy heads

Type	Rank order #	$^{87}Sr/^{86}Sr$	Difference from preceding sample
B	1	0.70548	N/A
B	2	0.70552	0.00004
B	3	0.70556	0.00004
B	4	0.70558	0.00002
B	5	0.70558	0.00000
B	6	0.70560	0.00002
B	7	0.70560	0.00000
B	8	0.70561	0.00001
B	9	0.70563	0.00002
B	10	0.70565	0.00002
B	11	0.70565	0.00000
B	12	0.70565	0.00000
B	13	0.70565	0.00000
B	14	0.70566	0.00001
B	15	0.70569	0.00003
B	16	0.70569	0.00000
B	17	0.70570	0.00001
B	18	0.70570	0.00000
B	19	0.70571	0.00001
B	20	0.70571	0.00000
B	21	0.70571	0.00000
B	22	0.70571	0.00000
B	23	0.70571	0.00000
B	24	0.70572	0.00001
B	25	0.70572	0.00000
B	26	0.70572	0.00000
B	27	0.70573	0.00001
B	28	0.70573	0.00000
B	29	0.70574	0.00001
B	30	0.70574	0.00000
B	31	0.70574	0.00000
B	32	0.70575	0.00001
B	33	0.70576	0.00001

continued

Table 6.4.—*continued*

Type	Rank order #	$^{87}Sr/^{86}Sr$	Difference from preceding sample
B	34	0.70576	0.00000
B	35	0.70577	0.00001
B	36	0.70579	0.00002
B	37	0.70580	0.00001
B	38	0.70583	0.00003
B	39	0.70584	0.00001
B	40	0.70586	0.00002
B	41	0.70587	0.00001
B	42	0.70589	0.00002
B	43	0.70591	0.00002
T	44	0.70596	0.00005
T	45	0.70601	0.00005
T	46	0.70607	0.00006
B	47	0.70610	0.00003
T	48	0.70613	0.00003
T	49	0.70615	0.00002
T	50	0.70616	0.00001
T	51	0.70626	0.00010
T	52	0.70626	0.00000
T	53	0.70627	0.00001
T	54	0.70632	0.00005
T	55	0.70633	0.00001
T	56	0.70640	0.00007
T	57	0.70648	0.00008
B	58	0.70673	0.00025
T	59	0.70678	0.00005
T	60	0.70719	0.00041
T	61	0.70729	0.00010
T	62	0.70762	0.00033
T	63	0.70821	0.00059
T	64	0.70831	0.00010
T	65	0.70881	0.00050
T	66	0.70923	0.00042
T	67	0.71013	0.00090
T	68	0.71020	0.00007

Type	Rank order #	$^{87}Sr/^{86}Sr$	Difference from preceding sample
B	69	0.71058	0.00038
T	70	0.71129	0.00071
T	71	0.71495	0.00366
T	72	0.71600	0.00105

Note: The rank order numbers correspond to those shown in figure 6.17.

ure 6.18). Tr-D ($^{87}Sr/^{86}Sr$=0.70719 and 0.70881) and Tr-F ($^{87}Sr/^{86}Sr$=0.70762 and 0.70831) have ratios consistent with those in Cusco, Ancon, Atacama, and possibly Tiwanaku, but they do not overlap with Nasca and Moquegua. Tr-N ($^{87}Sr/^{86}Sr$=0.70923 and 0.71020) is in the range expected for Tiwanaku but not other locales (at least based on what has been published thus far), and Tr-R ($^{87}Sr/^{86}Sr$=0.70626 and 0.70729) is consistent with those observed for Nasca and Moquegua. This is not meant to imply that they are from those particular areas; those nonlocal strontium isotope values may represent a combination of

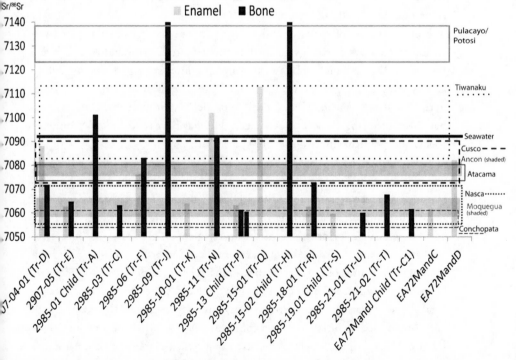

Figure 6.18. Strontium isotope ratios for bone-tooth pairs from Conchopata trophy heads. These are compared to strontium isotope ratios in other Andean regions. Among the 18 trophy head individuals, 14 fall outside the strontium isotope ratio associated with Conchopata and four are within the local range.

different geologic zones, or geologic zones not yet studied in the Andes. Instead, the salient point is that the trophy heads derive from a variety of regions, showing that individuals from diverse areas may have voluntarily migrated to the Wari heartland or Wari warriors took captives from several different geological zones and brought them back to Conchopata.

Trophy Heads Taken in Raids and Battles

Given that the majority of the trophy heads (14/18=78%) exhibit strontium isotope ratios outside the local range, it appears that Wari military agents occasionally traveled to distant locales to obtain captives, or just their heads. The victims were not isolated to adult men, decreasing the likelihood that the battlefield was the only context for obtaining captives and trophies. Rather, because nearly a quarter of the trophy heads come from children, it is probable that many were taken during village raids. Among the five child trophy heads/hands with known strontium isotope ratios, three come from regions outside the Wari heartland, suggesting that children were sometimes abducted from other communities. Thus, like the men, children were taken captive and brought back to Conchopata, or they were sometimes killed at the conflict site, where Wari warriors took their heads and hands as trophies.

Killing enemies' offspring or abducting them for later sacrifice may have been an intentional Wari strategy to further consolidate control and establish authority in diverse regions. This has been a common strategy for many ruling and aspiring ruling groups, from ancient Chinese dynasties to the Bolsheviks in the Russian revolution (Pipes 1991). In particular, the abducted children may have been offspring of local elites, a tactic that may have rendered Wari military agents and political elites all the more powerful.

Conversely, the child trophy heads may also represent children who were willingly "donated," perhaps for sacrifice, something akin to the Inka *capacocha*, in which children were sacrificed to mountain deities (Ceruti 2004; Gentile L 1996; Guaman Poma de Ayala et al. 1987 [1615]; Reinhard 2005) or to celebrate achievements by Inka lords, such as the new reign of an Inka ruler or a successful military campaign (Betanzos 1551; Sarmiento de Gamboa 1999 [1572]). In Inka society, the kin and community of the sacrificed children perceived the act as an honor, which also served to create political alliances between Inka rulers and local elites. If Wari children were similarly willingly sacrificed, the practice may have functioned to integrate those communities—whether local or foreign— into the Wari Empire, much as the Inka capacocha was meant to do. Although the osteological and strontium data do not clarify whether these children (and adults) were abducted or willingly sacrificed by donor communities, the ceramic iconography sheds some light on how they may have been obtained and used in rituals.

Coordinated Representations of Trophy Heads and Captives to Control the Body Politic

The art on Wari ceramics is spectacular, illuminating parts of the prisoner-taking process and showing how trophy heads could have been displayed. Strontium isotope data indicate that the majority of trophy heads are nonlocals—presumably enemies of the Wari state—so it may come as no surprise that Wari iconography shows Wari warriors and deities holding captives (figures 6.19 and 6.20). Figure 6.19 is a sherd from a large ceramic urn recovered by Isbell and Cook at Conchopata (Isbell and Cook 2002); it shows the Front Face Staff Deity holding a prisoner with hands bound behind the back. The Winged Profile Sacrificer, to its right, dangles a fleshed trophy head from a staff, physiognomy intact. This suggests that at least one phase of a trophy head's social life included its display while still recognizable by viewers. Apparently, in a subsequent ritual phase, some of the soft tissue and muscles (such as the masseter muscle) were cut off. (Not all musculature was removed, however. The burn patterns on

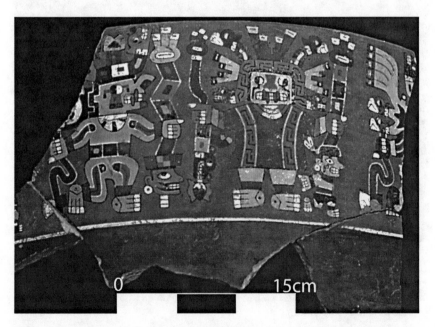

Figure 6.19. Front Face Staff Deity controlling a bound prisoner (*right*) and Winged Profile Sacrificer dangling a fleshed trophy head (*left*). (Courtesy of William Isbell and Anita Cook.)

Figure 6.20. Ceramic iconography showing Wari warriors holding captives.
Clockwise from top: Ceramic fragment from the Monqachayoq sector at Huari;
fragments from Conchopata (Sector A) showing prisoners led by rope; ceramic bottle
from Peruvian coastal site (from Museo de Antropología e Historia, Lima). (Photos
courtesy of José Ochatoma.)

one trophy head show that the temporalis muscle was still intact when it was partially burned.) The exact relationship between the bound prisoner and the trophy head is unknown, but it may well represent the process whereby captives were subsequently transformed into trophy heads.

Iconography on other Wari ceramics bolsters the notion that Wari individuals engaged in prisoner capture. On a sculpted bottle, a Wari warrior (identified as such based on the sun motif and other adornments [Ochatoma et al. 2008]) holds a prisoner by the hair, and on a ceramic cup fragment from the Monqachayoq sector at the capital site of Huari, a character identified as a Wari warrior is seen leading a prisoner by rope while he carries a weapon in the other hand (Ochatoma et al. 2008) (figure 6.20). Another example of a Wari captive depicted in the iconography is described by Ochatoma (2007). A fineware vessel was intentionally broken and placed in a pit in Sector A at Conchopata (on the west side of the modern road that runs to the airport), and it shows individuals wearing caps and facing forward. They have no visible face markings, they appear to be wearing loincloths with fringe, and their hands are tied with ropes (figure 6.20). As argued elsewhere (Ochatoma et al. 2008), the bound prisoners appear to be tied together in a line, reminiscent of the bound prisoners depicted in the Moche murals at Huaca del Brujo (Bourget 2006).

Another example of the parallels between art and activities can be seen on a ceramic fragment from the D-shaped ritual room (EA72). It shows a Wari warrior wearing a trophy head around his neck, with the trophy head face upright and facing forward. As noted earlier, a hole on the apex of a trophy head ensures that it dangles in this precise position. More notable, however, is that the warrior wears a tunic that resembles a jaguar pelt. Part of a jaguar paw with claws is also visible on the warrior's left shoulder (figure 6.21), leading to his identification as a "Jaguar Warrior" (Ochatoma and Cabrera 2002; Ochatoma et al. 2008), a familiar warrior-animal association, especially in the Aztec world (Benson 1998). As Cabrera (Ochatoma and Cabrera 2002) has suggested, jaguar behaviors, such as the act of defleshing and dismembering its victims, may have led Wari warriors to identify themselves with this animal. Indeed, the cut marks and chop marks on the trophy heads (described previously) indicate that these humans were defleshed and dismembered in a manner reminiscent of the feline predator. The spatial association between the physical remains of 10 human trophy heads—several of which were defleshed—and the ceramic urn depicting the Jaguar Warrior wearing a trophy head are astounding. All were recovered from the D-shaped structure (EA72). Thus, the shared behavioral qualities of the jaguar and Jaguar Warrior appear more than just artistic. Moreover, faunal analysis shows that feline skeletal parts are present at Conchopata in EA73N (Maita 2002).

Figure 6.21. *Top*: "Jaguar Warrior" wearing a fleshed trophy head around his neck. Note how the trophy head dangles facing forward; this would require a perforation on the apex of the cranial vault. A part of a jaguar's paw is visible on the warrior's left shoulder. *Bottom*: A disembodied head and hand depicted on a ceramic urn from the D-shaped ritual structure. (Both images by José Ochatoma.)

That a warrior is wearing the trophy head suggests that warriors were part of a ritual complex connected to military and physical prowess. The portrayal of these intact, strong bodies of warriors wearing disembodied heads demonstrates that they were both the "medium and the message," in much the same way that Yanomamo male bodies with their battle scars symbolized and generated aggressiveness (Scheper-Hughes and Lock 1987:25). Indeed, the Yanomamo male bodies, especially their heads (which were targeted in fights), were put "in the service of the body politic" (Scheper-Hughes and Lock 1987:25). For the Wari, the healthy, whole bodies of their own were in direct contrast to the defleshed and dismembered bodies of others, together creating a narrative of disciplined authority that led to power over "foreign" enemies and over its own populace as well. In short, the skeletal and iconographic evidence found together in a ritual space reflects a coordinated presentation of Wari warriors, their victims, and the valorization of the warriors' acts, a scene likely authored and promoted by Wari political, ritual, and military elites.

The hand phalanges recovered with the trophy heads also find a counterpart in Wari art. A ceramic urn fragment recovered from the D-shaped room displays a disembodied head and hand (Ochatoma and Cabrera 2002) (figure 6.21). This may suggest that disembodied heads and hands were perceived as the most valued body elements, given that both Wari artists and ritual specialists opted (or were instructed) to portray and physically modify those particular body parts.

As for many cultural groups, particular parts of the body may be perceived to house an individual's essence, whether the heart, head, or blood (Scheper-Hughes and Lock 1987). In Wari society, the head and hands may have been perceived in such a light. The dismemberment, display, and artistic depiction of those parts may have represented control over the entirety of the person. In a larger context, it may have been emblematic of Wari imperial control over the body politic. It was not, however, just an emblem of preexisting authority; the mangled and manipulated bodies also helped to generate authority, which Wari military personnel, ritual elites, and political leaders needed to govern, manage, and lead various Wari communities.

The images described above were not on small ceramic bowls produced in the home; rather, they were depicted on oversized ceramic urns likely produced by local master artisans for the state and its associates. They probably would have been fired in one of the large pit kilns or ovens (see Isbell and Cook 2002), requiring several adults to carry just one large urn. These beautiful urns were painted by master craftspeople, and some are so similar in design that Isbell and Cook (2002:263) have suggested that ceramics in different offering smashes may have been painted by the same master artist. In all, there is compelling evidence for savvy organization that coordinated various efforts to capture, dismember, display, artistically portray, and then ritually annihilate individual persons. This was achieved by focusing destructive acts on particular body parts that represented both the individual person and the social body. Furthermore, the braiding together of physical domination over bodies and their celebrations in art was further woven together with the representations of imposing, decorated warriors who carried out the violent acts. Together, these layered and coordinated media likely structured the behaviors and social and political norms of the Wari populace, further establishing imperial authority and its means of controlling the body politic.

Wari State Structures and the Agency of Military, Ritual, and Ceramic Specialists

Although single individuals could have been responsible for obtaining captives, processing their heads, and producing the fine polychrome ceramics, this seems unlikely. Instead, distinct classes of people with special skills may have been responsible for the various acts. The specialists involved may have included (1) military agents who conducted raids and engaged in battles to obtain captives and their heads; (2) a class of ritual specialists with knowledge of human anatomy and postmortem surgery who were viewed as having a special relationship to the supernatural; and (3) a group of artisans with mastery in ceramics, pigments, firing, and painting. Because each task likely required specialized knowledge and training, they were probably distinct classes of specialists. Although the impressive coordination between them could have been self-managed, their organization and standardization suggests oversight, perhaps by political elites. In other words, the three identifiable phases of trophy head creation were likely produced under the auspices of the Wari state. These state-sponsored activities may have included the coordination of military campaigns/raids and the maintenance of what appears to be an elite military class (Ochatoma and Cabrera 2002; Ochatoma et al. 2008), oversight and instruction on the detailed processing of trophy heads and elaborate trophy head rituals, and the production of ritual objects like the large polychrome ceramics depicting Wari deities, warriors, prisoners, and trophy heads.

State structuring of this sort, however, would not have precluded military personnel, ritual specialists, and master craftspeople from authoring social values and realizing their own agency. As Giddens (1984) has argued, structures both limit and enable action, such that actions that serve state goals might also serve one's self-interest and contribute to a self-inscribed identity. Violent actions by the individual military agents, and the performative valorizations of those acts (as shown in images of warriors in elaborate military garb wearing trophy heads around their necks), both signaled and created their own military prowess and authority. And while the creation of a military class may have been partly authored by high-level elites, it was also likely built upon preceding notions of value placed on military aptitude that the actors (warriors) themselves created and reinforced. Those within the military class thus likely played an active role in shaping and perpetuating state institutions and policies. In short, their acts could have been both self-serving and in the service of the state. Their aggressive acts represented the instantiation of such amorphous notions of Wari dominance, which in turn had real implications for the creation of certain social ideals and state policies. Those emergent structures (again) then reinforced and promoted the military class who engaged in prisoner capture and head taking, as well as the celebration of those violent acts.

In the same way that actions by the military class could be doubly impact-ful, ritual specialists could also carry out acts that served the self and the state. Cultural norms that cultivated a shared value regarding the significance of hu-man trophy heads imbued trophy head makers with ritual authority. As ritual specialists transformed living beings into sacred trophy head objects, they dem-onstrated their extraordinary knowledge, skills, and supernatural qualities and further enhanced the political and ritual value of trophy heads. Again, the ritual specialists who held these transformative powers may have been part of a greater state agenda that created a narrative of ritual exceptionalism within the Wari state, but their acts also highlighted their own ritual acumen and connections to the supernatural. This in turn would have been a powerful way to enhance their status within Wari communities.

The work of master artisans may have had a similar dual effect in which their arts were in the service of (and supported by) the Wari state, while also establishing their elite status as gifted artisans producing powerful imagery for elaborate rituals and ceremonies.

The Socially Generative Effect of Trophy Heads

While the agency of military, ritual, and artistic specialists may have been realized through their associations with Wari trophy heads, these corporeal objects were not merely passive symbols of preexisting authority for those who obtained them and made them. Thus, rather than viewing the trophy heads as simply a reflection of their elite status, they should be understood as objects that could create or generate authority for their makers. That is, trophy heads had a generative effect, or what Robb (2004) refers to as "effective agency." The trophy heads were socially generative, imbuing the ritual specialists with a unique identity and authoritative status. This does not mean, simply, that "objects have agency." Obviously, they do not have "conscious agency" or the volition of humans (Robb 2004). But these once-living subjects, who were ob-jectified in life and became permanent objects in death, were transformed into something wholly new: a ritual object with effective agency. This is a much more nuanced recognition of how objects can structure perceptions and shape future events; these ritual objects bestowed upon their handlers a particular kind of authority and legitimacy, enabling them to embody notions of Wari militarism and ritual exceptionalism.

The Foreign Female Sacrifice

Not all Wari captives may have been killed and transformed into trophy heads. For example, the 17–22-year-old female (B-1371-01.01), described in chapter 4, was buried alone in EA20 and exhibits a nonlocal strontium isotope ratio. Her body was deposited near the entrance of the D-shaped structure (EA72), suggesting that she may have been a sacrifice to sanctify the building and the rituals that occurred there. Her unique treatment and the fact that she was not transformed into a trophy head like the men and children suggests that Wari society may have structured the treatment of abducted individuals based on age and sex. That is, men and children may have been deemed appropriate for dismemberment and transformation into trophy heads, while females were kept wholly intact and ritually sacrificed and deposited in spaces external to the walled limits of the ritual buildings.

Majes Valley Trophy Heads

Trophy Heads at Beringa

Among the thousands of human skeletal remains recovered from Beringa, only one partial cranium exhibited modifications indicative of a trophy head. The post-mortem modification on the trophy head included one intentionally drilled hole on the center of the frontal bone. The rest of the cranium was absent, so the occipital bone could not be observed to determine if the foramen magnum had been enlarged to extract the brain. Given that only a portion of the frontal bone was present, its age could not be determined, but it was clearly not an infant or child. Observations for cranial wounds were not possible due to the poor preservation.

The presence of only one trophy head from the village site of Beringa is consistent with the archaeological data that indicate this was a community of agriculturalists and fishers, not a community of ritual specialists who engaged in the decapitation and mutilation of humans and human body parts.

Trophy Heads at La Real

La Real was quite distinct from Beringa in regard to the number of trophy heads. At La Real, there were at least seven adult trophy heads, which is not surprising given the ceremonial nature of the site. Although the Peruvian archaeologists who excavated La Real reliably described all of the trophy heads in their field notes, I personally observed only four of them.[2] Two of them still have the carrying cord threaded through the hole on the center of the frontal bone (figure 6.22). All trophy heads had an expanded foramen magnum, indicating that the occipital base was intentionally destroyed to extract the brain, similar to what has been described of trophy heads from Nasca (Browne et al. 1993; Silverman and Proulx 2002; Verano 1995; Williams et al. 2001).

The four examined trophy heads represent two males and two unsexed adults. One of the unsexed adults exhibits a gracile glabella and supraorbital

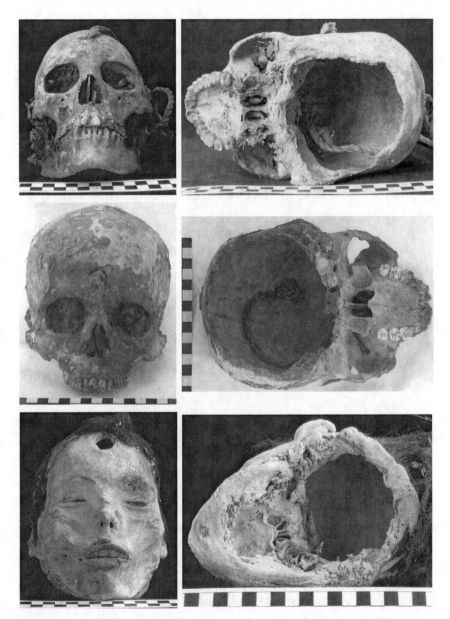

Figure 6.22. La Real trophy heads showing perforation on frontal bone and the enlarged foramen magnum.

margin (and could be interpreted as female), but the nuchal crest is intermediate and the mental eminence of the mandible is robust. Thus, it was not assigned a sex. The two males were 20–25 years old at the time of death. The other individuals were young adults. The age and sex of the three additional trophy heads described in the excavators' field notes are unknown.

Other Trophy Heads in the Majes Valley

Two trophy heads from the Majes valley museum in the town of Aplao were also examined, and because of the rarity of trophy heads, particularly outside of Nasca contexts, they are presented here for comparative purposes. Their exact provenience is unknown, but they were certainly collected by a local person from one of the archaeology sites in the middle Majes valley. While it is possible that the unprovenienced trophy heads derive from a pre–Middle Horizon context, this is unlikely given the dearth of early sites in the valley (de la Vera Cruz Chávez 1989; Garcia Márquez and Bustamante Montoro 1990). The first exhibits a hole on the center of the frontal bone, similar to those from Nasca, from which extends a carrying cord (figure 6.23). This trophy head victim was over 18 years old at the time of death, as indicated by the presence of third molars. The robust mandible indicates that this trophy head is a probable male. The facial skin and scalp are preserved, and the eyes are stuffed with raw cotton, a common botanical product included with mortuary remains during the Middle Horizon in the Majes valley. A red wig/headdress covers the individual's hair and the superior portion of the frontal bone and part of the parietals. The cranium has been cut slightly posterior to the coronal suture, such that the trophy head resembles a face mask. Cranial wounds were unobservable because of the preservation of soft tissue.

The second trophy head from the Majes valley museum exhibits an intentionally drilled hole slightly posterior to bregma, similar to those from Conchopata, and the occipital base shows intentional destruction, indicating that the brain was removed (figure 6.23). A knotted carrying cord is threaded through the hole at bregma, ensuring that the head could be displayed upright and looking forward. This trophy head is a middle-aged adult without any cranial wounds. No soft tissue is preserved, and because no cut marks were observed, it could have decomposed naturally. Notably, the cranium exhibits cranial modification in the tabular erect style, suggesting that the person derived from the yungas-coastal zone and was not likely from the highland region of the Wari heartland. Recent survey in the middle Majes valley has revealed another Wari-style trophy head (it has a perforation at bregma) from the site of Uraca: an adult male with a large healed wound on the left anterior of his cranium (Koontz 2011).

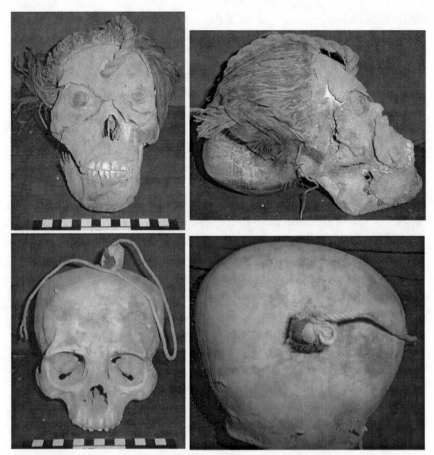

Figure 6.23. Trophy heads housed at the local museum in the town of Aplao. *Top:* Nasca-style trophy head "mask" from the middle Majes valley. The ceramic bowl supporting the skull in the side view is not part of the cranium. *Bottom:* Wari-style trophy head with hole drilled near bregma.

The presence of Wari-style trophy heads in the Majes valley suggests that the local Majes people were aware of the Wari trophy head style, one that was clearly distinct from their Nasca neighbors to the west. Further, those Wari-style trophy heads suggest intense interaction between Majes and Wari communities, interactions that may have been occasionally antagonistic in nature.

Conclusions: Wari Raids for Captives for Both Sacrifice and Trophy Heads

In the Wari heartland, current osteological and archaeological evidence indicate that Wari warriors traveled to foreign locales to obtain captives, likely for subsequent sacrifice rituals, and certainly to transform them into trophy heads. The demographic profile of the Wari trophy heads shows that adult men were preferred as trophies, though children were taken nearly a quarter of the time. This suggests that village raids at which young children were present were common contexts in which people were taken captive. Moreover, the cranial trauma frequency among trophy heads, though high (42%), is not significantly different from Conchopata and other Wari-affiliated populations in the south (Tung 2007b). This suggests that the trophy head victims were not a special class of warriors but commoner men who may have fought on occasion, perhaps during raids on their communities.

While some trophy heads could have been manufactured from naturally deceased community members or judicial killings of locals, this seems less likely in light of Wari iconography showing a bound captive and a trophy head together on a ritual urn and scenes of captives controlled by Wari warriors. Furthermore, the strontium isotope data indicate that a majority of the adult and child trophy heads were from foreign locales, likely taken captive by Wari warriors.

The Wari are not unique in their practice of captive taking. Amazonian groups and other native groups from the Americas took captives before European contact and during the colonial era (Cameron 2008; Fausto 2007; Trigger 1985). Archaeological and historical research has shown that raids and full-scale battles could lead to the capture of men, women, and children. In the Iroquoian and Huron culture area, for example, men were often taken captive and killed in a spectacularly brutal fashion, though they could also be adopted by the local community (Trigger 1985). At Conchopata, the data indicate that men were not incorporated into the local community. Women may have been brought into the community on rare occasions, albeit with a lower social standing, or only temporarily, until they could have been sacrificed, like the adolescent female in front of the D-shaped ritual building.

In all, Wari rituals may have included the sacrifice of prisoners, followed by their transformation into trophy heads. Given the plethora of evidence of human sacrifice in the Andes (Bourget 2001; Ceruti 2004; Cordy-Collins 2001; Gaither et al. 2008; Reinhard 1996; Verano 2001), the skeletal evidence for dismemberment and possible decapitation, and the prisoner/trophy head iconography on state-produced ceramics, the evidence that Wari engaged in sacrifice is compelling. Moreover, not only was human sacrifice part of the Wari ritual repertoire but, I also suggest, Wari state structures were used to facilitate and promote this ritual production and destruction of human bodies and trophy heads. These acts of violence against the body were not random or unplanned. Rather, they seem to have been well-orchestrated acts that brought together military elites who obtained prisoners and heads, ritual specialists with supernatural and technical skills to transform humans into trophy heads, and master artisans who could portray elaborately dressed warriors and deities with prisoners and trophy heads on large, state-produced urns.

The demographic pattern of the trophy head victims suggests that adult men may have been more valued as "symbols" or "substitutes" for the community at large (see Kelly 2000), but any individual body—a child, for example—could suffice as a stand-in for the whole community. Thus, the broken body of one could both symbolize and generate the breakdown of the social body of victim communities.

As the Wari Empire expanded into other domains, the act of so explicitly controlling and destroying the bodies of others aided in creating the authority necessary to subjugate particular populations. I am not suggesting that this was done in all regions; rather, there is compelling evidence that this was occasionally done to particular populations in the process of subjugating and incorporating them into the Wari domain. In this way, some communities were violently brought under the control of the Wari Empire, while others were incorporated more peaceably, perhaps through religious ritual and attendant feasts that strategically incorporated local belief systems into the Wari pantheon (Goldstein et al. 2009; Williams and Nash 2006). These different approaches to imperial expansion point to savvy and calculated strategies by Wari leaders, administrators, and military and religious elites. The presence of human trophy heads in Conchopata's ritual structures, as well as the artistic portrayals of how they were obtained and displayed, point to only one of several strategies employed by Wari elites to expand their rule throughout various Andean regions.

Conclusions

Life and Death in the Wari World

The policies and practices of the Wari Empire profoundly affected certain aspects of morbidity and lifestyle of both the conquering and the subject populations. They not only impacted disease and trauma rates but also affected ritual and mortuary practices and forms of social organization, resulting from and contributing to the reshuffling of political, social, and economic networks. The sociopolitical changes and related impacts on well-being and lifeways, however, were not always uniformly experienced by those within the Wari world. For some, the time of Wari imperial rule brought great opportunities for status enhancement, for example, among Wari military agents and ritual specialists. For others, however, Wari expansionist policies brought violence, and sometimes abductions and death, as seen in the remains of trophy head victims.

This study began with questions regarding how Wari imperialism affected various groups of people in the Wari heartland and southern hinterland and also inquired how peoples' actions and reactions affected the nature of Wari governance and strategies of control. These issues were addressed by placing the bioarchaeological body at the center of analysis and combining those insights with what was known from archaeological studies of the Wari Empire specifically, and archaic imperialism more generally. For example, prior to this bioarchaeological study, much was known about Wari domestic architecture (Isbell and McEwan 1991b), and we now have complementary information on the demographic profile and social organization of Wari-affiliated households and how those differed from one community to another.

Bioarchaeological research presented elsewhere (Tung and Del Castillo 2005) has also shown how ecological context and related dietary behaviors can affect physiological health status. In some areas of the southern Wari periphery, local ecology and foods created a more homogenous health profile for communities, despite social status differences, as was seen at Beringa and La Real in the Majes valley. There, similar percentages of individuals exhibited cribra orbitalia, an indicator of general physiological stress and poor nutrition (see Walker et al. 2009).

In contrast, the social contexts in which violence occurred seem to have differed among the groups in this study, though its frequency was notably similar. We have also gained a more intimate understanding of how ritual D-shaped buildings—identified by scholars decades ago—were used by imperial heartland elites. The skeletonized remains of broken bodies reveal a tale of Wari aggression deployed in a politically savvy manner, perhaps to ensure that these captive bodies were put in the service of promoting state supremacy and highlighting the exceptionalism of its military agents and ritual specialists.

Community Organization during the Wari Era

An intriguing observation gained from this study is the unbalanced sex profile at Conchopata, where women significantly outnumber men. The preliminary data on this trend (Tung 2001) led Isbell (2007; Isbell and Cook 2002) to posit that Conchopata was organized around elite polygynous households, to which he further noted—based on architectural data—that Conchopata was "a community of palaces," (Isbell 2001b) inhabited by a royal male or males and other elites. In contrast to Isbell, I have suggested that the unbalanced sex distribution is a result of men journeying on state projects, whether related to military or administrative purposes, thus leading to relatively lower numbers of men at the settlement. If extended family units were living at Conchopata but men were deployed elsewhere (as the foreign trophy heads at Conchopata suggest), then the observed sex distribution would be expected. Moreover, the rarity of nonlocal females at Conchopata (as indicated by strontium isotope data) further suggests that the unequal sex distribution is shaped more by the dearth of men than by the overabundance of women. The strontium isotope data also show that Conchopata was constituted of local people; it was not a cosmopolitan center to which foreigners migrated to settle. In short, the observed age-at-death and sex ratios at Conchopata have provided new views about how Wari heartland communities were organized.

Given that Conchopata was a center for the production of elaborate polychrome ceramics (Pozzi-Escot B. 1991), which were later intentionally destroyed in rituals (Cook and Glowacki 2003; Isbell and Cook 2002; Ochatoma and Cabrera 2002), perhaps these extended family groups included individuals who were high-end craft producers. The enormous and beautifully decorated ceramic urns, many of which were ritually destroyed in ritual spaces, indicate that a class of skilled artisans were producing these valuable goods for state ceremonies. Ritual specialists may have also resided with their families at the site, or they may have traveled there from the neighboring capital, located approximately 12 kilometers away. The ritual specialists likely prepared the trophy heads and oversaw many components of the rituals in the D-shaped structures, a role that would have garnered them high status in the local community and perhaps the core region more generally.

The Conchopata community may have also included deployable personnel, such as males engaged in military campaigns. Specifically, some Conchopata males may have been involved in raiding other settlements to obtain captives and trophy heads, just as the osteological, strontium, and iconographic data suggest. Some of these men may have never returned to their families living at Conchopata in order to receive proper burial.

The settlement at Beringa in the Majes valley comprises equal numbers of adult males and females, and nearly half of the skeletal population is represented by infants and children. Thus, the Beringa demographic profile appears to represent a single community settlement probably organized around extended-family households. This corresponds well with the archaeological data indicating Beringa was a village community that engaged in agricultural and textile production, as well as fishing and shrimping in the Majes River.

Beringa was a village where community members were buried over several generations. There is some archaeological evidence indicating that ceremonies occurred at the site, but they do not approach the ceremonial significance of the neighboring site of La Real, located eight kilometers downriver. That only one trophy head was recovered from Beringa is consistent with the archaeological context indicating that Beringa was a village of households with small-scale rituals; it does not appear to have been a major ritual center.

While the demographic profiles at Conchopata and Beringa may reflect the once-living populations that inhabited each site, the demographic distribution from La Real does not; it is not representative of a single-settlement community. Instead, it appears to represent an exclusive class of people from the nearby settlement, or from several settlements in the valley, who were selected for burial at this high-status ceremonial and funerary site. Based on the demographic profile, this exclusive mortuary class includes primarily adult men; the sex distribution at La Real shows significantly more males than females relative to a symmetrical sex distribution. Also, infants and children constitute only one-quarter of the burial population, suggesting that juveniles were infrequently selected for interment at La Real. Moreover, the high frequency of nonlethal cranial trauma among men suggests that their status may have been linked to prowess in battles ("real" or ritual) or physical conflict resolution. In short, their aggressive actions in life may have helped them earn distinction in death.

Heartland Living Better for Community Health

Although data on cribra orbitalia and porotic hyperostosis are not presented in detail in this volume, previous research shows that the highland Conchopata community exhibited significantly lower frequencies of porotic lesions than those in the southern hinterland (Tung 2003). This observation parallels other studies that have shown lower rates of porotic lesions among highland communities relative to lowland ones (Blom et al. 2004; Burgess 1999; Hrdlička 1914; Ubelaker 1992; Ubelaker and Newson 2002). This suggests that ecological factors may have contributed to the observed differences. Lowland, semitropical environments (yungas zones) that are low on the watershed may be more conducive to the spread of pathogens that lead to anemia or other nutritional and vitamin deficiencies; those physiological stressors could have led to the cranial lesions known as cribra orbitalia and porotic hyperostosis. In particular, contaminated water and river resources (such as crayfish) from the Majes River resulted in similar pathogen loads for the Majes populations, regardless of status. Thus, although there were differences in how the Beringa commoners versus La Real elites articulated with Wari imperial policies, parasite exposure from local resources appears to have swamped those distinctions and contributed to a similar disease experience—inasmuch as anemia and related physiological stressors were concerned—for those who lived in the Majes valley. Similarly, there were no differences between the sexes; both men and women in the Wari-era Majes valley exhibited similar rates of porotic lesions on the cranium. This appears to be one facet of health for which sex and social status had little effect; both communities consumed the contaminated water and river resources, and about half those who died before age 15 and a quarter of those who died in adulthood suffered the health consequences.

No Pax Wari in the Southern Wari Region

For those living in the Majes valley of Wari's southern domain, violence was a common occurrence; nearly one out of three adults exhibit cranial trauma, and both men and women were affected. It is difficult to establish whether this violence was a result of warfare and raids by Wari military agents from the imperial heartland, or whether it was conflict at the intravalley (local) level expressed through raids, tinku-like battles, and physical conflict resolution. The absence of Wari administrative centers in the middle Majes valley, however, suggests that Wari imperial agents (military or administrative) were not present; as such, it is unlikely that Wari warriors were attacking these communities. Nevertheless, the large quantity of Wari artifacts at Beringa and especially at La Real, as well as the locations of these sites en route to the Wari administrative outpost of Cerro Baúl in the Moquegua valley, indicate that middle Majes populations were tied into the Wari trade network and macroregional political economy. That, combined with the evidence for violence, suggests that Wari policies and actions contributed to the destabilization of political networks, social organization, and other social institutions among those in the southern periphery. In other words, although there is limited evidence that Wari warriors were personally inflicting injuries against Majes populations, Wari policies apparently destabilized some hinterland regions, adversely affecting areas without direct Wari administrative presence. While it is possible that widespread violence was the norm among Majes communities in the pre-Wari era, the evidence presented here shows that Wari rule did little to curb violence in the southern hinterland.

Gendered Violence

Percentages of persons with head trauma were similar among the three communities, and females from all sites showed a similar cranial trauma pattern—wounds on the posterior of the head. Based on this pattern, I suggest that there may have been a Middle Horizon pan-Andean concept regarding appropriate forms of physical abuse and corporeal punishment toward women and/or common techniques in subduing and injuring women in the context of raids. Across the three sites examined here, women sustained injuries in much the same manner. Injuries were nonlethal and likely sustained while women were fleeing from an attack or ducking their heads to avert an oncoming blow. That females were formally engaged in military conflicts is unlikely; they do not exhibit anterior wounds, and they are not depicted in military scenes in the iconography, though they are depicted in other contexts (for example, shown breast-feeding a jaguar [Isbell and Cook 2002]). It is also possible that some women were injured in intrahousehold disputes, either by their domestic partners or elder affines (such as a mother-in-law), as has been documented ethnographically among Quechua-speaking peasants in Bolivia (Van Vleet 2002). Also, there may have been some households in which primary or secondary wives or female domestic servants were beaten. Current data sets make it difficult to distinguish between those categories of women. For example, the elderly female with annular cranial modification who was buried alone at Conchopata was likely viewed as an outsider and frequently beaten; however, whether she was a servant, a wife, or both, who was beaten by her domestic partner or social superior is unknown. Despite the ambiguities in determining the details of the social contexts in which female-directed violence emerged, the salient point is that it was nonlethal, and the blows targeted areas other than the face.

While female patterns of trauma were similar, the location of head wounds among males was distinct at each site. This suggests that males in each community were involved in different kinds of violence. Injured males from Conchopata showed a more dispersed pattern of head wounds, and two men in particular exhibited anterior head wounds, as expected for those engaged in face-to-face conflicts. Beringa males displayed wounds primarily on the anterior and posterior of their skulls, and they showed the highest frequency of perimortem trauma among the three groups in this study. The wound locations and their lethality suggest that Beringa men may have been injured in raids on their village, though other contexts, such as intracommunity violence or formal battles, could have led to some of the injuries.

The wounded men from La Real showed the most consistent distribution of cranial trauma, whereby the significant majority was located on the frontal bone. Of those anterior wounds, 70 percent were located on the left side. As I have argued, this suggests that La Real men squared off in standardized forms of violent interaction such that the left side of the head was particularly vulnerable to a blow from a right-handed attacker. Notably, these head injuries were not fatal. While this could be evidence that the injured men successfully defended their lives during warfare battles, it is also possible that the perpetrators struck them without lethal intent. A similar pattern of nonlethal trauma among prehistoric Chumash males from central coastal California led Walker (1989) and Lambert (1994) to suggest that the injuries resulted from physical conflict resolution in which men squared off in physical combat. This form of ritualized violence has also been documented among the Yanomamo and the Oro-Warí of Amazonia. It is possible that the La Real men sustained these nonfatal injuries in a similar manner.

Overall, the slight differences in head wound frequency and the significant distinctions in head wound distribution between the sexes indicate that violence emerged in unique social contexts for men versus women. In particular, adult males were more often in situations where they faced their attackers, resulting in the numerous anterior cranial wounds. Women, in contrast, were commonly injured while fleeing or positioning their body in a defensive posture (for example, lowering the head) to avoid an oncoming blow.

Masculine Identity in the Wari Empire

These bodily patterns of injury reveal much about gender roles in Wari society, showing that physical assertiveness may have been a behavioral norm for men, something that was inculcated into them through discourse, imagery, and daily observations of other men. Certainly, as the military iconography from Conchopata and Huari shows, a warrior identity that emphasized aggressiveness (carrying weapons, trophy heads, and prisoners) was a quality that was celebrated in art and presumably in ceremonies. This served to turn men into warriors, likely in the service of state goals but also in the service of their own social advancement. The ways in which Wari warriors were valorized in iconography suggest that this was at least one means for status enhancement for men. Militaristic actions may well have been an integral part of masculine identity in Wari society.

That I propose this does not make it a blind assumption of what Vandkilde (2003:137) calls the "myth of the courageous warrior." That is, I am not assuming that an ideology promoting the valorization of a brave male warrior is a natural outcome. I agree with Vandkilde (2003) that attitudes toward warriors and their belligerent actions may not have always been celebrated. Rather, a shared ideology that links masculine identity with the qualities of a successful warrior must be constructed and maintained, sometimes in the face of competing discourses. In the case of Wari society, there is ample evidence to demonstrate that aggressive actions by warriors were valorized and socially valued; this is not an a priori assumption but a conclusion based on several lines of data.

For example, based on violence-related trauma, male warrior iconography, enemy trophy heads (mostly from men from distant locales), and an unbalanced sex profile in which Conchopata men are missing, I argue that there was a concerted effort to valorize the male warrior and his risky and violent actions. Part of this celebrated warrior narrative emanated from those in and near the urban capital who controlled the complex production of huge, polychrome ceramic urns that were decorated by master artisans. Those finely produced urns (and other vessels) had colorful depictions of Wari warriors engaged in hostile acts, such as wielding weapons, wearing human trophy heads, and holding prisoners by their hair. This iconographic propaganda was produced by those with the means to acquire the necessary raw materials and the technological know-how to build large, high-temperature kilns and fire the elaborately decorated oversized vessels. Those engaged in the ceramic production may have been elite individuals who were well integrated into the Wari state apparatus. Indeed, this production process would have served to further enmesh them within the state system. That is, with each urn produced and prominently displayed in a ceremony, the significant roles of ceramic producers and master artisans were solidified and folded into Wari society, as were narratives about the characters (warriors) portrayed on the urns. In this way, we gain a glimpse into the ways that ceramic production and ceremonies may have served to promote warriorhood in Wari society.

This should not imply, however, that the normalizing narratives about warrior identity were top-down only, or that the men who adopted warrior identities were dupes of Wari imperial policy, blindly carrying out tasks in the interest of the state. Instead, they may have been active agents in the construction of these discourses, perhaps contributing to a dominant notion of what it took to be perceived as a valued member of Wari society. In other words, the social (and state) structures enabled action and opportunity for a subgroup of men in Wari society, and the militaristic actions of the men themselves contributed to the notions that military prowess was a "natural" path to power and status. Their acts also demonstrated "normal" ways of being in Wari society, especially for men.

Although the structures of Wari society may have enabled or promoted certain kinds of actions (such as militaristic violence) for particular groups of people, these structures also limited options. Clearly, this harkens back to Giddens's (1984) point on how social structures can be simultaneously enabling and constraining. By their very definition, social structures structure access to opportunities, resources, and mates, for example, as well as structuring behaviors, attitudes, and beliefs, among other things. Thus, through the celebrated Wari warrior, we can see how attributes of the warrior identity were tied to militaristic achievements that served state goals; however, the warrior identity may have also limited the paths that men could take to enhance and maintain their standing in Wari society. Was warriorhood the only way to gain status in Wari society? Probably not. Master artisans and other social or occupational categories also may have been status-enhancing positions; they are just not as visible based on the data sets explored in this book. As such, I do not mean to imply that warriorhood was the *only* means for social recognition, but these data hint that there may have been a narrow range of opportunities and limited options for individuals to gain social, spiritual, or material advancements in Wari society. Moreover, the value placed on warrior status may have been accessible by only a small group of individuals; for example, females were apparently excluded from pursuing this role, at least as communicated in Wari art and based on the patterning of female head trauma, in which the absence of anterior wounds suggests violence in nonmilitary contexts.

While the perspective of the valiant warrior dominates aspects of Wari material culture and site layout (such as prominent ritual buildings where warriors and their trophy head victims were displayed), attitudes toward Wari warriors could have varied internally (see Vandkilde 2003), both by the warriors themselves and by others in society. Counternarratives to the valorized male warrior identity may be seen in the large numbers of males with no trauma, suggesting that a significant portion of men buried at Conchopata did not engage in activities that were promoted through prominent ceremonies and iconography. It is unclear whether some men were simply excluded (as noted above) or opted out of militaristic activities by choice, perhaps taking up other valued roles in Wari society (for example, master artisan, ritual specialist, parent, or some other role). Nonetheless, the demographic and trauma data demonstrate that only a portion of adults were directly tied into the Wari military apparatus, highlighting it as a relatively unique role in Wari society, one that was apparently valued and worthy of being singled out and portrayed in Wari art.

Indeed, ceramic iconography suggests that the various styles of military garb, body positioning, and weaponry are a reflection of an exclusive military class akin to military officers (Ochatoma et al. 2008). As discussed in chapters 5 and 6, there appear to be at least three warrior groups, or military subclasses, identified based on shared characteristics depicted in iconography. One of the most intriguing is the Jaguar Warrior (Ochatoma et al. 2008), distinct from but not unlike those in the Aztec realm (Benson 1998). The Wari Jaguar Warrior is named as such because of his jaguar pelt, the jaguar paw on his left shoulder, and his association with the dismembered human trophy head. Like the feline predator, the Jaguar Warrior dismembers and defleshes his victims. The defleshed and dismembered human trophy heads were found in the same ritual room as the ceramic fragment showing the Jaguar Warrior wearing a trophy head; this provides compelling evidence for the linkages between the idealized behaviors of the Jaguar Warrior and those actions that he actually carried out.

Together, the iconographic and osteological data suggest that the emergence of a military class was part of a larger Wari imperial program that both emanated from it and simultaneously helped to produce it. The military class and its ranks may have been partly authored by high-level political elites, but it was also likely built upon preceding notions of value placed on military skill that the actors (warriors) themselves created and reinforced. Those within the military class thus probably played an active role in shaping and perpetuating state institutions and policies, making it difficult to differentiate between military and political authority. The establishment and maintenance of Wari imperial authority may have been born of the indivisibility of military might and political legitimacy. The data presented here, then, support the notion that the expansion of Wari was likely related to an ideology of dominance, some of which was reified through the emergence of a military class, the material markers that identified them, and the attendant rituals that celebrated their exploits, as when prisoners were paraded, captive bodies were dismembered, and the disembodied heads of enemies were displayed and worn as trophies.

Wari Militarism and Ritualism and Their Roles in Imperial Expansion

Wari leaders created a militaristic apparatus emboldened by ritual legitimation that enabled imperial expansion and maintenance of Wari authority throughout much of the Peruvian Andes. The evidence for this comes from various lines of data, one of which is the significant dearth of male burials at Conchopata, suggesting that men were sent away on military and administrative campaigns. Furthermore, osteological and iconographic evidence suggests the presence of a military program with elite warriors, some of whom may have engaged in prisoner capture, bringing captives home for transformation into trophy heads.

Given that there were two ritual structures with trophy heads used at different times, from the late Huarpa/early Wari era (EA143) to the middle to late Wari era (EA72), the practice of taking enemy captives and dismembering their bodies to create trophy heads was not a one-time occurrence. Indeed, in order to maintain a militaristic ideology, this act needed to be repeated again and again, reflecting and affirming Wari values while simultaneously creating them. Moreover, the coordinated repetition of iconography depicting warriors, weapons, and trophy heads served a similar purpose, as did the rituals in which these heads were displayed. Creating and sustaining an ideology that supports policies of imperial expansion and militarism is not an easy feat, yet savvy Wari leaders seem to have achieved some success in promoting this ideology and attendant policies during the Middle Horizon.

In addition to the militarism, ritual practices and the supernatural legitimacy that those rituals provided to the practitioners appear to have been a coordinated aspect of constructing and maintaining Wari supremacy. While there could have been tensions and plays for political power between military and ritual leaders, the osteological and iconographic evidence may suggest more coordination than conflict, at least within the realm of ritual acts involving trophy heads made from enemies' bodies. That is, the presence of human trophy heads and mutilated body parts in Wari ritual structures suggests coordination between military personnel, who were likely responsible for obtaining enemy prisoners, and ritual specialists who dismembered the enemy bodies and transformed them into trophies for use in ritual ceremonies. With each prisoner (or head) captured, the status of that military agent likely increased, as exemplified in Wari art showing the Jaguar Warrior wearing a trophy head around his neck as he brandishes a weapon.

In the same way that a warrior's status increased by obtaining a captive or head, the ritual specialist's authority increased with each new head that s/he processed. The very act of creating a trophy head legitimated the ritual practitioner's expertise, knowledge, and ritual acumen. Drawing from a social practice perspective, I suggest that the act of preparing the trophy head served to establish and affirm the legitimacy of that person to carry out the important task. Thus, the ritual specialists were tightly linked to the military agents who supplied the bodies; these were the corporal entities through which ritual practitioners could demonstrate their ritual exceptionalism. Reciprocally, the military personnel were tied to ritual leaders who aided in authoring narratives of military prowess and reaffirmed the military agents' integral status in the Wari state system. The military and ritual players are unlikely to have been one and the same, as each class would have required immense specialization and knowledge within each realm; thus, a negotiated coordination was a likely strategy. The nature of their relationships with political elites, however, is unknown, as is the possibility that political elites were constituted by military and/or ritual specialists. That is, it is unclear whether political power was consolidated by military or ritual leaders, such that distinctions between them are undetectable. This would not have been a unique form of political organization relative to other times and places, as theocracies and despotic rulers throughout history have shown. Nonetheless, future research is needed to explore whether or not military elites or ritual specialists (or both) constituted the political leadership in Wari society, or whether these classes functioned as distinct entities, constantly negotiating collaborations and perhaps entering into conflict with each other. Although the reasons for the Wari demise are as of yet unknown, future investigations may find evidence of these internal conflicts and the partial role they may have played in the eventual decline of Wari imperial authority around AD 1000–1100.

Other Tools of Imperial Expansion

Although much of the data from this study reveals aspects of Wari militarism, this does not mean that this was the only means for consolidating power. Of course, to observe the violence-related trauma, the foreign trophy heads, and the militaristic iconography and then not discuss the role of Wari militarism would have been to selectively ignore a prominent aspect of Wari society, at least as it is apparent through the body and in art depicted on vessels used in rituals. Clearly, if food refuse or utilitarian wares or skeletal metric data had been the focus of this study, the points being emphasized in this conclusion would be quite different. As such, this study should not be taken as evidence that militarism and ritualism were the *only* means of establishing and maintaining Wari authority. As research at Cerro Baúl (an administrative and ceremonial Wari site) and other Wari sites in the Moquegua valley have shown (Feldman 1998; Moseley et al. 1991; Nash 2002; Williams 2001; Williams 2002; Williams and Nash 2006), Wari imperial elites may have colonized this region, setting up an "embassy-like enclave" (Moseley et al. 2005:17264). Perhaps these Wari ambassadors constructed diplomatic relations with Tiwanaku communities through activities such as feasting ceremonies. Elaborate feasts certainly occurred at Cerro Baúl, in which they consumed large quantities of protein (camelid, vizcacha, deer, and marine fish) and chicha (chicha de maize and chicha de molle), most or all of which was produced in the Cerro Baúl brewery, the largest pre-Inkan brewery in the Americas (Moseley et al. 2005). Whether or not non-Wari people (such as Tiwanaku elites) were invited to these feasts as part of a Wari imperial strategy that included diplomacy is unclear, but the hybrid ceramic forms from Cerro Baúl suggest some form of interaction between Wari and Tiwanaku (Williams 2002). Although this interaction has been described as a militaristic encounter such that the Wari intrusion drove Tiwanaku out of the middle valley (Goldstein 1989), Williams has suggested that Wari took control in parts of the valley through "hydraulic superiority" (Williams 2002:366). That is, in the mid-seventh century AD, Wari engineers developed a better water canal system that improved water flow, enabling them to work larger areas of agricultural land. This, combined with the fact that the new Wari canals cut into water availability for Tiwanaku communities downstream, particularly during the decade-long drought circa AD 640, prevented the continuation of Tiwanaku agricultural practices in the middle valley (Williams 2002). As Williams cogently describes it, "[T]he Wari investment in agricultural infrastructure [in the upper Moquegua valley] is a conquest by hydraulic superiority, accomplished through economic rather than military means" (Williams 2002:366). Thus, when perspectives from the heartland and different parts of the hinterland are combined, we can see the savvy deployment of diverse Wari strategies, likely resulting from various state goals and adaptations they had to make in their encounters with different groups.

Ancient States and Empires

The study presented here focuses on the presentation and discussion of bioarchaeological data to gain insights into the ancient Wari Empire of the Peruvian Andes. This focused work, however, speaks to larger issues related to how state and imperial policies and practices can affect the lives of those within their domain. Certain effects may not be uniformly experienced by all peoples within a community, as in the case of who was targeted for prisoner taking or head taking by Wari warriors. As the demographic profile of the trophy heads shows, adult men were particularly vulnerable to this kind of attack, as were young children, though to a much lesser degree. Women were rarely, if ever, targeted for this kind of violent treatment that resulted in the mutilation of their bodies after death.

This research also demonstrates how Wari political elites, and others with decision-making power, smartly developed, implemented, and negotiated various state strategies depending on local circumstances. That is, various studies on the Wari show that it is inaccurate to characterize Wari expansionism as purely militaristic or based solely on religious indoctrination or economic dominance. In some cases, all these tactics, and perhaps others, may well have been used to subjugate or incorporate populations and/or extract resources and labor. As Williams (2002) has suggested, Wari dominance in the upper Moquegua valley was achieved through engineering supremacy, not military subjugation. And although the nature of that Wari-Tiwanaku interaction needs to be more fully deduced—Was the usurpation of water rights in the upper Moquegua valley void of conflict?—current data suggest that Wari personnel simply filled an empty niche and exploited it without the need for violent intervention (Williams 2002), which would have been costly and risky, especially that far from the Wari heartland. If engineering innovation combined with local negotiation was indeed the method, this clearly demonstrates sophisticated diplomacy deployed in a particular place with a particular polity, designed to achieve particular ends. This impressive feat of tapping into previously unused agricultural lands and taking over a prominent ritual point on the landscape (Cerro Baúl is on the most visible mesa with commanding views of the valley and distant mountain deities [Williams and Nash 2006]) speaks to successful implementation of Wari policies without heavy-handed military intrusion.

The view from the heartland, in contrast, indicates that militaristic techniques were used in the conquest of some nonlocal peoples. Thus, it is not that the Wari never utilized militarism; rather, it appears that Wari leaders selectively used military might, depending on the state agenda and local conditions.

Like the elites of many other empires that dominated regions for centuries, political leaders among the Wari had to smartly deploy resources and develop flexible strategies, which often led to varied policies and practices that were highly contingent and related to state goals, state means, local landscapes, and specific social circumstances. In this way, we can see how imperial policies and practices are never purely defined by political elites or other leaders. They too must operate within a complex field of social relations, political alliances, environmental constraints, and local perceptions of the expanding polity. As such, it is apparent that the process of imperial expansion is an ongoing, dynamic interaction in which relationships are negotiated and renegotiated, leading, at times, to variable conditions that differentially impact the lifeways and health status of those living in the region. If we are to document this process—and not just from the top-down view of the state—then it is through bioarchaeological investigations that examine the bony diary of a person's life that we can begin to reconstruct, and perhaps understand, the lives of individuals and their families who lived under imperial rule centuries ago.

Notes

Chapter 3. The Wari Empire in the Andean World

1. Garcia and Bustamante refer to this area as Sector A. This area was not given a designation in my study, nor was any part of this area mapped or collected, because some of it had since been washed into the Majes River.

2. Garcia and Bustamante refer to this area as Sector B, but my study refers to it as Sector A.

Chapter 4. Wari Community Organization

1. As Premo (2000) has documented, although population relocation projects may have begun as temporary, many migrants never returned home, thus altering the original demographic composition of the origin community.

2. However, Drusini (2001:170) assumes that the Wari-era peoples living in Nasca were not locals but individuals who migrated there from the Wari heartland, an assumption that he admits must be tested with additional studies.

3. It also possible that they were related through both biology and marriage, for we know that the later Inka lords married their sisters. As such, we should not wholly exclude the possibility of polygeny for Wari men of elite status.

4. Although the Inka state often sent husbands and wives together on military campaigns or state farming projects, young, single men were often relocated, but not young woman (D'Altroy 2002).

Chapter 5. Violence and Skeletal Trauma among Wari Communities

1. All bones from Tomb 1 (1977 excavations) were placed in the same box and labeled as "Entierro 1" (Burial 1). However, there were actually two nearly complete female skeletons and the arm bones of a third person near/within this tomb. Therefore, determining to which person the fractured right radius belongs is impossible. All bones are generally equal in size, and all show similar taphonomic changes.

2. In short, females trace their ancestry through their mothers, and males trace their ancestry through their fathers (i.e., sex-specific parallel descent).

3. It is possible that these eight adults had more than one rib fracture, but all of their ribs were not recovered or well enough preserved to observe for breaks.

4. Although there are a total of 53 cranial wounds, the location of one wound is unknown

because some skeletal material had been removed for museum display before I completed data collection.

5. In this particular statistical test, Fisher's exact could not be performed to determine significance. Instead, Wald's chi-square, an approximation of Fisher's exact test, was used.

6. The Oro-Warí are a modern group from southern Amazonia, and although they are commonly called the Warí, I use their self-referent, Oro-Warí (Beth Conklin, pers. comm. 2009) to clearly distinguish them from the Middle Horizon Wari.

7. Kellner's (2002) rich data set presents trauma frequencies for Early, Middle, and Late Nasca periods, but for the purposes of this summary, I collapsed the three Nasca time periods. This does not alter the general pattern, whereby trauma frequencies are essentially similar during all Nasca phases in the Early Intermediate Period.

Chapter 6. Corporeal Icons of Wari Imperialism

1. A skull includes two parts: cranium and mandible. A cranium has no associated mandible.

2. One trophy head was removed from the storage facility, apparently to put it on display at some other locale, so I had no access to the specimen, and the other one has not yet been located in the storage room at the Institute of National Culture in Arequipa.

References

Abu-Lughod JL. 1989. Before European hegemony: The world system, A.D. 1250–1350. New York: Oxford University Press.

Alcock SE, D'Altroy TN, Morrison KD, and Sinopoli CM. 2001. Empires: Perspectives from archaeology and history. Cambridge: Cambridge University Press.

Allen CJ. 1988. The hold life has: Coca and cultural identity in an Andean community. Washington, D.C.: Smithsonian Institution Press.

Allen MW, and Arkush EN. 2006. Introduction: Archaeology and the study of war. In: Arkush EN, and Allen MW, editors. The archaeology of warfare: Prehistories of raiding and conquest. Gainesville: University of Florida Press. Pp. 1–22.

Anders MB. 1989. Evidence for the dual socio-political organisation and administrative structure of the Wari state. In: Czwarno RM, Meddens FM, and Morgan A, editors. The nature of Wari: A reappraisal of the Middle Horizon period in Peru. BAR International Series 525. Oxford: British Archaeological Reports. Pp. 35–52.

Anders MB. 1991. Structure and function at the planned site of Azangaro: Cautionary notes for the model of Huari as a centralized secular state. In: Isbell WH, and McEwan GF, editors. Huari administrative structure: Prehistoric monumental architecture and state government. Washington, D.C.: Dumbarton Oaks. Pp. 165–97.

Anderson B. 1991. Imagined communities: Reflections on the origins and spread of nationalism. London: Verso.

Andrushko VA. 2007. The bioarchaeology of Inca imperialism in the heartland: An analysis of prehistoric burials from the Cuzco region of Peru [Ph.D. dissertation]. Santa Barbara: University of California.

Andrushko VA. n.d. Skeletal evidence for Inca warfare from Cuzco, Peru. Manuscript in review.

Angel LJ. 1947. The length of life in ancient Greece. Journal of Gerontology 2(1):18–24.

Arkush E, and Stanish C. 2005. Interpreting conflict in the ancient Andes: Implications for the archaeology of warfare. Current Anthropology 46(1):3–28.

Arkush EN. 2008. War, chronology, and causality in the Titicaca Basin. Latin American Antiquity 19(4):339–73.

Armelagos GJ. 1994. You are what you eat. In: Sobolik KD, editor. Paleonutrition: The diet and health of prehistoric Americans. Carbondale: Center for Archaeological Investigations, Southern Illinois University at Carbondale. Pp. 235–44.

Arutinov SA. 2002. The diaspora as a process. Anthropology and Archaeology of Eurasia 41(1):89–96.

Baraybar JP. 1987. Cabezas trofeo Nasca: Nuevas evidencias. Gaceta Arqueológica Andina 15:6–10.

Barfield TJ. 2001. The shadow of empires: Imperial state formation along the Chinese-Nomad frontier. In: Alcock SE, D'Altroy TN, Morrison KD, and Sinopoli CM, editors. Empires: Perspectives from archaeology and history. Cambridge: Cambridge University Press. Pp. 10–41.

Bastien JW. 1985. Qollahuaya-Andean body concepts: A topographical-hydraulic model of physiology. American Anthropologist 87(3):595–611.

Bauer BS. 1992. The development of the Inca state. Austin: University of Texas Press.

Bauer BS, and Covey RA. 2002. Processes of state formation in the Inca heartland (Cuzco, Peru). American Anthropologist 104(3):846–64.

Bawden G. 1996. The Moche. Oxford, U.K.: Blackwell Publishers.

Bawden G, and Conrad GW. 1982. The Andean heritage: Masterpieces of Peruvian art from the collections of the Peabody Museum. Cambridge, Mass.: Peabody Museum Press, distributed by Harvard University Press.

Bennett WC. 1954. Excavaciones en Wari, Ayacucho, Peru. Revista, Museo Nacional:198–211.

Benson EP. 1998. The Lord, the ruler: Jaguar symbolism in the Americas. In: Saunders NJ, editor. Icons of power: Feline symbolism in the Americas. London: Routledge. Pp. 53–76.

Bentley RA, Price TD, and Stephan E. 2004. Determining the "local" 87Sr/86Sr range for archaeological skeletons: A case study from Neolithic Europe. Journal of Archaeological Science 31:365–75.

Betanzos Jd. 1551. Narrative of the Incas. Austin: University of Texas Press.

Biasca N, Wirth S, and Tegner Y. 2002. The avoidability of head and neck injuries in ice hockey: An historical review. British Journal of Sports Medicine 36:410–427.

Blacker JC. 2001. Growing up Huari: An analysis of architectural style, technique, and history at the Middle Horizon site of Conchopata, Ayacucho, Peru [master's thesis]. Binghamton: Binghamton University, State University of New York.

Blom DE. 2005. Embodying borders: Human body modification and diversity in Tiwanaku society. Journal of Anthropological Archaeology 24(1):1–24.

Blom DE, Buikstra JE, Keng L, Tomczak P, Shoreman E, and Stevens-Tuttle D. 2004. Anemia and childhood mortality: Latitudinal patterning along the coast of pre-Columbian Peru. American Journal of Physical Anthropology 2:152–69.

Blom DE, Keng L, and Shoreman E. 2003. Health and variation in Moquegua's Tiwanaku settlements. Paper presented at the 68th Annual Meeting for the Society of American Archaeology. Milwaukee.

Bocquet-Appel J, and Masset C. 1982. Farewell to paleodemography. Journal of Human Evolution 11:321–33.

Bolin I. 1998. Rituals of respect: The secret of survival in the high Peruvian Andes. Austin: University of Texas Press.

Bourdieu P. 1977. Outline of a theory of practice. Cambridge: Cambridge University Press.

Bourdieu P. 1994. Structures, habitus, power: Basis for a theory of symbolic power. In: Dirks NB, Eley G, and Ortner SB, editors. Culture/power/history: A reader in contemporary social theory. Princeton: Princeton University Press. Pp. 155–99.

Bourget S. 2001. Children and ancestors: Ritual practices at the Moche site of Huaca de la Luna, north coast of Peru. In: Benson EP, and Cook AG, editors. Ritual sacrifice in ancient Peru. Austin: University of Texas Press. Pp. 93–118.

Bourget S. 2006. Sex, death, and sacrifice in Moche religion and visual culture. Austin: University of Texas Press.

Bowers N. 1971. Demographic problems in montane New Guinea. In: Polgar S, editor. Culture and population: A collection of current studies. Chapel Hill: Carolina Population Center. Pp. 11–31.

Brachetti A. 2001. La Batalla de Chiaraje: Una pelea ritual en los Andes del Sur de Peru. Anales 9:59–77.

Bragayrac E. 1991. Archaeological excavations in the Vegachayoq Moqo sector of Huari. In: Isbell WH, and McEwan GF, editors. Huari administrative structure: Prehistoric monumental architecture and state government. Washington, D.C.: Dumbarton Oaks. Pp. 71–80.

Brewster-Wray CC. 1989. Huari administration: A view from the capital. In: Czwarno RM, Meddens FM, and Morgan A., editors. The nature of Wari: A reappraisal of the Middle Horizon Period in Peru. BAR International Series 525. Oxford: British Archaeological Reports. Pp. 23–33.

Browne DM, Silverman H, and García R. 1993. A cache of 48 Nasca trophy heads from Cerro Carapo, Peru. Latin American Antiquity 4(3):274–94.

Brumfiel EM. 1992. Distinguished lecture in archaeology: Breaking and entering the ecosystem—gender, class, and faction steal the show. American Anthropologist 94:551–67.

Brumfiel EM. 1996. Figurines and the Aztec state: Testing the effectiveness of ideological domination. In: Wright RP, editor. Gender and archaeology. Philadelphia: University of Pennsylvania Press. Pp. 143–66.

Brumfiel EM. 2001. Aztec hearts and minds: Religion and the state in the Aztec empire. In: Alcock SE, D'Altroy TN, Morrison KD, and Sinopoli CM, editors. Empires. Cambridge: Cambridge University Press. Pp. 283–310.

Buikstra JE. 1991. Out of the appendix and into the dirt: Comments on thirteen years of bioarchaeological research. In: Powell ML, Bridges PS, and Wagner Mires AM, editors. What mean these bones? Studies in southeastern bioarchaeology. Tuscaloosa: University of Alabama Press. Pp. 172–88.

Buikstra JE, and Ubelaker DH. 1994. Standards for data collection from human skeletal remains. Fayetteville: Arkansas Archaeological Survey.

Burbank VK. 1994. Fighting women: Anger and aggression in Aboriginal Australia. Berkeley: University of California Press.

Burger R, Asaro F, Salas G, and Stross F. 1998. The Chivay obsidian source and the geological origin of Titicaca Basin–type obsidian artifacts. Andean Past 5:203–23.

Burger RL. 1992. Sacred center of Chavín de Huántar. In: Townsend RF. Ancient Americas: Art from sacred landscapes. Chicago: Art Institute of Chicago. Pp. 264–77.

Burger RL, Mohr Chavez KL, and Chavez SJ. 2000. Through the glass darkly: Prehispanic obsidian procurement and exchange in southern Peru and northern Bolivia. Journal of World Prehistory 14(3):267–362.

Burgess SD. 1999. Chiribayan skeletal pathology on the south coast of Peru: Patterns of production and consumption [Ph.D. dissertation]. Chicago: University of Chicago.

Bynum CW. 1991. Fragmentation and redemption: Essays on gender and the human body in medieval religion. New York: Zone Books, distributed by MIT Press.

Caldwell JC, and Caldwell P. 1977. The role of marital sexual abstinence in determining fertility: A study of the Yoruba in Nigeria. Population Studies 31:193–217.

Cameron CM. 2008. Invisible citizens: Captives and their consequences. Salt Lake City: University of Utah Press.

Carmichael PH. 1988. Nasca mortuary customs: Death and ancient society on the south coast of Peru [Ph.D. dissertation]. Calgary: University of Calgary.

Carneiro RL. 1970. A theory of the origin of the state. Science 169:733–38.

Carr TEF, Harrison GE, Loutit JF, and Sutton A. 1962. Movement of strontium in the human body. British Medical Journal:773–75.

Carrasco D. 1995. Give me some skin: The charisma of the Aztec warrior. History of Religions 35(1):1–26.

Ceruti C. 2004. Human bodies as objects of dedication at Inca mountain shrines (north-western Argentina). World Archaeology 36(1):103–22.

Chacon R, Chacon Y, and Guandinango A. 2004. Blood for the earth: The Inti Raimi festival among the Cotacachi and Otavalo Indians of highland Ecuador. Paper presented at the 69th Annual Meeting of the Society for American Archaeology. Montreal.

Chacon RJ, and Dye DH. 2007. The taking and displaying of human trophies by Amerindians. New York: Springer.

Chagnon NA. 1992. Yanomamo. New York: Holt, Reinhart and Winston.

Chagnon NA, and Bugos PE Jr. 1979. Kin selection and conflict: An analysis of a Yanamamo ax fight. In: Chagnon NA, and Irons W, editors. Evolutionary biology and human social behavior: An anthropological perspective. North Scituate, Mass.: Duxbury Press. Pp. 213–37.

Cobo B. 1892 [1653]. Historia del nuevo mundo. In: Jiménez de la Espada M, editor. Seville: Sociedad de bibliófilos Andaluces.

Cobo BRH. 1990 [1653]. Inca religion and customs. Austin: University of Texas Press.

Cohen R. 1984. Warfare and state formation: Wars make states and states make war. In: Ferguson BR, editor. Warfare, culture, and environment. Orlando, Fla.: Academic Press. Pp. 329–58.

Comar C, Russell RS, and Wasserman RH. 1957. Strontium-calcium movement from soil to man. Science 126(3272):485–92.

Conklin BA. 2001. Consuming grief: Compassionate cannibalism in an Amazonian society. Austin: University of Texas Press.

Conrad GW. 1981. Reply to Paulsen and Isbell. American Antiquity 46(1):38–42.

Cook AG. 1992. Stone ancestors: Idioms of imperial attire and rank among Huari figurines. Latin American Antiquity 3(4):341–64.

Cook AG. 1994. Wari y Tiwanaku: Entre el estilo y la imagen. Lima, Peru: Pontificia Universidad Católica del Perú.

Cook AG. 2001. Huari D-shaped structures, sacrificial offerings, and divine rulership. In: Benson E, and Cook AG, editors. Ritual sacrifice in ancient Peru. Austin: University of Texas Press. Pp. 137–63.

Cook AG, and Benco N. 2002. Vasijas para la fiesta y la fama: Producción artesanal en un centro urbano Wari. In: Kaulicke P, and Isbell WH, editors. Boletín de arqueología PUCP: Wari y Tiwanaku: Modelos y evidencias. Lima: Fondo Editorial, Pontífica Universidad Católica del Perú. Pp. 489–504.

Cook AG, and Glowacki M. 2003. Pots, politics, and power: Wari ceramic assemblages and imperial administration. In: Bray T, editor. The archaeology and politics of food and feasting in early states and empires. New York: Kluwer Academic/Plenum Publishers. Pp. 173–202.

Cook AG, and Tung TA. 2006. Expressing life through death: mortuary rituals in Huari society. Paper presented at the 71st Annual Meeting of the Society for American Archaeology. San Juan, Puerto Rico.

Cordy-Collins A. 2001. Decapitation in Cuspisnique and early Moche societies. In: Benson EP, and Cook AG, editors. Ritual sacrifice in ancient Peru. Austin: University of Texas Press. Pp. 21–34.

Costin CL, Earle TK, Owen B, and Russell GS. 1989. Impact of Inka conquest on local technology in the upper Mantaro Valley, Peru. In: van der Leeuw SE, and Torrence R, editors. What's new? A closer look at the process of innovation. London: Unwin and Allen. Pp. 107–39.

Counts DA, Brown JK, Campbell J, and Duke Endowment Health Care Division. 1999. To have and to hit: Cultural perspectives on wife beating. Urbana: University of Illinois Press.

Czwarno RM, Meddens FM, and Morgan A. 1989. The nature of Wari: A reappraisal of the Middle Horizon Period in Peru. BAR International Series 525. Oxford: British Archaeological Reports.

Dagget RE. 1987. Toward the development of the state on the north central coast of Peru. In: Haas J, Pozorski S, and Pozorski T, editors. The origins and development of the Andean state. Cambridge: Cambridge University Press. Pp. 70–82.

D'Altroy TN. 1992. Provincial power in the Inka Empire. Washington, D.C.: Smithsonian Institution Press.

D'Altroy TN. 2002. The Incas. Malden, Mass.: Blackwell Publishers.

de la Vega E, Frye KL, and Tung TA. 2005. The cave burial from Molino-Chilacachi. In: Stanish C, Cohen A, and Aldenderfer M, editors. Advances in the archaeology of the Titicaca Basin. Los Angeles: Cotsen Institute of Archaeology Press, UCLA. Pp. 185–96.

de la Vera Cruz Chávez P. 1989. Cronología y corología de la cuenca del río Camaná—Majes—Colca—Arequipa [licentiature thesis]. Arequipa: Universidad Católica Santa María.

de la Vera Cruz Chávez P. 1996. El papel de la sub region norte de los valles occidentales en la articulacion entre los Andes centrales y los Andes centro sur. In: Albó X, editor. Integracion Surandina: Cinco siglos despues. Arica: Corporación Norte Grande Taller de Estudios Andinos. Pp. 135–57.

de la Vera Cruz Chávez P, and Yépez Alvarez W. 1995. Informe preliminar de las excavaciones de La Real, valle de Majes. Arequipa: Instituto Nacional de Cultura, Arequipa.

Dillehay TD. 1995. Introduction. In: Dillehay TD, editor. Tombs for the living: Andean mortuary practices. Washington, D.C.: Dumbarton Oaks. Pp. 1–26.

Dirkmaat DC, Cabo LL, Ousley SD, and Symes SA. 2008. New perspectives in forensic anthropology. Yearbook of Physical Anhropology 51:33–52.

Dobres M-A, and Robb JE. 2000. Agency in archaeology. London: Routledge.

Donnan CB. 1997. Deer hunting and combat: Parallel activities in the Moche world. In: Berrin K, editor. The spirit of ancient Peru: Treasures from the Museo Arqueológico Rafael Larco Herrera. New York: Thames and Hudson and the Fine Arts Museums of San Francisco. Pp. 51–59.

Donnan CB, and Mackey CJ. 1978. Ancient burial patterns of the Moche Valley, Peru. Austin: University of Texas Press.

Doutriaux MA. 2004. Imperial conquest in a multiethnic setting: The Inka occupation of the Colca valley, Peru [Ph.D. dissertation]. Berkeley: University of California.

Dower JW. 1986. War without mercy: Race and power in the Pacific war. New York: Pantheon Books.

Drusini AG. 2001. Paleodemography of the Nasca valley: Reconstruction of the human ecology in the southern Peruvian coast. Homo 52(2):157–72.

Earle TC. 1997. How chiefs come to power: The political economy in prehistory. Stanford: Stanford University Press.

Edwards, MJ. 2010. Archaeological investigation at Pataraya: A Wari outpost in the Nasca valley of southern Peru [Ph.D. dissertation]. Santa Barbara: University of California.

Fausto C. 2007. Feasting on people: Eating animals and humans in Amazonia. Current Anthropology 48:497–530.

Fausto-Sterling A. 1993. The five sexes: Why male and female are not enough. The Sciences (March/April):20–25.

Featherstone M, Hepworth M, and Turner BS. 1998. Ageing, the life course and the sociology of embodiment. In: Higgs P, and Scambler G, editors. Modernity, medicine and health: Issues confronting medical sociology. London: Routledge. Pp. 147–75.

Feinman GM, and Marcus J. 1998. Archaic states. Santa Fe, N.Mex.: School of American Research Press.

Feldman RA. 1989. Speculative hypothesis of Wari southern expansion. In: Czwarno RM, Meddens FM, and Morgan A, editors. The nature of Wari: A reappraisal of the Middle Horizon Period in Peru. BAR International Series 525. Oxford: British Archaeological Reports. Pp. 72–97.

Feldman RA. 1998. La cuidadela Wari de Cerro Baul en Moquegua. In: Wise K, editor. Moquegua: Los primeros doce mil años. Arequipa, Peru: Policrom. Pp. 59–65.

Ferguson RB. 2004. Tribal warfare. In: Scheper-Hughes N, and Bourgois P, editors. Violence in war and peace: An anthology. Malden, Mass.: Blackwell Publishing. Pp. 69–73.

Ferguson RB, and Whitehead NL. 1992. War in the tribal zone: Expanding states and indigenous warfare. Sante Fe, N.Mex.: School of American Research Press.

Finnegan M. 1978. Non-metric variation of the infracranial skeleton. Journal of Anatomy 125:23–37.

Finucane B, Maita P, and Isbell WH. 2006. Human and animal diet at Conchopata, Peru: Stable isotope evidence for maize agriculture and animal management practices during the Middle Horizon. Journal of Archaeological Science 33:1766–76.

Forgey K. 2005. Osteological and ancient DNA analyses of human trophy heads and comparative skeletal material from the south coast of Peru: Origins and function in early Nasca society (AD 1–450) [Ph.D. dissertation]. Chicago: University of Illinois.

Foucault M. 1977. Discipline and punish: The birth of the prison. New York: Pantheon Books.

Frame M. 2001. Blood, fertility, and transformation: Interwoven themes in the Paracas Necropolis embroideries. In: Elizabeth Benson AGC, editor. Ritual sacrifice in ancient Peru. Austin: University of Texas Press. Pp. 55–92.

Fried M. 1961. Warfare, military organization, and the evolution of society. Anthropologica 3:134–47.

Gade DW, and Escobar M. 1982. Village settlement and the colonial legacy in southern Peru. Geographical Review 72:430–49.

Gaither C, Kent J, Vásquez Sánchez V, and Rosales Tham T. 2008. Mortuary practices and human sacrifice in the middle Chao Valley of Peru: Their interpretation in the context of Andean mortuary patterning. Latin American Antiquity 19(2):107–21.

Galloway A. 1999. Broken bones: Anthropological analysis of blunt force trauma. Springfield, Ill.: Charles C. Thomas.

Garcia Márquez M, and Bustamante Montoro R. 1990. Arqueología del valle de Majes. Gaceta Arqueológica Andina 18/19:25–40.

Garenne M, and van de Waller E. 1989. Polygyny and fertility among the Sereer of Senegal. Population Studies 43:267–83.

Gentile ME. 1996. Dimension sociopolitica y religiosa de la capacocha del cerro Aconcagua. Bulletin, Institut Francais d'Etudes Andines 25(1):43–90.

Giddens A. 1976. New rules of sociological method: A positive critique of interpretative sociologies. London: Hutchinson.

Giddens A. 1984. The constitution of society: Outline of the theory of structuration. Berkeley: University of California Press.

Gifford D, Hoggarth P, Flores A, and Valeriano S. 1976. Carnival and coca leaf: Some traditions of the Peruvian Quechua Ayllu. Edinburgh: Scottish Academic Press.

Gladwell RR. 2003. Animals among the dead: The zooarchaeology of the Wari Middle Horizon site of Beringa, Majes Valley, Peru. Paper presented at the 68th Annual Meeting of the Society for American Archaeology. Milwaukee.

Glencross B, and Sawchuk L. 2003. The person-years construct: Aging and the prevalence of health related phenomena from skeletal samples. International Journal of Osteoarchaeology 13:369–74.

Glowacki M. 2002. The Huaro archaeological site complex: Rethinking the Huari occupation of Cuzco. In: Isbell WH, and Silverman H, editors. Andean archaeology I: Variations in sociopolitical organization. New York: Kluwer Academic/Plenum Publishers.

Glowacki M. 2005. Dating Pikillacta. In: McEwan GF, editor. Pikillacta: The Wari empire in Cuzco. Iowa City: University of Iowa Press.

Goldstein DB. 2003. Conservators report to the Conchopata Archaeological Project.

Goldstein DJ, Goldstein RCC, and Williams PR. 2009. You are what you drink: A socio-cultural reconstruction of prehispanic fermented beverage use at Cerro Baúl, Moquegua, Peru. In: Jennings JJ, and Bowser B, editors. Drink, power, and society in the Andes. Gainesville: University Press of Florida. Pp. 133–66.

Goldstein P. 2005. Andean diaspora: The Tiwanaku colonies and the origins of South American empire. Gainesville: University Press of Florida.

Goldstein PS. 1989. Omo, a Tiwanaku provincial center in Moquegua, Peru [doctoral dissertation]. Chicago: University of Chicago.

Gordon CC, and Buikstra JE. 1981. Soil pH, bone preservation, and sampling bias at mortuary sites. American Antiquity 48:566–71.

Gose P. 2003. Converting the ancestors: Indirect rule, settlement consolidation, and the struggle over burial in colonial Peru, 1532–1614. In: Mills K, and Grafton A, editors. Conversion: Old worlds and new. Rochester: University of Rochester Press. Pp. 140–74.

Grupe G, Price TD, Schröter P, Söllner F, Johnson CM, and Beard BL. 1997. Mobility of Bell Beaker people revealed by strontium isotope ratios of tooth and bone: A study of southern Bavarian skeletal remains. Applied Geochemistry 12:517–25.

Guaman Poma de Ayala F, Murra JV, Adorno R, and Urioste J. 1987 [1615]. Nueva corónica y buen gobierno. Madrid: Historia 16.

Harner MJ. 1972. The Jívaro, people of the sacred waterfalls. Garden City, N.Y.: Published for the American Museum of Natural History by Doubleday/Natural History Press.

Harrison S. 2006. Skull trophies of the Pacific War: Transgressive objects of remembrance. Journal of the Royal Anthropological Institute 12:817–36.

Hartmann R. 1972. Otros datos sobre las llamadas "batallas rituales." Actas y Memorias del XXXIX Congreso Internacional de Americanistas 6:125–35.

Hassig R. 1988. Aztec warfare: Imperial expansion and political control. Norman: University of Oklahoma Press.

Hern WM. 1992. Shipibo polygyny and patrilocality. American Ethnologist 19(3):501–22.

Hickerson H. 1960. The feast of the dead among the seventeenth century Algonkians of the upper Great Lakes. American Anthropologist 62(1):81–107.

Hill K, and Hurtado AM. 1996. Aché life history: The ecology and demography of a foraging people. New York: Aldine de Gruyter.

Hobbs CJ. 1984. Skull fracture and the diagnosis of abuse. Archives of Disease in Childhood 59:246–52.

Hodges RM, MacDonald NS, Nusbaum R, Stearns R, Ezmirlian F, Spain P, and MacArthur C. 1950. The strontium content of human bones. Journal of Biological Chemistry 185:519–24.

Holmberg AR. 1950. Nomads of the long bow: The Siriono of eastern Bolivia. Washington, D.C.: U.S. Government Printing Office.

Hoppa RD, and Vaupel JW. 2002. Paleodemography: Age distribution from skeletal samples. Cambridge: Cambridge University Press.

Howell TL, and Kintigh KW. 1996. Archaeological identification of kin groups using mortuary and biological data: An example from the American Southwest. American Antiquity 61(3):537–54.

Hrdlička A. 1914. Anthropological work in Peru in 1913, with notes on pathology of ancient Peruvians. Smithsonian Miscellaneous Collections 61:1–69.

Huss-Ashmore R, Goodman AH, and Armelagos GJ. 1982. Nutritional inference from paleopathology. Advances in Archaeological Method and Theory 5:395–474.

Isbell WH. 1977. The rural foundation for urbanism: Economic and stylistic interaction between rural and urban communities in eighth-century Peru. Urbana: University of Illinois Press.

Isbell WH. 1984. Huari urban prehistory. In: Kendall A, editor. Current archaeological projects in the central Andes. BAR International Series 210. Oxford: British Archaeological Reports. Pp. 95–131.

Isbell WH. 1989. Honcopampa: Was it a Huari administrative centre? In: Czwarno RM, Meddens FM, and Morgan A, editors. The nature of Wari: A reappraisal of the Middle Horizon Period in Peru. BAR International Series 525. Oxford: British Archaeological Reports. Pp. 98–114.

Isbell WH. 1991. Conclusion: Huari administration and the orthogonal cellular architecture horizon. In: Isbell WH, and McEwan GF, editors. Huari administrative structure: Prehistoric monumental architecture and state government. Washington, D.C.: Dumbarton Oaks. Pp. 293–315.

Isbell WH. 1997a. Mummies and mortuary monuments: A postprocessual prehistory of central Andean social organization. Austin: University of Texas Press.

Isbell WH. 1997b. Reconstructing Huari: A cultural chronology for the capital city. In: Manzanilla L, editor. Emergence and change in early urban societies. New York: Plenum Press. Pp. 181–227.

Isbell WH. 2000. Repensando el Horizonte Medio: El caso de Conchopata, Ayacucho Perú. Boletín de Arqueología PUCP 4(Huari y Tiwanaku: Modelos vs. Evidencias, Primera Parte):9–68.

Isbell WH. 2001a. Huari: Crecimiento y desarrolo de la capital imperial. In: Museo Nacional de Antropología y Arqueología. Wari: Arte precolombino Peruano. Sevilla: Centro Cultural el Monte. Pp. 99–172.

Isbell WH. 2001b. Conchopata: A Middle Horizon community of palaces? Paper presented at the 66th Annual Meeting of the Society for American Archaeology. New Orleans.

Isbell WH. 2004. Mortuary preferences: A Wari culture case study from Middle Horizon, Peru. Latin American Antiquity 15(1):3–32.

Isbell WH. 2007. A community of potters or multicrafting wives of polygynous Lords? In: Shimada I, editor. Craft production in complex societies: Multicraft and producer perspectives. Salt Lake City: University of Utah Press. Pp. 68–96.

Isbell WH, Brewster-Wray C, and Spickard LE. 1991. Architecture and spatial organization at Huari. In: Isbell WH, and McEwan GF, editors. Huari administrative structure: Prehistoric monumental architecture and state government. Washington, D.C.: Dumbarton Oaks. Pp. 19–54.

Isbell WH, and Cook AG. 1987. Ideological origins of an Andean conquest state. Archaeology 40(4):26–33.

Isbell WH, and Cook AG. 2002. A new perspective on Conchopata and the Andean Middle Horizon. In: Silverman H, and Isbell WH, editors. Andean archaeology II: Art, landscape, and society. New York: Kluwer Academic Press. Pp. 249–305.

Isbell W, and Groleau A. 2010. The Wari brewer women: Feasting, gender, offerings, and memory. In: Klarich E, editor. Inside ancient kitchens: New directions in the study of daily meals and feasts: University of Colorado Press.

Isbell WH, and McEwan GF. 1991a. A history of Huari studies and introduction to current interpretations. In: Isbell WH, and McEwan GF, editors. Huari administrative structure: Prehistoric monumental architecture and state government. Washington, D.C.: Dumbarton Oaks. Pp. 1–18.

Isbell WH, and McEwan GF, eds. 1991b. Huari administrative structure: Prehistoric monumental architecture and state government. Washington, D.C.: Dumbarton Oaks Research Library and Collection.

Isbell WH, and Schreiber KJ. 1978. Was Huari a state? American Antiquity 43(3):372–89.

Isla Cuadrado J. 2009. From hunters to regional lords: Funerary practices in Palpa, Peru. In: Reindel M, and Wagner GA, editors. New technologies for archaeology: Multidisciplinary investigations in Palpa and Nasca, Peru. Berlin: Springer. Pp. 119–39.

Jackes M. 1992. Paleodemography: Problems and techniques. In: Saunders SR, and Katzenberg MA, editors. Skeletal biology of past peoples: Research methods. New York: Wiley-Liss. Pp. 189–224.

Janusek JW. 1999. Craft and local power: Embedded specialization in Tiwanaku cities. Latin American Antiquity 10(2):107–31.

Janusek JW. 2008. Ancient Tiwanaku: Civilization in the high Andes. Cambridge: Cambridge University Press.

Jennings J. 2002. Prehistoric imperialism and cultural development in the Cotahuasi Valley, Peru [Ph.D. dissertation]. Santa Barbara: University of California.

Jennings JJ. 2007. In the shadows of Wari: Preliminary results of the 2006 excavations at Collota and Tenahaha in the Cotahuasi valley, Peru. Paper presented at the 72nd Annual Meeting of the Society for American Archaeology. Austin, TX.

Jennings JJ. n.d. (in press). Una reevaluación del horizonte medio en Arequipa. In: Jennings JJ, and Castillo Butters LJ, editors. Interacciones interregionales en el horizonte medio de los Andes centrales. Lima: Fondo Editorial de la Pontificia Universidad Católica del Perú.

Jennings JJ, and Craig N. 2001. Politywide analysis and imperial political economy: The relationship between valley political complexity and administrative centers in the Wari Empire of the central Andes. Journal of Anthropological Archaeology 20:470–502.

Joyce RA. 2003. Making something of herself: Embodiment in life and death at Playa de los Muertos, Honduras. Cambridge Archaeological Journal 13(2):248–61.

Judd MA. 2008. The parry problem. Journal of Archaeological Science 35:1658–66.

Karsten R. 1949 [1969 trans.]. Das altperuanische Inkareich und seine Kulture [A totalitarian state of the past: The civilization of the Inca Empire in ancient Peru]. Leipzig: F. A. Brockhaus.

Kellner CM. 2002. Coping with environmental and social challenges in prehistoric Peru: Bioarchaeological analyses of Nasca populations [Ph.D. dissertation]. Santa Barbara: University of California, Santa Barbara.

Kellner CM, and Schoeninger MJ. 2008. Wari's imperial influence on local Nasca diet: The stable isotope evidence. Journal of Anthropological Archaeology 27:226–43.

Kelly RC. 2000. Warless societies and the origin of war. Ann Arbor: University of Michigan Press.

Kemp BM, Tung TA, and Summar M. 2009. Genetic continuity after the collapse of the Wari empire: Mitochondrial DNA profiles from Wari and post-Wari populations in the ancient Andes. American Journal of Physical Anthropology 140(1):80–91.

Ketteman WG. 2002. New dates from the Huari Empire: Chronometric dating of the prehistoric occupation of Conchopata, Ayacucho, Peru [master's thesis]. Binghamton: Binghamton University, State University of New York.

Knudson KJ, and Blom DE. 2009. The complex relationship between Tiwanaku mortuary identity and geographic origin in the south central Andes. In: Knudson KJ, and Stojanowski CM, editors. Bioarcheaology and identity in the Americas. Gainesville: University Press of Florida. Pp. 194–211.

Knudson KJ, and Price TD. 2007. The utility of multiple chemical techniques in archaeological residential mobility studies: Case studies from Tiwanaku- and Chiribaya-affiliated sites in the Andes. American Journal of Phyical Anthropology 132:25–39.

Knudson KJ, Price TD, Buikstra JE, and Blom DE. 2004. The use of strontium isotope analysis to investigate Tiwanaku migration and mortuary ritual in Bolivia and Peru. Archaeometry 46:5–18.

Knudson KJ, and Tung TA. 2007. Using archaeological chemistry to investigate the geographic origins of trophy heads in the central Andes. In: Glascock MD, Speakman RJ, and Popelka-Filcoff R, editors. Archaeological chemistry: Analytical techniques and archaeological interpretation. Washington, D.C.: American Chemical Society. Pp. 99–113.

Knudson KJ, Williams SR, Osborn R, Forgey K, and Williams RP. 2009. The geographic origins of Nasca trophy heads using strontium, oxygen, and carbon isotope data. Journal of Anthropological Archaeology 28(2):244–57.

Koch K. 1974. War and peace in Jalemo. Cambridge, Mass.: Harvard University Press.

Kohl PL. 1987. The use and abuse of world systems theory: The case of the pristine West Asian state. Advances in Archaeological Method and Theory 11:1–35.

Koontz CB. 2011. Pre-Wari and Wari health, trauma, and tradition in the Majes and Siguas valleys, Department of Arequipa, Peru. Nashville, Tenn.: Center for Latin American Studies Graduate Student Conference, Vanderbilt University.

Kulp JL, and Schulert AR. 1962. Strontium-90 in man V. Science 136(3516):619–32.

Kurin DS. n.d. Violence related trauma and trepanation among the Chanka of Peru. Manuscript in preparation.

Lambert PM. 1994. War and peace on the western front: A study of violent conflict and its correlates in prehistoric hunter-gatherer societies of coastal southern California [Ph.D. dissertation]. Santa Barbara: University of California at Santa Barbara.

Lambert PM. 1997. Patterns of violence in prehistoric hunter-gatherer societies of coastal California. In: Martin DL, and Frayer DW, editors. Troubled times: Violence and warfare in the past. Amsterdam: Gordon and Breach Publishers. Pp. 77–109.

Larco Hoyle R. 1948. Cronología arqueológico del norte del Perú. Buenos Aires: Sociedad Geográfica Americana.

Larsen CS. 1997. Bioarchaeology: Interpreting behavior from the human skeleton. Cambridge: Cambridge University Press.

Leoni JB. 2001. Kilns and houses: Ceramic production and its social contexts at the site of Conchopata, Ayacucho, Peru. Paper presented at the 66th Annual Meeting of the Society for American Archaeology. New Orleans.

Leoni JB. 2004. Ritual, place, and memory in the construction of community identity: A diachronic view from Ñawinpukyo (Ayacucho, Peru) [Ph.D. dissertation]. Binghamton: State University of New York.

Levinson D. 1989. Family violence in cross cultural perspective. Newbury Park, Calif.: Sage Publications.

Lewis CM, Buikstra JE, and Stone AC. 2007. Ancient DNA and genetic continuity in the south central Andes. Latin American Antiquity 18(2):145–60.

Lewis CM, Tito RY, Lizarraga B, and Stone AC. 2005. Land, language, and loci: mtDNA in Native Americans and the genetic history of Peru. American Journal of Physical Anthropology 127(3):351–60.

Lovell NC. 1997. Trauma analysis in paleopathology. Yearbook of Physical Anthropology 40:139–70.

Lumbreras LG. 1974. The peoples and cultures of ancient Peru. Washington, D.C.: Smithsonian Institution Press.

Lumbreras LG. 2000a. Las formas históricas del Perú, vol. 5: El proceso de regionalización. Lima: IFEA and Lluvia Editores.

Lumbreras LG. 2000b. Las formas históricas del Perú, vol. 8: El imperio Wari. Lima: IFEA and Lluvia Editores.

MacCurdy GG. 1923. Human skeletal remains from the highlands of Peru. American Journal of Physical Anthropology 6:217–329.

Maita P. 2002. Reporte de restos faunisticos de Conchopata.

Málaga Medina A. 1974. Las reducciones en el Peru (1532–1600). Historia y Cultura (8):141–72.

Malpass MA. 1998. Final report of 1996 summer grant for faculty research "Test excavations at the site of Sonay, Camana Valley, Peru." Ithaca, N.Y.: Ithaca College.

Malpass MA. 2001. Sonay: Un centro Wari celular ortogonal en el valle de Camana, Perú. Boletín de Arqueología PUCP, Lima 5:51–68.

Manrique Valdivia J, and Cornejo Zegarra M. 1990. Visión sobre la arqueología del valle de Camaná. Gaceta Arqueológica Andina 5(18/19):21–24.

Martin DL. 1997. Violence against women in the La Plata River valley (A.D. 1000–1300). In: Martin DL, and Frayer DW, editors. Troubled times: Violence and warfare in the past. Amsterdam: Gordon and Breach Publishers. Pp. 45–75.

Martin DL, and Fryer DW. Troubled times: Violence and warfare in the past. Amsterdam: Gordon and Breach Publishers.

Massey VK, and Steele DG. 1997. A Maya skull pit from the Terminal Classic Period, Colha, Belize. In: Whittington SL, and Reed DM, editors. Bones of the Maya. Washington, D.C.: Smithsonian Institution Press. Pp. 62–77.

Mathien FJ, McGuire RH, and Southern Illinois University at Carbondale Center for Archaeological Investigations. 1986. Ripples in the Chichimec Sea: New considerations of southwestern-Mesoamerican interactions. Carbondale: Southern Illinois University Press.

Mays S. 2003. Bone strontium: Calcium ratios and duration of breastfeeding in a mediaeval skeletal population. Journal of Archaeological Science 30(6):731–41.

McDowell N. 1991. The Mundugumor: From the field notes of Margaret Mead and Reo Fortune. Washington, D.C.: Smithsonian Institution Press.

McEwan G. 1983. Investigaciones en Pikillaqta: Una ocupacion Wari en el Cusco. Gaceta Arqueologica Andina 2(8):4–5.

McEwan GF. 1991. Investigations at the Pikillacta site: A provincial Huari center in the valley of Cuzco. In: Isbell WH, and McEwan GF, editors. Huari administrative structure: Prehistoric monumental architecture and state government. Washington, D.C.: Dumbarton Oaks. Pp. 93–119.

McEwan GF. 1996. Archaeological investigations at Pikillacta, a Wari site in Peru. Journal of Field Archaeology 23(2):169–86.

McEwan GF. 2005. Pikillacta: The Wari Empire in Cuzco. Iowa City: University Press of Iowa.

Meddens F. 1991. A provincial perspective of Huari organization viewed from the Chicha/Soras Valley. In: Isbell WH, and McEwan GF, editors. Huari administrative structure: Prehistoric monumental architecture and state government. Washington, D.C.: Dumbarton Oaks. Pp. 215–31.

Meddens F. 1994. Mountains, miniatures, ancestors, and fertility: The meaning of a Late Horizon offering in a Middle Horizon structure in Peru. Institute of Archaeology Bulletin 31:127–50.

Menzel D. 1964. Style and time in the Middle Horizon. Nawpa Pacha 2:1–105.

Menzel D. 1968. New data on the Huari empire in Middle Horizon Epoch 2A. Nawpa Pacha 6:47–114.

Menzel D. 1977. The archaeology of ancient Peru and the work of Max Uhle. Berkeley, Calif.: R. H. Lowie Museum of Anthropology.

Milner GR, Anderson E, and Smith VG. 1991. Warfare in late prehistoric west-central Illinois. American Antiquity 56(4):581–503.

Milner GR, Larsen CS, Hutchinson DL, Williamson MA, and Humpf DA. 2000. Conquistadors, excavators, or rodents: What damaged the King site skeletons? American Antiquity 65(2):355–63.

Milner GR, Wood JW, and Boldsen JL. 2000. Paleodemography. In: Katzenberg MA, and Saunders SR, editors. Biological anthropology of the human skeleton. New York: Wiley-Liss. Pp. 467–97.

Moore SF. 1958. Power and property in Inca Peru. Morningside Heights, N.Y.: Columbia University Press.

Moore SF. 1973. Power and property in Inca Peru. Westport, Conn.: Greenwood Press.

Moseley ME. 1978. The evolution of Andean civilization. Ancient Native Americans:491–541.

Moseley ME, Feldman RA, Goldstein PS, and Watanabe L. 1991. Colonies and conquest: Tiahuanaco and Huari in Moquegua. In: Isbell WH, and McEwan GF, editors. Huari administrative structure: Prehistoric monumental architecture and state government. Washington, D.C.: Dumbarton Oaks. Pp. 121–40.

Moseley ME, Nash DJ, Williams RP, deFrance SD, Miranda A, and Ruales M. 2005. Burning down the brewery: Establishing and evacuating an ancient imperial colony at Cerro Baúl, Peru. Proceedings of the National Academy of Science 102(48):17,264–71.

Moyer J. 1989. Human skeletal remains. In: Todd I, editor. Vasilikos Valley Project 3: Kalavassos-Ayios Dhimitrios II: Ceramics, tombs, specialist studies. Goteborg: Paul Atröms Förlag.

Murphy MS. 2004. From bare bones to mummified: Understanding health and disease in an Inca community [Ph.D. dissertation]. Philadelphia: University of Pennsylvania.

Murúa Md. 1946 [1590]. Historia del origen y genealogía real de los reyes inças del Perú. In: Bayle C, editor. Biblioteca "missionalia hispanica," vol. 2. Madrid: Consejo Superior de Investigaciones Científicas Instituto Santo Toribio de Mogrovejo.

Murúa Md. 2004 [16th century]. Códice Murúa: Historia y genealogía de los reyes incas del Perú del padre mercedario Fray Martín de Murúa. Madrid: Testiminio Compañía Editorial.

Nash DJ. 2002. The archaeology of space: Places of power in the Wari empire [Ph.D. dissertation]. Gainesville: University of Florida.

Nystrom KC. 2004. Trauma y identidad entre los Chachapoya. Proceedings of the Primera Conferencia Internacional sobre el Arte, la Arqueología y la Etnohistoria de los Chachapoya, Leymebamba, Perú: Sian 15:20–21.

Ochatoma JA. 2007. Alfereros del imperio Huari: Vida cotidiana y areas de actividad en Conchopata. Ayacucho: Universidad Nacional de San Cristóbal de Huamanga Facultad de Ciencias Sociales.

Ochatoma JA, and Cabrera MR. 2000. Arquitectura y áreas de actividad en Conchopata. In: Isbell WH, and Kaulike P, editors. Huari y Tiwanaku: Modelos vs evidencias. Lima: Pontificia Universidad Católica del Perú. Pp. 449–88.

Ochatoma JA, and Cabrera MR. 2001. Poblados rurales Huari: Una vision desde Aqo Wayqo. Lima: CANO asociados SAC.

Ochatoma JA, and Cabrera MR. 2002. Religious ideology and military organization in the iconography of a D-shaped ceremonial precinct at Conchopata. In: Silverman H, and Isbell WH, editors. Andean archaeology II: Art, landscape, and society. New York: Kluwer Academic Press. Pp. 225–47.

Ochatoma JA, Tung TA, and Cabrera M. 2008. The emergence of a Wari military class as viewed through art and the body. Paper presented at the 73rd Annual Meeting of the Society for American Archaeology. Vancouver, B.C.

Ogburn DE. 2007. Human trophies in the late Prehispanic Andes: Striving for status and maintaining power among the Incas and other societies. In: Chacon R, and Dye DH, editors. The taking and displaying of human trophies by Amerindians. New York: Springer Press. Pp. 501–18.

Orlove B. 1994. Sticks and stones: Ritual battles and play in the southern Peruvian Andes. In: Poole D, editor. Unruly order: Violence, power, and cultural identity in the high provinces of southern Peru. Boulder, Colo.: Westview. Pp. 133–64.

Ortner DJ, and Putschar WGJ. 1981. Identification of pathological conditions in human skeletal remains. Washington, D.C.: Smithsonian Institution Press.

Osterholtz A. 2010. Hobbling and torment at sacred ridge: Perimortem damage to the feet as a mechanism of social and physical control. Paper presented at the 79th Annual Meeting of the American Association of Physical Anthropologists. Albuquerque, N.Mex.

Owen B. 2002. Marine carbon reservoir effects on radiocarbon ages of human bone from south coastal Peru. Final report to National Science Foundation for Award # 9982152.

Owen B. 2007. The Wari heartland on the Arequipa Coast: Huamanga ceramics from Beringa, Majes. Andean Past 8:287–373.

Owsley DW. 1994. Warfare in Coalescent Tradition populations of the Northern Plains. In: Owsley DW, and Jantz RJ, editors. Skeletal biology in the Great Plains: Migration, warfare, health, and subsistence. Washington, D.C.: Smithsonian Institution Press. Pp. 333–43.

Paine RR. 1989. Model life tables as a measure of bias in the Grasshopper Pueblo skeletal series. American Antiquity 54:820–824.

Paine RR, and Boldsen JL. 2002. Linking age-at-death distributions and ancient population dynamics: A case study. In: Hoppa RD, and Vaupel JW, editors. Paleodemography: Age distributions from skeletal samples. Cambridge: Cambridge University Press. Pp. 169–80.

Paine RR, and Harpending HC. 1996. Assessing the reliability of paleodemographic fertility estimators using simulated skeletal distributions. American Journal of Physical Anthropology 101:151–59.

Pereira G. 2005. The utilization of grooved human bones: A reanalysis of artificially modified human bones excavated by Carl Lumholtz at Zacapu, Michoacan, Mexico. Latin American Antiquity 16(3):293–312.

Pipes R. 1991. The Russian Revolution. New York: Vintage Books.

Plog FT. 1983. Political and economic alliances on the Colorado Plateaus, AD 400–1450. In: Wendorf F, and Close A, editors. Advances in world archaeology. New York: Academic Press. Pp. 289–330.

Pozzi-Escot BD. 1991. Conchopata: A community of potters. In: Isbell WH, and McEwan GF, editors. Huari administrative structure: Prehistoric monumental architecture and state government. Washington, D.C.: Dumbarton Oaks. Pp. 81–92.

Premo B. 2000. From the pockets of women: The gendering of the mita, migration, and tribute in colonial Chucuito, Peru. The Americas 57(1):63–94.

Price TD, Johnson CM, Ezzo JA, Ericson J, and Burton JH. 1994. Residential mobility in the prehistoric southwest United States: A preliminary study using strontium isotope analysis. Journal of Archaeological Science 21:315–30.

Proulx DA. 1989. Nasca trophy heads: Victims of warfare or ritual sacrifice? Cultures in conflict: Current archaeological perspectives. Calgary: Archaeological Association, University of Calgary. Pp. 73–85.

Proulx DA. 2001. Ritual uses of trophy heads in ancient Nasca society. In: Benson EP, and Cook AG, editors. Ritual sacrifice in ancient Peru. Austin: University of Texas Press. Pp. 119–36.

Ratti de Luchi Lomellini M, and Zegarra Arenas A. 1987. Reconocimiento del yacimiento arqueológico de Beringa [bachiller en ciencias arqueológicas]. Arequipa: Universidad Católica Santa María.

Rehnberg G, Strong A, Porter C, and Carter M. 1969. Levels of stable strontium in milk and the total diet. Environmental Science and Technology 3(2):171–73.

Reinhard J. 1996. Peru's ice maidens: Unwrapping the secrets. National Geographic 189(6):62–81.

Reinhard J. 2005. The Ice Maiden: Inca mummies, mountain gods, and sacred sites in the Andes. Washington, D.C.: National Geographic Society.

Robb J. 1997. Violence and gender in early Italy. In: Martin DL, and Frayer DW, editors. Troubled times: Violence and warfare in the past. Amsterdam: Gordon and Breach Publishers. Pp. 111–44.

Robb J. 2004. The extended artefact and the monumental economy: a methodology for material agency. In: DeMarrais E, Gosden C, and Renfrew C, editors. Rethinking materiality: The engagement of mind with the material world. Cambridge, U.K.: McDonald Institute for Archaeological Research. Pp. 131–39.

Roberts C. 2000. Trauma in biocultural perspective: Past, present and future work in Britain. In: Cox M, and Mays S, editors. Human osteology in archaeology and forensic science. Cambridge: Cambridge University Press. Pp. 337–56.

Rosaldo R. 1980. Ilongot headhunting, 1883–1974: A study in society and history. Stanford: Stanford University Press.

Rowe JH. 1946. Inca culture at the time of the Spanish conquest. In: Steward JH, editor. Handbook of South American Indians. Washington, D.C.: Smithsonian Institution Bureau of American Ethnology. Pp. 183–330.

Rowe J. 1956. Archaeological explorations in southern Peru, 1954–1955. American Antiquity 22(2):135–51.

Rowe JH. 1966. Diffusionism and archaeology. American Antiquity 31(3):334–37.

Rowe JH, Collier D, and Willey GR. 1950. Reconnaissance notes on the site of Huari, near Aycucho, Peru. American Antiquity:120–37.

Sallnow MJ. 1987. Pilgrims of the Andes: Regional cults in Cusco. Washington, D.C.: Smithsonian Institution Press.

Salomon F. 1995. "The beautiful grandparents": Andean ancestor shrines and mortuary ritual as seen through colonial records. In: Dillehay T, editor. Tombs for the living: Andean mortuary practices. Washington, D.C.: Dumbarton Oaks. Pp. 315–54.

Sarmiento de Gamboa P. 1999 [1572]. History of the Incas. New York: Dover Publications.

Sattenspiel LR, and Harpending HC. 1983. Stable populations and skeletal age. American Antiquity 48:489–98.

Scheper-Hughes N, and Lock MM. 1987. The mindful body: A prolegomenon to future work in medical anthropology. Medical Anthropology Quarterly 1(1):6–41.

Schreiber KJ. 1987. Conquest and consolidation: A comparison of the Wari and Inka occupations of highland Peruvian valley. American Antiquity 52(2):266–84.

Schreiber KJ. 1991a. Association between roads and polities: Evidence for Wari roads in Peru. In: Trombold CD, editor. Ancient road networks and settlement hierarchies in the New World. Cambridge: Cambridge University Press. Pp. 243–52.

Schreiber KJ. 1991b. Jincamocco: A Huari administrative center in the south central highlands of Peru. In: Isbell WH, and McEwan GF, editors. Huari administrative structure: Prehistoric monumental architecture and state government. Washington, D.C.: Dumbarton Oaks. Pp. 199–214.

Schreiber KJ. 1992. Wari imperialism in Middle Horizon Peru. Ann Arbor: Museum of Anthropology, University of Michigan.

Schreiber KJ. 1998. Nasca research since 1926. In: Carmichael PH, editor. The archaeology and pottery of Nazca, Peru. Walnut Creek, Calif.: Altamira Press. Pp. 261–70.

Schreiber KJ. 1999. Regional approaches to the study of prehistoric empires: Examples from Ayacucho and Nasca, Peru. In: Billman BR, and Feinman GM, editors. Settlement pattern studies in the Americas: Fifty years since Virú. Washington, D.C.: Smithsonian Institution Press. Pp. 160–71.

Schreiber KJ. 2001. The Wari empire of Middle Horizon Peru: The epistemological challenge of documenting an empire without documentary evidence. In: Alcock SE, D'Altroy TN, Morrison KD, and Sinopoli CM, editors. Empires. Cambridge: Cambridge University Press. Pp. 70–92.

Schreiber KJ, and Gibson J. 2002. Sacred landscapes and imperial power. Paper presented at the 101st Annual Meeting of the American Anthropological Association. New Orleans.

Schroeder HH, Tipton IH, and Nason AP. 1972. Trace metals in man: Strontium and barium. Journal of Chronic Diseases 25:491–517.

Schuller W, and Petermann H. 1992. Land des condores. Detmold: Screen Verlag.

Schultz JJ. 1988. Close encounters [master's thesis]. London: London School of Economics.

Schurr TG. 2004. The peopling of the New World: Perspectives from molecular anthropology. Annual Review of Anthropology 33:551–83.

Sciscento MM. 1989. Imperialism in the high Andes: Inka and Wari involvement in the Chuquibamba valley, Peru [Ph.D. dissertation]. Santa Barbara: University of California, Santa Barbara.

Sewell WH. 2005. Logics of history: Social theory and social transformation. Chicago: University of Chicago Press.

Shady R, and Ruiz A. 1979. Evidence for interregional relationships during the Middle Horizon on the north-central coast of Peru. American Antiquity 44(4):676–84.

Shady Solis R. 1982. Cultura Nieveria y la interaccion social en el mundo Andino en la epoca Huari. Arqueologicas 19:5–108.

Shady Solis R. 1988. Epoca Huari como interaccion de las sociedades regionales. Revista Andina 6(1):67–99.

Shady Solis R. 1989. Cambios significativos ocurridos en el mundo andino durante el Horizonte Medio. In: Czwarno RM, Meddens FM, and Morgan A, editors. The nature of Wari: A reappraisal of the Middle Horizon Period in Peru. BAR International Series 525. Oxford: British Archaeological Reports. Pp. 1–22.

Shea D. 1969. Wari Wilka: A central Andean oracle site [Ph.D. dissertation]. Madison: University of Wisconsin.

Shimada I. 1990. Cultural continuities and discontinuities on the northern North Coast of Peru, Middle–Late Horizons. In: Moseley ME, and Cordy-Collins A, editors. Northern dynasties: Kingship and statecraft in Chimor. Washington, D.C.: Dumbarton Oaks. Pp. 297–392.

Shimada I, Shinoda K-i, Farnum J, Corruccini R, and Watanabe H. 2004. An integrated analysis of pre-Hispanic mortuary remains: A Middle Sican case study. Current Anthropology 34(3):369–402.

Shinoda K-i, Adachi N, Guillen S, and Shimada I. 2006. Mitochondrial DNA analysis of ancient Peruvian highlanders. American Journal of Physical Anthropology 131:98–107.

Silverman H. 1993. Cahuachi in the ancient Nasca world. Iowa City: University of Iowa Press.

Silverman H. 2002. Ancient Nasca settlement and society. Iowa City: University of Iowa Press.

Silverman H, and Isbell WH. 2002. Introduction: Landscapes of power. In: Silverman H, and Isbell WH, editors. Andean archaeology II: Art, landscape, and society. New York: Kluwer Academic/Plenum Publishers. Pp. 181–88.

Silverman H, and Proulx DA. 2002. The Nasca. Malden, Mass.: Blackwell Publishers.

Simpson GR. 1990. Wallerstein's world-systems theory and the Cook Islands: A critical examination. Pacific Studies 14:73–94.

Sinopoli CM. 1994. The archaeology of empires. Annual Review of Anthropology 23:159–80.

Smith MO. 2003. Beyond palisades: The nature and frequency of late prehistoric deliberate violent trauma in the Chickamauga Reservoir of east Tennessee. American Journal of Physical Anthropology 121(4):303–18.

Sofaer JR. 2006. The body as material culture: A theoretical osteoarchaeology. Cambridge: Cambridge University Press.

Solano F, and Guerrero V. 1981. Estudio arqueológico en el sector de Monqachayoq-Wari [bachelor's thesis]. Universidad Nacional de San Cristóbal de Huamanga.

Speal SC. 2006. The social implications of Younge Complex mortuary ritual: A survey of postmortem skeletal modifications from Riviere au Vase, Michigan. Archaeology of Eastern North America 34:1–28.

Standen VG, and Arriaza BT. 2000. Trauma in the Preceramic coastal populations of northern Chile: Violence or occupational hazards? American Journal of Physical Anthropology 112(2):239–49.

Stein G. 2002. From passive periphery to active agents: Emerging perspectives in the archaeology of interregional interaction. American Anthropologist 104(3):903–16.

Stone-Miller R, and McEwan GF. 1990. Representation of the Wari state in stone and thread: A comparison of architecture and tapestry tunics. Res 19–20:53–80.

Stone-Miller R, Paul A, Niles SA, and Young-Sánchez M. 1992. To weave for the sun: Andean textiles in the Museum of Fine Arts, Boston. Boston: Museum of Fine Arts.

Stothers DM, Graves JR, Bechtel SK, and Abel TJ. 1994. Current perspectives on the late prehistory of the western Lake Erie region: An alternative to Murphy and Ferris. Archaeology of Eastern North America 22:135–96.

Tello JC. 1970. Las ruinas de Huari. In: 100 años de arqueología en el Perú. Fuentes e investigaciones para la historia del Perú, 3. Lima: Instituto de Estudios Peruanos (IEP). Pp. 519–25.

Tierney P. 2001. Darkness in El Dorado: How scientists and journalists devastated the Amazon. New York: Norton.

Tomasto EC. 2009. Talking bones: Bioarchaeological analysis of individuals from Palpa. In: Reindel M, and Wagner GA, editors. New technologies for archaeology: Multidisciplinary investigations in Palpa and Nasca, Peru. Berlin: Springer. Pp. 141–58.

Topic JR. 1991. Huari and Huamachuco. In: Isbell WH, and McEwan GF, editors. Huari administrative structure: Prehistoric monumental architecture and state government. Washington, D.C.: Dumbarton Oaks. Pp. 141–64.

Topic JR, and Topic TL. 1985. Horizonte Medio en Huamachuco. Revista del Museo Nacional 47:13–52.

Topic JR, and Topic TL. 1992. The rise and decline of Cerro Amaru: An Andean shrine during the Early Intermediate Period and Middle Horizon. In: Goldsmith AS, editor. Ancient images, ancient thought: The archaeology of ideology. Calgary: University of Calgary Archaeological Association. p 167–80.

Topic TL. 1991. The Middle Horizon in northern Peru. In: Isbell WH, and McEwan GF, editors. Huari administrative structure: Prehistoric monumental architecture and state government. Washington, D.C.: Dumbarton Oaks. Pp. 233–46.

Torres-Rouff C. 2002. Cranial vault modification and ethnicity in Middle Horizon San Pedro de Atacama, Chile. Current Anthropology 43(1):163–71.

Treacy JM. 1989. The fields of Coporaque: Agricultural terracing and water management in the Colca valley, Arequipa, Peru [Ph.D. dissertation]. Madison: University of Wisconsin–Madison.

Trigger BG. 1969. The Huron farmers of the North. New York: Holt.

Trigger BG. 1985. Natives and newcomers: Canada's "Heroic Age" reconsidered. Kingston: Mc-Gill-Queen's University Press.

Tung TA. 2001. Health, disease, and diet in the Wari heartland: A bioarchaeological analysis of the Conchopata population. Paper presented at the 66th Annual Meeting of the Society for American Archaeology. New Orleans.

Tung TA. 2003. A bioarchaeological perspective on Wari imperialism in the Andes of Peru: A view from heartland and hinterland skeletal populations [Ph.D. dissertation]. Chapel Hill: University of North Carolina.

Tung TA. 2007a. From corporeality to sanctity: Transforming bodies into trophy heads in the prehispanic Andes. In: Chacon RJ, and Dye DH, editors. The taking and displaying of human trophies by Amerindians. New York: Springer Press. Pp. 477–500.

Tung TA. 2007b. Trauma and violence in the Wari Empire of the Peruvian Andes: Warfare, raids, and ritual fights. American Journal of Physical Anthropology 133(3):941–56.

Tung TA. 2007c. The village of Beringa at the periphery of the Wari Empire: A site overview and new radiocarbon dates. Andean Past 8:253–86.

Tung TA. 2008a. Dismembering bodies for display: A bioarchaeological study of trophy heads from the Wari site of Conchopata, Peru. American Journal of Physical Anthropology 136:294–308.

Tung TA. 2008b. Life on the move: Bioarchaeological contributions to the study of migration and diaspora communities in the Andes. In: Silverman H, and Isbell W, editors. Handbook of South American archaeology. New York: Springer. Pp. 671–80.

Tung TA, and Cook AG. 2006. Intermediate elite agency in the Wari empire: The bioarchaeological and mortuary evidence. In: Elson C, and Covey AR, editors. Intermediate elites in pre-Columbian states and empires. Tucson: University of Arizona Press. Pp. 68–93.

Tung TA, and Del Castillo M. 2005. Una visión de la salud comunitaria en el valle de Majes durante la época Wari. In: César Olaya C, and Romero Bernales MA, editors. Muerte y evidencias funerarias en los Andes Centrales: Avances y perspectivas. Lima: Universidad Nacional de Federico Villarreal. p 149–72.

Tung TA, and Knudson KJ. 2008. Social identities and geographical origins of Wari trophy heads from Conchopata, Peru. Current Anthropology 49(5):915–25.

Tung TA, and Schreiber KJ. 2010. Morbidity patterns in ancient Nasca, Peru. Poster presented at the 75th Annual Meeting of the Society for American Archaeology. St. Louis, Mo.

Ubelaker DH. 1992. Porotic hyperostosis in prehistoric Ecuador. In: Stuart-Macadam P, and Kent S, editors. Diet, demography, and disease: Changing perspectives on anemia. New York: Aldine de Gruyter. Pp. 201–17.

Ubelaker DH, and Newson LA. 2002. Patterns in health and nutrition in prehistoric and historic Ecuador. In: Steckel RH, and Rose JC, editors. The backbone of history: Health and nutrition in the western hemisphere. Cambridge: Cambridge University Press.

Ubelaker DH, and Ripley CE. 1999. The ossuary of San Francisco Church, Quito, Ecuador: Human skeletal biology. Washington, D.C.: Smithsonian Institution Press.

Valencia Zegarra A. 2005. Wari hydraulic works in the Lucre Basin. In: McEwan GF, editor. Pikillacta: The Wari Empire in Cuzco. Iowa City: University of Iowa Press. Pp. 85–97.

Valera B. 1945 [1585]. Las costumbres antiguas del Perú y la historia de los Incas: Los pequeños grandes libros de historia Americana. Lima: Miranda.

Vandkilde H. 2003. Commemorative tales: Archaeological responses to modern myth, politics, and war. World Archaeology 35(1):126–44.

Van Vleet KE. 2002. The intimacies of power: Rethinking violence and affinity in the Bolivian Andes. American Ethnologist 29(3):567–601.

Vaughn KJ. 2004. Households, crafts, and feasting in the ancient Andes: The village context of early Nasca craft consumption. Latin American Antiquity 15(1):61–88.

Verano JW. 1995. Where do they rest? The treatment of human offerings and trophies in ancient Peru. In: Dillehay TD, editor. Tombs for the living: Andean mortuary practices. Washington, D.C.: Dumbarton Oaks. Pp. 189–227.

Verano JW. 2001a. War and death in the Moche world: Osteological evidence and visual discourse. In: Pillsbury J, editor. Moche art and archaeology in ancient Peru. Washington, D.C.: National Gallery of Art. Pp. 111–26.

Verano JW. 2001b. The physical evidence of human sacrifice in ancient Peru. In: Benson EP, and Cook AG, editors. Ritual sacrifice in ancient Peru. Austin: University of Texas Press. Pp. 165–84.

Verano JW. 2003. Human skeletal remains from Machu Picchu: A reexamination of the Yale Peabody Museum's collections. In: Burger RL, and Salazar LC, editors. The 1912 Yale Peruvian Scientific Expedition Collections from Machu Picchu. New Haven, Conn.: Yale University Publications. Pp. 65–117.

Wachtel N. 2001. El regreso de los antepasados: Los indios urus de Bolivia, del siglo XX al XVI. Mexico City: El Colegio de México.

Waldron T. 1996. Legalized trauma. International Journal of Osteoarchaeology 6(1):114–18.

Walker PL. 1989. Cranial injuries as evidence of violence in prehistoric southern California. American Journal of Physical Anthropology 80:313–23.

Walker PL. 1997. Wife beating, boxing, and broken noses: Skeletal evidence for the cultural patterning of violence. In: Martin DK, and Frayer DW, editors. Troubled times: Violence and warfare in the past. Amsterdam: Gordon and Breach Publishers. Pp. 145–79.

Walker PL. 2001. A bioarchaeological perspective on the history of violence. Annual Review of Anthropology 30:573–96.

Walker PL, Bathurst RR, Richman R, Gjerdrum T, and Andrushko VA. 2009. The causes of porotic hyperostosis and cribra orbitalia: A reappraisal of the iron-deficiency-anemia hypothesis. American Journal of Physical Anthropology 139(2):109–25.

Walker PL, and Cook DC. 1998. Gender and sex: Vive la difference. American Journal of Physical Anthropology 106(2):255–59.

Walker PL, Johnson J, and Lambert PM. 1988. Age and sex biases in the preservation of human skeletal remains. American Journal of Physical Anthropology 76:183–88.

Walker PL, and Long J. 1977. An experimental study of the morphological characteristics of toolmarks. American Antiquity 42:605–16.

Walker PL, Miller KP, and Richman R. 2008. Time, temperature, and oxygen availability: An experimental study of the effects of environmental conditions on the color and organic content of cremated bone. In: Schmidt CW, editor. Burned bone. Burlington, Mass.: Elsevier Press.

Wallerstein IM. 1974a. Capitalist agriculture and the origins of the European world-economy in the sixteenth century. New York: Academic Press.

Wallerstein IM. 1974b. The modern world-system. New York: Academic Press.

Wallerstein IM. 1990. World systems analysis: The second phase. Review 13:287–93.

Wapler U, Crubézy E, and Schultz M. 2004. Is cribra orbitalia synonymous with anemia? Analysis and interpretation of cranial pathology in Sudan. American Journal of Physical Anthropology 123(4):333–39.

Watters DAK, and Dyke T. 1996. Trauma in Papua New Guinea: What do we know and where do we go? PNG Medical Journal 39:121–25.

Webb S. 1995. Palaeopathology of aboriginal Australians: Health and disease across a hunter-gatherer continent. New York: Cambridge University Press.

Webster D. 1975. Warfare and the evolution of the state: A reconsideration. American Antiquity 40(4):464–70.

Wernke SA. 2003. An archaeo-history of Andean community and landscape: The late pre-hispanic and early colonial Colca valley, Peru [Ph.D. dissertation]. Madison: University of Wisconsin.

Wilkinson RG, and Van Wagenen KM. 1993. Violence against women: Prehistoric skeletal evidence from Michigan. Midcontinental Journal of Archaeology 18:190–216.

Willey GR. 1991. Horizontal integration and regional diversity: An alternating process in the rise of civilizations. American Antiquity 56(2):197–215.

Williams PR. 2001. Cerro Baúl: A Wari center on the Tiwanaku frontier. Latin American Antiquity 12(1):67–83.

Williams PR. 2002. Rethinking disaster-induced collapse in the demise of the Andean highland states: Wari and Tiwanaku. World Archaeology 33(3):361–74.

Williams PR, and Nash DJ. 2005. Architecture and power: Relations on the Wari-Tiwanaku frontier. In: Vaughn K, Conlee C, and Ogburn D, editors. The foundations of power in the prehispanic Andes. Arlington, Va.: American Anthropological Association. Pp. 151–74.

Williams PR, and Nash DJ. 2006. Sighting the apu: A GIS analysis of Wari imperialism and the worship of mountain peaks. World Archaeology 38(3):455–68.

Williams SR. 1990. The skeletal biology of Estuquiña: A Late Intermediate Period site in southern Peru [Ph.D. dissertation]. Chicago: Northwestern University.

Williams SR, Forgey K, and Klarich E. 2001. An osteological study of Nasca trophy heads collected by A. L. Kroeber during the Marshall field expeditions to Peru. Chicago: Field Museum of Natural History.

Wise JM. 2004. Geology of the Ayacucho intermontane basin, central Peru [doctoral thesis]. University of Nevada, Reno.

Wolff B. n.d. Wari ceramic production. Washington, DC: Catholic University of America.

Worth JE. 2001. The ethnohistorical context of bioarchaeology in Spanish Florida. In: Larsen CS, editor. Bioarchaeology of Spanish Florida: The impact of colonialism. Gainesville: University Press of Florida. Pp. 1–21.

Wright LE. 2005. Identifying immigrants to Tikal, Guatemala: Defining local variability in strontium isotope ratios of human tooth enamel. Journal of Archaeological Science 32:555–66.

Yépez Álvarez WJ, and Jennings J. 2010. La Real: A Middle Horizon mortuary site in southern Peru. Paper presented at the 75th Annual Meeting of the Society for American Archaeology. St. Louis, Mo.

Zuidema RT. 1977. The Inca kinship system: A new theoretical view. In: Bolton R, and Mayer E, editors. Andean kinship and marriage. Washington, D.C.: American Anthropological Association. Pp. 240–92.

Index

Page numbers in italics indicate figures and tables.

Tiffiny A. Tung is associate professor in the Department of Anthropology at Vanderbilt University.

Bioarchaeological Interpretations of the Human Past: Local, Regional, and Global Perspectives

EDITED BY CLARK SPENCER LARSEN

This series examines the field of bioarchaeology, the study of human biological remains from archaeological settings. Focusing on the intersection between biology and behavior in the past, each volume will highlight important issues, such as biocultural perspectives on health, lifestyle and behavioral adaptation, biomechanical responses to key adaptive shifts in human history, dietary reconstruction and foodways, biodistance and population history, warfare and conflict, demography, social inequality, and environmental impacts on population.

Ancient Health: Skeletal Indicators of Agricultural and Economic Intensification, edited by Mark Nathan Cohen and Gillian M. M. Crane-Kramer (2007; first paperback edition, 2012)

Bioarchaeology and Identity in the Americas, edited by Kelly J. Knudson and Christopher M. Stojanowski (2009; first paperback edition, 2010)

Island Shores, Distant Pasts: Archaeological and Biological Approaches to the Pre-Columbian Settlement of the Caribbean, edited by Scott M. Fitzpatrick and Ann H. Ross (2010)

The Bioarchaeology of the Human Head: Decapitation, Decoration, and Deformation, edited by Michelle Bonogofsky (2011)

Bioarchaeology and Climate Change: A View from South Asian Prehistory, by Gwen Robbins Schug (2011)

Violence, Ritual, and the Wari Empire: A Social Bioarchaeology of Imperialism in the Ancient Andes, by Tiffiny A. Tung (2012; first paperback edition, 2013)

The Bioarchaeology of Individuals, edited by Ann L. W. Stodder and Ann M. Palkovich (2012)

The Bioarchaeology of Violence, edited by Debra L. Martin, Ryan P. Harrod, and Ventura R. Pérez (2012)

Bioarchaeology and Behavior: The People of the Ancient Near East, edited by Megan A. Perry (2012)

Paleopathology at the Origins of Agriculture, edited by Mark Nathan Cohen and George J. Armelagos (2013)

CPSIA information can be obtained at www.ICGtesting.com
Printed in the USA
LVOW132054100413

328390LV00005B/14/P